# The Cultural Marxism Conspiracy

# The Cultural Marxism Conspiracy

## Why the Right Blames the Frankfurt School for the Decline of the West

A.J.A. Woods

VERSO
London • New York

First published by Verso 2026
© A.J.A. Woods 2026

All rights reserved

The manufacturer's authorized representative in the EU for product safety (GPSR) is LOGOS EUROPE, 9 rue Nicolas Poussin, 17000, La Rochelle, France
contact@logoseurope.eu

The moral rights of the author have been asserted

1 3 5 7 9 10 8 6 4 2

**Verso**
UK: 6 Meard Street, London W1F 0EG
US: 207 East 32nd Street, New York, NY 10016
versobooks.com

Verso is the imprint of New Left Books

ISBN-13: 978-1-8042-9696-7
ISBN-13: 978-1-8042-9699-8 (US EBK)
ISBN-13: 978-1-8042-9698-1 (UK EBK)

**British Library Cataloguing in Publication Data**
A catalogue record for this book is available from the British Library

**Library of Congress Cataloging-in-Publication Data**
A catalog record for this book is available from the Library of Congress

Typeset in Sabon by MJ & N Gavan, Truro, Cornwall
Printed and bound by CPI Group (UK) Ltd, Croydon CR0 4YY

# Contents

# Introduction

*Social life is essentially practical. All mysteries which mislead theory to mysticism find their rational solution in human practice and in the comprehension of this practice.*

—Karl Marx, *Theses on Feuerbach*

In December 2021, the term "Cultural Marxism" was added to the Oxford English Dictionary. It was, according to the OED, a phrase with a sinister and controversial past. Its etymology could allegedly be traced to 1930s Nazi propaganda; its first recorded English-language use was in a 1938 issue of a British Union of Fascists magazine. Despite its dark history, this expression has recently surged in popularity. College campuses and city streets have been plastered with stickers that urge passersby to "smash" Cultural Marxism. Prominent US Republicans, such as Texas Senator Ted Cruz and Defense Secretary Pete Hegseth, have written book-length polemics to blame America's decline on Cultural Marxist ideologies. Leaders in Latin America, like Brazil's former President Jair Bolsonaro and Argentina's President Javier Milei, have vowed to rid their governments of this left-wing scourge. In the United Kingdom, Conservative Party MPs have said that Cultural Marxists are "destroying" children's souls and "snuffing out" the right to free speech. Even the world's richest man, tech-mogul-turned-Trumpian Elon Musk, has voiced concerns about a Wikipedia article that dismisses Cultural Marxism as a "conspiracy theory." This buzzword has now become a fixture in the lexicon of the contemporary right—but what does it mean?

"Cultural Marxism," or the "Cultural Marxism conspiracy theory," is the political right's attempt to explain why the culture of Western societies has changed over the past sixty years. According to this theory, a group of German thinkers known as the Frankfurt School (or the Institute for Social Research) invented the "ideologies" of multiculturalism, feminism, and environmentalism to trigger the demise of Western civilization. When Theodor Adorno, Herbert Marcuse, and other Frankfurt School theorists fled Nazi Germany, they traveled to the United States and successfully injected their ideas into the 1960s student movement. In the late twentieth century, their indoctrinated disciples performed a "long march through the institutions" (a phrase coined by German New Left activist Rudi Dutschke) to promote Cultural Marxism in education, the media, the government, and the church. More recently, right-wing activists and conservative pundits have used this theory to understand the rise of the Black Lives Matter movement, the increased visibility of LGBTQ+ communities, and the efforts to tackle the climate emergency. Even in countries outside the United States, conservatives have engaged in a "culture war" to defend their societies from this menace.

What is *cultural* about this Cultural Marxism? What is *Marxist* about cultural change? Conservative critics speculate that the Frankfurt School developed a fresh strategy of communist subversion in the 1930s. Instead of building a vanguardist party or seizing the factories, the Frankfurt School decided to infiltrate the cultural apparatus of bourgeois society to undermine Western capitalism. Once ensconced in these positions of power, Cultural Marxists catered to the petulant demands of various minority groups—Black people, LGBTQ+ people, feminists—and dismantled the civilizational inheritance of the (white) majority. The Frankfurt School apparently believed that this strategy would cause a Marxist egalitarian utopia to emerge from the ruins of Western culture. As the art historian Sven Lütticken observes, this alternative intellectual history relies on a theory of culture that mixes "conservative essentialism" with "schematic superstructuralism."[1] Culture, according to this right-wing conception, naturally reflects the values of a native populace. These values fuse a nation's citizens into a harmonious unity that annuls antagonism and difference. Yet this essentialist notion of culture cannot account for the drastic social changes that have taken place since the 1960s, because it treats the subordination of minorities as "natural" (or, even, as virtuous). Consequently, conservatives must conclude that an outside agent has seized the organs of cultural production to destroy the West. In an act of self-defense, the opponents of Cultural Marxism propose to eliminate every instance of "political correctness" or "wokeness" in public life through legislative reform, lifestyle changes, or violence. In this version of global events, the Frankfurt School and their devotees are blessed with a magical level of agency that can overcome all contradictions and countervailing forces.

Of course, no one can deny the historical existence and importance of the Frankfurt School. In 1923, the Institute for Social Research was established at the University of Frankfurt as an institutional base for Marxist scholarship. The Institute's thinkers synthesized Hegelian philosophy, Marxist political economy, and Freudian psychoanalysis to produce a form of sociological critique called Critical Theory. Their work offered powerful insights into the nature of modern capitalist civilization, the dynamics of fascist propaganda, and the commodification of art and culture. Many members of the Frankfurt School escaped the Nazi regime in the thirties and found refuge, research positions, and professorships in the United States. During the 1960s, Marcuse became an enthusiastic supporter of the student protest movement and earned a reputation in the American media as the "Guru of the New

1 Sven Lütticken, "Cultural Marxists Like Us," *Afterall: A Journal of Art, Context, and Inquiry* 46 (Autumn/Winter 2018): 68.

Left." Some of the Frankfurt School's students went on to have successful academic careers. A few of them became major left-wing activists, such as Angela Davis and Abbie Hoffman. Even in the 2020s, the texts of the Frankfurt School continue to be reprinted and reread.

This is not a book on the history of the Institute for Social Research, however. I will not be discussing the scholarly uses of the term "Cultural Marxism" in the work of Trent Schroyer, Dennis Dworkin, or Douglas Kellner. I will not be addressing the relatively sober critiques of the Frankfurt School made by conservative authors such as Paul Gottfried, Christopher Lasch, and Roger Scruton. Instead, this book is a study of those who argue that the Frankfurt School's Cultural Marxism is ultimately responsible for civilizational decline. It is an attempt to work out a series of critical puzzles. Why does this narrative of cultural degeneration focus so much on a collective of German Marxists? How does it continue to convince and excite the forces of political reaction? What is the genealogy of this idea we call the "Cultural Marxism conspiracy theory"?

Other scholars have tried to tackle these questions. They suggest that "Cultural Marxism" is simply an updated version of older antisemitic conspiracy theories like "Judeo-Bolshevism" or "cultural Bolshevism." The term "Judeo-Bolshevism" refers to the idea that communism is a Jewish conspiracy. Those who spread this belief revived the conspiracist hoax *The Protocols of the Elders of Zion* to portray the communist revolutions in Russia and elsewhere as the initial maneuvers of a secret Jewish plan to destroy Christendom. Like Judeo-Bolshevism, the Nazi's interwar propaganda about "cultural Bolshevism," or *Kulturbolschewismus*, supposed that Jews were trying to destroy European culture. This concept stemmed from Adolf Hitler's remarks on race and culture in *Mein Kampf* and Nazi theorist Alfred Rosenberg's notion of "racial aesthetics." It represented aesthetic modernism, or "degenerate art," as a tool of Jewish communist subversion.

Of course, there are some eerie parallels between these earlier ideas and "Cultural Marxism." The British Union of Fascists translated *Kulturbolschewismus* as "Cultural Marxism" in 1938, even if their use of the term was long forgotten by the time it was "recoined" in the early 1990s. Contemporary far-right activists and authors tend to emphasize that several members of the Frankfurt School were Jewish, as if to suggest that these thinkers were genetically predisposed to operate as agents of cultural degeneracy. Even more damningly, the fascist online encyclopedia *Metapedia* once maintained an entry on Cultural Marxism that presented the term as interchangeable with "cultural Bolshevism."

It is ahistorical, however, to claim that "Cultural Marxism" is nothing more than a rebranding of these previous tropes. This argument presupposes that Judeo-Bolshevism, cultural Bolshevism, and Cultural Marxism are substantially identical, as though they share a transcendental essence that precedes their historical manifestations. It ignores the distinct trajectories of these ideas and implies that all right-wing politics are fundamentally the same: The right is the right is the right. The phrase "Cultural Marxism," as well as the conspiratorial narratives about the Frankfurt School that it often denotes, had its own bizarre history long before it ended up in the neo-Nazi thesaurus as a synonym for cultural Bolshevism. Comparisons between Judeo- or cultural Bolshevism and Cultural Marxism reveal very little about this complex story. Only when we ignore these analogies can we better understand the unique histories of the so-called Cultural Marxism conspiracy theory.

Before we delve into these histories, we must first think critically about our own terminology. In many ways, the term "Cultural Marxism conspiracy theory" is a misleading and unhelpful abstraction. In his 2008 book *Conspiracy Panics: Political Rationality and Popular Culture*, the media theorist

Jack Bratich tried to figure out why some ideas are called "conspiracy theories." Building on the work of Michel Foucault, Bratich argued that "conspiracy theories are defined not merely by their strictly denotative inherent properties, but by their discursive position in relation to a 'regime of truth.'"[2] Regimes of truth govern the discourses, institutions, and apparatuses that are empowered to make and distribute "true" statements. Foucault originally developed this concept to understand battles over "the status of truth and the economic and political role it plays."[3] Instead of seeking to verify or debunk the facts of specific conspiracy theories, this Foucauldian approach encourages us to interrogate the norms and techniques that establish the boundary between valid research and conspiracist nonsense.

Bratich coined the term "conspiracy panic discourse" to describe the procedures that brand an idea as a conspiracy theory. Conspiracy panic discourse preserves the division between the production of legitimate knowledge and the fashioning of paranoid narratives. The practitioners of this discourse tend to be trusted intellectuals, such as trained journalists or university-affiliated academics, who rank highly in the current regime of truth. They are responsible for identifying the "conspiracy theories" that threaten to poison "our" mainstream consensus. Bratich contends that this practice is "not separate from conspiracy theories; it is constitutive of them."[4] In other words, a conspiracy theory does not exist as a discernible object until conspiracy panic discourse captures and categorizes it. "Conspiracy theory" is an assigned status within a regime of truth rather than a thing with intrinsic structural properties.

---

2 Jack Bratich, *Conspiracy Panics: Political Rationality and Popular Culture* (Albany: State University of New York Press, 2008), 3.

3 Michel Foucault, *Power/Knowledge: Selected Interviews and Other Writings 1972–1977* (New York: Pantheon Books, 1980), 132.

4 Bratich, *Conspiracy Panics*, 19.

Bratich's provocation raises a serious theoretical problem for anyone who plans to write about the history of a so-called conspiracy theory. Conspiracy panic discourse is a sorting mechanism that extracts a whole variety of arguments and narratives from their original contexts and lumps them together under the name of a particular conspiracy theory. It assumes that all the proponents of this theory are conspiracy theorists who lurk beyond the boundaries of mainstream society rather than specific political actors with varying degrees of power, legitimacy, and influence. What would it mean to go against the automatic reflexes of this conspiracy panic discourse? How should we think about the ideas that have been automatically pigeonholed as this or that conspiracy theory? What are we missing in our existing accounts of Cultural Marxism?

This book will show that there is no such thing as the "Cultural Marxism conspiracy theory." As the scholar John E. Richardson points out, Cultural Marxism is a "discursive will-o'-the-wisp" whose "meaning shifts according to the rhetorical, political and contextual conditions of its use."[5] Consequently, it is more appropriate to discuss plural Cultural Marxisms.[6] Whereas conspiracy panic discourse diagnoses conspiracy theories from an external standpoint, this book offers a patchwork history that radically contextualizes the separate expressions of Cultural Marxism/s. I argue that Cultural Marxism/s is not a generic conspiracy theory but, rather, an ever-changing combination of narrative elements that possesses different meanings and functions in various political contexts. Such an approach

5 John E. Richardson, "'Cultural Marxism' and the British National Party: A Transnational Discourse," in *Cultures of Post-War Fascism*, ed. Nigel Copsey and John E. Richardson (Croydon, UK: Routledge, 2015), 222.

6 I want to make a terminological note for clarity. I use "Cultural Marxism/s" to refer to the political narratives that are usually described as the "Cultural Marxism conspiracy theory," whereas I use "Cultural Marxism" to denote the supposed social and political phenomenon that these narratives seek to explain.

helps us to understand how right-wing authors and activists adapted earlier narratives of Cultural Marxism/s to suit new audiences and meet fresh political challenges.

In this book, I draw on conjunctural analysis as a method of contextualization. Conjunctural analysis is a methodological approach that comes from a particular reading of Antonio Gramsci's *Prison Notebooks*. The pioneers of British cultural studies, such as Stuart Hall, turned to Gramsci's writings to develop a form of Marxist analysis that could identify the complex relationships between politics, culture, and the economy in a certain historical moment. Many of Marx's concepts, such as the "capitalist mode of production," tend to function at a high level of abstraction to reveal the fundamental features of capitalist society. Conjunctural analysis, however, works in a historico-concrete register to examine the conditions of a society at specific stages in the development of capitalism. A conjuncture is neither a period (the Victorian era) nor an epoch (feudalism). It is a moment at which different forces and factions come together to occupy or transform the terrain on which political and ideological struggle takes place.

The practice of conjunctural analysis rests on Gramsci's distinction between the organic and the conjunctural. The organic refers to the relatively permanent features of a social formation. Organic facts are the taken-for-granted relationships and routines that underpin day-to-day life in each society, such as labor relations, economic infrastructure, government institutions, cultural norms, and legal frameworks. These elements are stable enough to outlast fleeting moments of political scandal and market fluctuation. The organic, to put it simply, is the status quo.

The conjunctural is the terrain of struggle that opens up whenever this status quo encounters crises. An organic crisis is a heightened expression of the inherently antagonistic and crisis-ridden development of capitalism. It disrupts the "normal" order of things, challenges established practices and patterns and unsettles conventional wisdom. Hegemonic forces enter this conjunctural terrain to conserve the status quo and fix these crises (within certain limits). They may propose policies to mitigate urgent social problems, enhance policing powers to deal with unrest, or announce public sector cuts to manage budget deficits. They may even devise compromises or form coalitions with other groups to secure an equilibrium. Alternative or oppositional political movements can use these conjunctural moments to present their own solutions to the crisis. The success of these efforts, as Gramsci writes, "can be estimated by the extent to which they are convincing and shift the previously existing disposition of social forces."[7] The level of the conjunctural consists of all these attempts to establish a new balance of forces, or a new hegemonic order, and to stabilize an increasingly turbulent society.

How can we use conjunctural analysis to understand the history of Cultural Marxism/s? We must always remember that Cultural Marxism/s did not randomly pop into someone's head. These narratives were forged in the heat of conjunctural struggle. They were designed to perform ideological work for specific political forces: to tell people why a crisis was happening and to persuade them to support a particular vision for a "better" society. Conjunctural analysis can illuminate the terrain on which these forces emerged and mobilized. It can show how specific forces developed their own kind of politics and why they decided to confront certain issues or problems. Furthermore, it can provide a level of analytical specificity that has been absent from other historical accounts of the "Cultural Marxism conspiracy theory."

Admittedly, this book cannot offer a full-scale conjunctural analysis. As the cultural theorist John Clarke points out, this form of investigation requires a collaborative effort of thinking

7 Antonio Gramsci, *Selections from the Prison Notebooks of Antonio Gramsci* (New York: Lawrence & Wishart, 1980), 178.

and writing. No single researcher, Clarke warns, "can grasp the multiplicity of forces, pressures, tendencies, tensions, antagonisms and contradictions that make up a conjuncture."[8] Even though I draw extensively on the long-standing tradition of conjunctural analysis, my own study of conjunctures remains partial and provisional. In this book, I use these ways of conjunctural thinking to understand how it became possible for the ideas of Cultural Marxism/s to be produced and propagated. Inevitably, I have set myself strict chronological and geographical limits. In the open and collective spirit of conjunctural analysis, I hope that others will extend, deepen, and complicate the arguments and interpretations that I put forward. After all, the story of Cultural Marxism/s is far from over.

Where do we start? While I recognize the parallels between cultural Bolshevism and Cultural Marxism/s, I do not think that the story begins in the 1920s or 1930s. For me, the 1960s is a better starting point for our analysis. The history of Cultural Marxism/s cannot be understood unless we reflect on the many overlapping shifts and realignments that stemmed from the sixties. We must remember not to limit our notion of that decade to the spectacular images of May 1968 or Woodstock. As many scholars now agree, the 1960s were *long*—some claim that the 1960s lasted from 1955 to 1974—and *global*. It was a conjuncture that opened possibilities for revolution, dissent, and counterculture. However, it also involved the exercise of vast political power to defend social and racial hierarchies, control subversive energies, and protect modes of domination and exploitation. As Tamara Chaplin and Jadwiga E. Pieper Mooney put it, the 1960s were a "global crucible" in which "politics and social protests—over race, gender, class, sexuality,

8 John Clarke, "Doing the Dirty Work: The Challenges of Conjunctural Analysis," in *Stuart Hall: Conversations, Projects and Legacies*, ed. J. Henriques, D. Morley and V. Goblot (London: Goldsmith's Press), 84.

and generation—collided with new forms of technology, a growing mass media, and expanding commercial markets."[9]

In his groundbreaking essay "Periodizing the 60s," the cultural critic Fredric Jameson argues that the beginning of what would become known as the 1960s can be traced back to the struggles for national liberation and decolonization that broke out in 1950s Africa.[10] Events in the Global South, such as the independence of Ghana and the Algerian War, ignited nearly two decades of struggle that shook the postwar global order. Radicals in America and Western Europe drew inspiration from the successes of revolutionary and anti-imperialist movements around the world. They read Frantz Fanon's *The Wretched of the Earth*, Mao Zedong's *The Little Red Book*, and Che Guevara's *Guerrilla Warfare*. Students in the American New Left marched in the streets, held teach-ins, and occupied university buildings to protest their government's military interventions in Vietnam, Cambodia, and Laos. The truly global nature of this 1960s revolt, with all its fissures and contradictions, gave rise to the hope that the "marginalized" and "minoritized" of the Earth were at the forefront of an unstoppable worldwide revolution. The days of an all-supreme Western civilization looked like they were coming to an end.

The 1960s saw the flourishing of new social and political categories of race, gender, and sexuality. Traditional modes of class-based struggle had lost their radical edge. The Taft-Hartley Act of 1947, as well as the merger between AFL and CIO, tamed the labor movement in the United States and integrated unions into the anti-communist Cold War consensus. Uprisings against bureaucratic communism in the Soviet

---

9 Tamara Chaplin and Jadwiga E. Pieper Mooney, "Introduction," in *The Global 1960s: Convention, Contest, and Counterculture*, ed. Tamara Chaplin and Jadwiga E. Pieper Mooney (Abingdon, UK: Routledge, 2018), 7.

10 Fredric Jameson, "Periodizing the 60s," *Social Text*, no. 9/10 (Spring–Summer 1984): 178–209.

Bloc—Hungary, Poland, Czechoslovakia—demonstrated the need for a non-Stalinist and antiauthoritarian left. New ways of doing politics were tested and elaborated. The slogan "the personal is political," popularized by second-wave feminism, emphasized the importance of finding the links between individual experiences and wider structures of repression. Movements for Black power, women's liberation, and gay liberation introduced a vibrant politics of identity that fused potent critiques of the existing order with daring visions of a liberated future. They exposed the social exclusions, subordinations, and restrictions that underpinned the status quo of postwar capitalist societies. In the United States, these movements fought for the establishment of women's studies, Black studies, and ethnic studies departments in American universities. Racial, sexual, and gender identities were embraced as epistemological bases for developing new forms of knowledge that could identify the multiple dimensions of power and oppression. In the decades following the 1960s, many countries experienced something of a social and cultural revolution as women, racial minorities, and LGBTQ+ people acquired civil rights and started to play a more active and visible role in the public sphere. While these forms of equality and inclusion were usually partial and contradictory, they represented a significant liberalization of social life and an unsettling of old hierarchies.

One of the most significant developments of the 1960s was the drastic expansion of "culture." In the middle of the twentieth century, many "developed" countries transitioned from a predominantly industrial model of production to a largely service- and information-based one. During the rise of the post-industrial economy, culture burst into the foreground of day-to-day life.[11] The mass media—film, television, music, fashion, advertising, newspapers, and magazines—started to exert tremendous power and influence over the rhythms of

11 Michael Denning, *Culture in the Age of Three Worlds* (New York: Verso, 2004), 1.

everyday existence. The growing demographic of teenagers and young adults became an eager audience for the offerings of a new and exciting "youth culture." The rise of this youth-oriented popular culture even altered conventional habits of speech, dress, and behavior. These rapid changes spurred a "cultural turn" in humanities and social sciences scholarship. The thinkers of British cultural studies drew on the resources of Gramscian theory to rethink the nature of cultural production and consumption in postwar capitalist societies. Instead of assuming that mass culture turned people into passive consumers, these cultural theorists suggested that popular culture, especially youth subculture, constituted a site of potentially subversive political struggle. As the forces of Western Marxism cut ties with Moscow, these intellectuals engaged with other radical causes and movements to promote a broad and populist form of cultural politics. Since the 1960s, cultural questions have become increasingly central to political debate.

It would be a mistake to believe that the 1960s were nothing but an outburst of liberal acceptance and youthful rebellion. From right-wing coups and neo-colonial economic policies to police repression and state surveillance, the 1960s featured the use of extraordinary force to preserve arrangements of power and privilege. Various right-wing and reactionary political movements ventured into this conjunctural terrain to defend the existing hierarchies of a pristine Western civilization. These forces required intellectuals who could explain away the causes of perceived cultural decline, organize their supporters into a coherent political identity, and offer compelling visions of conservative revival. All Cultural Marxism narratives derive from these efforts to resist and reverse the social changes that started to unfold in the long and global 1960s. It is important to understand how these intellectuals operated within their own political movements. How might we investigate the function and activity of these intellectuals? What kind of theory would illuminate the specific ideological practices that shaped their approaches to this cultural tumult? What this task requires, I suggest, is a return to Gramsci's theory of intellectuals.

A central theme of Gramsci's *Prison Notebooks* is a sustained and innovative rethinking of the concept of the intellectual. In a letter to his sister-in-law Tatiana Schucht, Gramsci remarked that he wanted to extend this concept beyond the limits of "the current notion that refers only to the preeminent intellectuals."[12] Instead of sticking to this abstract notion, Gramsci examined how specific types of intellectual were formed historically and how they functioned politically. The sociologist Jerome Karabel describes this reorientation as a shift from a normative framework, which "treats intellectuals not as they actually are, but as they should be," to an analytical one that identifies "the conditions and processes that shape the actual political consciousness and actions of different groups of intellectuals."[13] In the *Prison Notebooks*, Gramsci started from the "immediate, direct, and vivid impression"—the details of social practice and material circumstance—to reveal larger historical patterns.[14] His entries on intellectuals included several reminders about the importance of grounding one's research in material reality. He specified that the formation and elaboration of intellectual strata did not "take place on the terrain of abstract democracy, but in accordance with very concrete traditional historical processes."[15] In this book, I follow Gramsci's example and show that the propagators of Cultural Marxism/s are neither stereotypical conspiracy theorists nor generic intellectuals. Rather, they are active practitioners of certain kinds of ideological struggle that arise from very particular relationships

12 Antonio Gramsci, *Letters from Prison: Volume II* (New York: Columbia University Press, 1994), 67.

13 Jerome Karabel, "Toward a Theory of Intellectuals and Politics," *Theory and Society* 25, no. 2 (April 1996): 205–6.

14 Antonio Gramsci, *Letters from Prison: Volume I* (New York: Columbia University Press, 1994), 233.

15 Gramsci, *Selections from the Prison Notebooks*, 11.

between social classes, political forces, and superstructural institutions. Each articulation of Cultural Marxism/s must be studied concretely.

This book is not a single timeline that follows the development of an idea from its origins to its later adaptations but, rather, an effort to capture what the philosopher Vittorio Morfino would call the "plural temporality" of Cultural Marxism/s.[16] It is a tale of detours and discontinuities. It untangles the strands of history that have taken on physical form in the flesh of a megalomaniacal cult leader, in the corridors of a conservative think tank, and in the footage of a Christian right documentary. The elements of cultural Marxism/s have been deconstructed and reconfigured time and time again as reactionary political forces across the world search for new ways to justify their opposition to equality, democracy, and justice. We will never understand these stories if we cling to the language of individual pathology. Our approach to Cultural Marxism/s must be rooted in the institutional, the conjunctural, and the structural. As Gramsci once put it, "ideas and opinions are not spontaneously born in each individual brain: They have had a center of formation, of irradiation, of dissemination, of persuasion [that] has developed them and presented them in the political form of current reality."[17] This is a book that de-centers the individual brain and focuses on those centers that made the popularization of Cultural Marxism/s possible.

This book does not "debunk" Cultural Marxism/s. It would be impossible—and uninteresting—to refute all the claims that every critic of Cultural Marxism has made. After all, most Cultural Marxism narratives include several factual observations, such as Marcuse's endorsement of the "long march

16 Vittorio Morfino, "The Layers of History and the Politics of Gramsci," in *A Companion to Antonio Gramsci: Essays on the History and Theories of History, Politics, and Historiography*, ed. Davide Cadeddu (Chicago: Haymarket Books, 2020), 47–56.

17 Gramsci, *Selections from the Prison Notebooks*, 192–3.

through the institutions" as a potential strategy for the post-1960s New Left. Yet these little facts are rarely used to provide us with an accurate account of either the Frankfurt School's influence or contemporary social realities. Instead, they are mobilized to fuel political campaigns that seek to denigrate and disempower certain groups. This is not a scholarly disagreement about the legacy of the Frankfurt School; it is a struggle to determine what kind of world we want to live in. The right has declared war on Cultural Marxism. Only when we understand the practices—and weaknesses—of those reactionaries who have signed up for this war can we hope to resist their attacks and fight for a better future.

# 1

# Lyndon LaRouche: From the New Left to the New Dark Age

*I still like to think that some of my research was validly conducted and useful. However, I see very clearly that the whole enterprise—and especially the conclusions—was hopelessly deformed by self-censorship and the desire to in some way to support Mr. LaRouche's crack-brained world-view. So, in that sense, I do not stand by what I wrote, and I find it unfortunate that it is still remembered.*

—Michael J. Minnicino[1]

On June 17, 1969, the French German radical Daniel Cohn-Bendit interrupted Herbert Marcuse's lecture at the Teatro Eliseo in Rome to ask why this "Father of the New Left" accepted payments from the CIA. According to newspaper reports, Marcuse ignored this question and hurriedly exited the theater. Cohn-Bendit had likely come across the accusation that Marcuse was a clandestine CIA agent from an issue of the West German left-wing publication *Berliner Extra-Dienst*. The peddler of this peculiar claim—a journalist named Leo Matthias—speculated that Marcuse, who once worked for the Office of Strategic Services (the precursor to the CIA) and the State Department, was currently employed by the US government to manipulate the New Left. In an open letter to *Der Spiegel*, Marcuse condemned these allegations as shabby

1 Quoted in Martin Jay, "Dialectic of Counter-Enlightenment: the Frankfurt School as Scapegoat of the Lunatic Fringe," *Salmagundi*, no. 168/169 (Fall 2010/Winter 2011): 34.

tricks that tarnished the New Left's reputation. Seventeen members of the West German student movement, including Rudi Dutschke and Oskar Negt, signed another open letter to denounce this anti-Marcuse witch hunt. Rumors about Marcuse's background had initially been sparked by a 1968 *Pravda* exposé that revealed the theorist's past connections to the intelligence community.[2] Yet this new rumor—that Marcuse was *still* one of the CIA's prime operatives—did not originate in Soviet Russia. It came from an American Maoist organization called the Progressive Labor Party (PL).

"Marcuse: Cop-out or Cop?," an anonymous article in the February 1969 issue of *Progressive Labor* magazine, accused the German philosopher of helping the CIA to dampen the revolutionary fervor of student protest.[3] At the time, criticisms of Marcuse were not uncommon in PL publications. The previous issue of *Progressive Labor* featured an article, "Herbert Marcuse and His Philosophy of Copout," that described the Frankfurt School thinker as "thoroughly anti-social and profoundly reactionary."[4] In a 1968 speech, PL's National Student Organizer Jeff Gordon surmised that Marcuse's famous book *One-Dimensional Man* was part of a mass media campaign to convince students that American workers were passive and counterrevolutionary.[5] PL's denunciations of Marcuse were linked to a broader theoretical debate between factions in the Students for a Democratic Society (SDS)—the largest organization in the American New Left—over the strategy of building a "worker-student alliance." PL theorized that students could not perform the same revolutionary role as the traditional

2 Yuri Zhukov, "Oborotni," *Pravda*, May 30, 1968, 4.

3 "Marcuse: Cop-out or Cop?," *Progressive Labor* 6, no. 6 (February 1969): 61–6.

4 Jared Israel and William Russel, "Herbert Marcuse and His Philosophy of Copout," *Progressive Labor* 6, no. 5 (October 1968): 61.

5 Jeff Gordon, "SDS: An Analysis," *Progressive Labor* 6, no. 5 (October 1968).

industrial working class. They argued that members of the student movement needed to "proletarianize" themselves, join the workers on the factory floor, and establish a firm political alliance with their fellow laborers to overthrow capitalist hegemony. Yet the seriousness of this debate is not reflected in "Marcuse: Cop-Out or Cop?," which advances the spurious hypothesis that Marcuse's supposed endorsement of "love-ins" was a CIA-orchestrated ploy to distract American youngsters from real political work. Ultimately, PL's anti-Marcuse stance was dismissed by New Left activists as a thoughtless display of embarrassing sectarianism.

Following the split of SDS at its 1969 annual convention, PL rushed to lead the American student movement. Many rank-and-file members of SDS, however, were unenthusiastic about PL's proposed worker-student alliance. Whereas PL condemned the Black Panther Party and the Viet Cong as revisionist and nationalistic, most young radicals were sympathetic to these movements. Other students were simply turned off by PL's moralistic stances on drug use and sexual promiscuity—they would rather fool around and smoke a joint than adopt the spartan lifestyle of a full-time revolutionist. Whatever their reasons, students abandoned the PL-led SDS. Within eighteen months of PL stewardship, SDS went from 304 chapters to 10. In a certain sense, PL played a much greater role in the collapse of the organized student movement than the supposed CIA asset Marcuse.

As PL fizzled slowly into political irrelevance, New Left activists drifted into other vanguard organizations. Around this time, some students severed ties with PL to join a new faction that had developed within an SDS chapter in New York City. The leader of this group—an older leftist intellectual named Lyn Marcus—dazzled these bright recruits with his theoretical and strategic insights. During the early 1970s, this faction would become known as the National Caucus of Labor Committees (NCLC), and Marcus would acquire a strange kind of notoriety as the pseudo-Leninist-turned-conspiracist cult leader Lyndon LaRouche.

In 1974, LaRouche and NCLC recycled PL's old claims about Marcuse to discredit their opponents and assert that they were the only revolutionary organization that could save humanity from what they called "Rockefeller Fascism." Marcuse and other Frankfurt School thinkers—along with a revolving cast of co-conspirators like Queen Elizabeth II and Henry Kissinger—popped up repeatedly in LaRouche's writings in the subsequent decades. Why did LaRouche and his followers believe that the Frankfurt School wanted to implement a global fascist regime? Why were these kinds of conspiratorial polemics so integral to their ideology? What historical circumstances gave rise to this disciplined and authoritarian cult of personality that churned out narratives of suspicion at such a prolific rate? The key to answering these questions lies in studying how NCLC was organized and how it functioned. LaRouchean polemics were not simply the inventions of a charismatic crank but, rather, the products of a specific ideological practice that emerged from NCLC's organizational framework and political experience.

These anti–Frankfurt School narratives were embedded in what Gramsci would call the "arbitrary ideology" of the LaRouche cult. For Gramsci, arbitrary ideologies spring from the "formally constructive will of one personality or of a group that is driven to propose [them] by its own fanatical philosophical or religious convictions."[6] In other words, an arbitrary ideology performs a socializing function within cult-like groups.[7] The members of a cult must demonstrate familiarity with, and fidelity to, their leader's teachings. They

---

6 Antonio Gramsci, *Subaltern Social Groups: A Critical Edition of Prison Notebook 25* (New York: Columbia University Press, 2021), 86.

7 Dennis Tourish and Tim Wohlforth, *On the Edge: Political Cults Left and Right* (Armonk, NY: M. E. Sharpe, 2000), 6.

are taught to distrust all other sources of information and engage only in the forms of knowledge that the leader permits. Their vocabulary shifts as they start to integrate cult-authorized terms and expressions into their everyday speech. They find it increasingly difficult to communicate with nonmembers. To the wider public, the cult's beliefs may come across as kooky or implausible. The isolating effects of these ideologies tend to produce what could be called an *arbitrary intellectual*: an individual who devotes their energies to preserving and propagating a set of cultic ideas.

Gramsci contrasts arbitrary ideologies with "organic" ones along a spectrum of historical effectiveness. When an ideology obtains a deep psychosocial validity, it becomes organic to a social structure. An organic ideology can forge links between different groups and combine them into a new bloc. All ideologies organize social life, even if some of them never organize anything larger than a small cult. Whereas an organic intellectual would work to unify various struggles into a coherent political force, the arbitrary intellectual pushes a fanatical agenda that does not meaningfully resonate with most people. As Gramsci would put it, arbitrary ideologies express a purely "willed" force rather than a political movement "that corresponds to the conditions that are present or are in the course of formation."[8] Those who place their faith in these esoteric doctrines are often condemned to a life of semi-obscurity on the fringes of the political spectrum.

What was the arbitrary ideology of the LaRouche movement? The central organizing element of LaRoucheanism was *elitism*. Whether he described them as Marxist-Leninist revolutionaries or Neoplatonist philosopher-kings, LaRouche always maintained that his followers constituted a political elite that would shepherd humanity into a new Golden Age. LaRouche also believed that his movement was fighting an oligarchical

8 Antonio Gramsci, *Prison Notebooks, Volume III* (New York: Columbia University Press, 2007), 277.

conspiracy that wanted to reverse technological progress and eradicate the world's population. According to the LaRouchites, the Frankfurt School helped this counter-elite to brainwash the masses. Various allegations about the Frankfurt School littered the pages of LaRouchean journals: Marcuse had turned Angela Davis into a CIA "zombie," Adorno masterminded the rock-drug-sex counterculture of the 1960s, and Horkheimer invented the concept of the "authoritarian personality" to undermine Judeo-Christian civilization. Although these claims may baffle an outside observer, they contributed to the ideological coherence of the LaRouchean cult. As this chapter unfolds, I will illuminate the circumstances and dynamics that gave rise to the LaRouche movement's self-conception as an elite and demonstrate why these polemics about the Frankfurt School became a component of their practice. Without NCLC's attacks on the Frankfurt School, the ideas of Cultural Marxism/s as they stand today would likely not exist. And one cannot understand these attacks without first learning about the history of the LaRouche movement.

## The Rise of a Pseudo-Leninist

In 1965, a spindly and bearded forty-three-year-old Trotskyist named Lyn Marcus—LaRouche's Marxist *nom de guerre*—penned an Internal Discussion Bulletin for the Socialist Workers Party (SWP) entitled "The Coming American Socialist Revolution." In this document, LaRouche urged the SWP to recruit "Leninist 'boomers'" from the radical student movement.[9] Under his leadership, these new party members would reread Lenin's *What Is to Be Done?* and master Marxist dialectics. For LaRouche, only a party with a disciplined cadre of young,

9 Lyn Marcus and C. Lawrence, "The Coming American Socialist Revolution: A Draft Resolution on Strategic Perspectives," *SWP Discussion Bulletin* 25, no. 6 (1965): xv.

theory-minded intellectuals could hope to lead a successful socialist revolution in the United States.

LaRouche's fellow Trotskyists interpreted his proposal as little more than a recipe for a pseudo-revolutionary and pseudo-intellectual cult of personality. A rival Trotskyist publication offered a surprisingly penetrating critique of LaRouche's vision. In "Spartacist and Leninist Politics: The Flight of the Middle-Class Intellectual," an anonymous author characterized LaRouche's strategy as "the very essence of petit-bourgeois arrogance."[10] The author also lampooned LaRouche's condescending attitude toward the proletariat: "It is the task of the workers to follow and of the Marcus-es to lead. Ah, but no one follows when Marcus leads. What dumb brutes the workers are!"[11] According to this nameless critic, LaRouche desired followers rather than comrades. Although this critique is smug and uncharitable, it was prescient in identifying LaRouche's ambition to become the supreme leader of his own organization. By the summer of 1966, LaRouche had left the fringes of the Trotskyist movement to build his own following in the New Left's blossoming activist subculture in New York City.

The New Left was a movement of protest, voluntarism, and nonconformity. Inspired by the civil rights movement of the 1950s and the non-hierarchical structure of the Students Non-Violent Coordinating Committee, SDS favored the egalitarian principle of "participatory democracy" over the Old Left ideal of democratic centralism. The fluid and non-exclusionary nature of SDS attracted students who were driven by a sense of moral justice to campaign against racial inequality, social alienation, and US imperialism. Strangely enough, this politics of outrage was a contradictory by-product of the very society that these students condemned.

---

10 Anonymous, "Spartacist and Leninist Politics: The Flight of the Middle-Class Intellectual," *Bulletin* 2, no. 34 (August–September 1966): 16.

11 Ibid., 17.

In the quarter century following World War II, American universities received an extraordinary amount of funding. Substantial public and philanthropic investment in the higher education system, as well as bold government legislation (the GI Bill, for instance), spurred an unprecedented growth in college enrollment. During the golden years of postwar prosperity, many upwardly mobile and financially secure families could afford full-time study for their offspring. By 1969, the number of college students amounted to 35 percent of the eighteen-to-twenty-four-year-old population. This demographic upsurge compounded the sense that students were an inchoate historical subject that could be organized into an effective political force.

Nonetheless, the expansion of the university system and the enlargement of the student population does not wholly explain the rise of the New Left. As the historian Henry Heller identifies, this student revolt erupted from the contradiction between the role of the university as a site of critical knowledge and as an adjunct to capitalism.[12] In the postwar years, higher education was set up to function as an ideological factory to produce a reliable supply of managers, teachers, and salaried professionals. University administrators welcomed corporate and government funding for research that served the interests of capital and the national security state. Drawing on Gramscian terminology, Heller describes this educational system as a classic example of non-coercive force—a means of making people consent to the power of the ruling class.[13] These universities, and the students who attended them, were supposed to preserve the hegemony of American capitalism.

Yet the apparent equilibrium of the bourgeois hegemonic order is always unstable, insufficient, and incomplete.

---

12 Henry Heller, *The Capitalist University: The Transformation of Higher Education in the United States since 1945* (London: Pluto Press, 2016), xiii.

13 Ibid., 10.

Contradictions within this order can generate sites for alternative political aspirations. The major contradiction in the US higher education system of the 1960s emerged from the tension between the ideological function of the university and the subversive promise of the liberal arts education that many American students received. Professors and administrators assumed that a humanistic education would teach students to respect their national institutions, yet it tended to expose the horrifying discrepancies between the normative claims of American democracy and the realities of the American state. The moral politics of the student movement sprang from this unsettling realization that the United States was failing to live up to its purported ideals of freedom and democracy.

A handful of writers and activists anticipated that students would come to play a significant role in the social movements of the 1960s. C. Wright Mills's memorable 1960 "Letter to the New Left" argued that the most pressing task of political reflection was to identify the agent of historical change.[14] Whereas conventional Marxist thinkers continued to place their hopes in the diminishing revolutionary potential of the working class, Mills encouraged leftists to abandon the traditional tenets of Marxism and acknowledge that the young intelligentsia had become the new vanguard. Citing the examples of anti-authoritarian protestors in Poland, Hungary, and Japan, Mills announced that these student intellectuals were emerging as a significant political force.

In June 1962, fifty-nine members of SDS gathered at a labor union resort on the shores of Lake Huron to draft a manifesto for their generation. Tom Hayden, the lead author of what would become known as *The Port Huron Statement*, was profoundly influenced by Mills's conception of a New Left. The final version of the *Statement* offers an invigorating and deeply existential critique of American society as an impersonal,

14 C. Wright Mills, "Letter to the New Left," *New Left Review*, no. 5 (September–October 1960).

bureaucratic, and militaristic system that stifled individual self-fulfilment and democratic participation. The authors of the *Statement* sought to replace this grey and alienating mass society with a participatory democracy that provided citizens with a sense of purpose and community. Like Mills, SDS saw the university as a potential base from which to build a new American left. They wanted to release the critical impulses of the university from the sprawling academic bureaucracy that accepted funds from private financial interests and compartmentalized knowledge into narrow research specialisms. *The Port Huron Statement*—and the massive student movement that it anticipated—appeared to answer Mills's call for a generation of student intellectuals that could remake society.

To spread their message, the New Left used an old-fashioned medium: the printed word. Students wrote position papers, bulletins, essays, and comic strips that were published in *New Left Notes*, *Radical America*, and other publications. The availability of cheaper printing devices and services—the slogan "Our Founder, the Mimeograph" was a handwritten motto on the walls of the SDS national office—facilitated the widespread dissemination of political knowledge throughout the movement. The New Left's inclusive style of decision-making, as the historian John McMillian argues, partly "grew out of the social processes surrounding the production, distribution, and transmission of its written texts."[15] And so, SDS's student intellectuals felt that their print culture intimated an alternative way of life that would eventually supplant the alienation of American mass society. The cylinders of SDS's mimeographs would be the cogs that powered a social revolution.

Not everyone was convinced that these student intellectuals could function as a new revolutionary agent. The average SDS

15 John McMillan, "'Our Founder, the Mimeograph Machine': Participatory Democracy in Students for a Democratic Society's Print Culture," *Journal for the Study of Radicalism* 2, no. 2 (2008): 87.

activist stood, as Eric Hobsbawm reflected, "at an awkward angle to the rest of society."[16] Despite their opposition to the values and practices of bourgeois America, many SDS members came from relatively affluent and conventional backgrounds. The ambivalent class position of these student radicals produced a sense of guilt about their predominantly white petit-bourgeois origins and generated a feeling of frustration about their structural isolation from working class and marginalized communities. Some students sought to reconcile their political commitments with the facts of their social standing. Some of them even decided that they needed to serve as an auxiliary to the real revolutionary subject: the working class, anti-imperialist guerrilla fighters, and Black militants. The combination of white guilt and workerism ignited a pseudo-Leninist turn in SDS. PL urged students to join workers on the factory floor and form a worker-student alliance; the Weathermen encouraged their cadre to hang out with working-class youth and talk to them about revolution. Each of these SDS factions ached to be part of the revolutionary vanguard, even though, as a former member of PL recalls, their efforts were essentially misguided attempts to "shoehorn the square pegs of theory into the round holes of reality."[17]

What distinguishes pseudo-Leninism from more advanced varieties of Marxism and Leninism is its failure to respond to the conjunctural forces, determinations, and tempos of a concrete situation. The sociologist and ex–student radical Janja Lalich observes that "the conditions specific to the USSR at the time were rarely taken into consideration with any seriousness by the US activists who adopted the Marxist-Leninist organizational

---

16 Eric Hobsbawm, *The Age of Extremes: 1914–1991* (London: Abacus, 2006), 301.

17 Eddie Goldman, "PL, the Struggle at Columbia, and the Road to Irrelevance," in *You Say You Want a Revolution: SDS, PL, and Adventures in Building a Worker-Student Alliance*, ed. John F. Levin and Earl Silbar (San Francisco: 1741 Press, 2019), 200.

model for their own purposes."[18] The absence of this serious comparative analysis prevented pseudo-Leninist radicals from developing a useful strategic perspective on what needed to be done to prepare for revolution in the United States. In fact, as Max Elbaum retorts, these pseudo-Leninists were guilty of the very myopia that Lenin condemned in *Left-Wing Communism: An Infantile Disorder*—the use of unpopular and alienating tactics, an overreliance on cliché-ridden revolutionary rhetoric, the rejection of strategic alliances and compromises. Instead of overcoming these limitations, the pseudo-Leninists cultivated a "dogmatic mindset" that "reduced the complex task of building a mass-based radical party into the more formulaic process of building political sects."[19]And these sects were often only a charismatic individual away from degenerating into intense and fearful cults.

LaRouche entered the orbit of the student movement during the initial stirrings of this lurch toward Old Left ideologies and strategies. He was ready to become the pseudo-Lenin of SDS's pseudo-Leninist turn. Contrary to PL's strict workerism and the Weathermen's quixotic actionism, LaRouche offered to mold student radicals into a Marxist intelligentsia that could enlighten the working class. The magnetic LaRouche persuaded a small group of students that he was the sole possessor of the only correct revolutionary doctrine—the road map to the coming American socialist revolution. He started to train this cadre of intellectuals and build the membership of what would become NCLC in a class called the "Elementary Course in Marxist Economics" at the Free School of New York.

The Free School, known as FUNY, was established and operated by members of the May Second Movement, PL's student

18 Janja Lalich, *Bounded Choice: True Believers and Charismatic Cults* (Berkeley and Los Angeles: University of California Press, 2004), 116.

19 Max Elbaum, *Revolution in the Air: Sixties Radicals Turn to Lenin, Mao and Che* (London: Verso, 2018), 7–8.

organization, in a run-down loft above a café on East Fourteenth Street in Manhattan. The school's founders saw that American universities were complicit in the Vietnam War and hostile to socialist thought. Although many student activists felt that the university could be a base for social change, they recognized that American colleges were still deeply embedded in the US imperialist machine. In their well-known exposés, the radical left-wing magazine *Ramparts* revealed that Michigan State University had assisted counterinsurgency efforts in Vietnam and that the CIA was secretly funding the National Student Association. Left-wing students were eager to find alternative institutions where they could escape the influence of state propaganda and receive a real political education. FUNY satisfied this need and served as a haven for renegade left-wing intellectuals, such as LaRouche, who could teach classes on radical history, Marxist theory, and revolutionary praxis.

FUNY's summer 1966 catalogue lists LaRouche's class as an introductory seminar on Marxist economics. The reading list for this course included all three volumes of Marx's *Capital*, Hegel's *Science of Logic*, Rosa Luxemburg's *The Accumulation of Capital*, Lawrence Kubie's *Neurotic Distortion of the Creative Process*, the mathematical ideas of Kurt Gödel, and writings about the influence of cybernetics on American labor. LaRouche's idiosyncratic and polymathic approach to Marxist thought captivated his students. Drawing on the ideas of Marx and Luxemburg, he argued that the "reindustrialization" of America—and a new Industrial Revolution in the Third World—would solve the crises of capitalism. If the world's leaders did not listen to LaRouche's economic theories, then the capitalist system would face permanent stagnation and mass starvation.

At first glance, it may seem implausible to posit this seminar as the start of conspiratorial mutterings in the LaRouchean sect. After all, many people read Marx and Hegel without suddenly propagating dubious narratives about the Frankfurt School. Yet, as Gramsci understood, the "doctrinal" character of a group can spring more from their "concrete activity" than the "abstract content" of their doctrine.[20] Regardless of the texts on the reading list, the purpose of LaRouche's seminar was the selection and preparation of a sect. What started as a pedagogical relation between teacher and student gradually hardened into an ideological bond between guru and disciple.

LaRouche picked his recruits carefully. He filled his syllabus with complex and demanding texts to deter the uncommitted. He set an upper age limit of twenty-five, because he felt that almost all graduate students had already fallen victim to "the mind-destroying features of most liberal PhD training."[21] The older the student, the more integrated into the apparatus of the capitalist university. Once LaRouche had attracted a set of devotees, he aimed to transform them from "an inwardly frightened, alienated petit-bourgeois into a person of self-conscious moral identity and enhanced powers of general intelligence."[22] They were discouraged from enjoying the earthly delights of the 1960s counterculture, such as Bob Dylan and free love, to distinguish themselves from the rest of the student movement. LaRouche's followers needed to reject these petit-bourgeois diversions to prove that, one day, they would be capable of mobilizing the masses during a period of crisis. When he decided that his recruits were ready, LaRouche coordinated organizing efforts, or "laboratory work," to test whether they could put his revolutionary theories into practice. Yet what counted as "readiness" in this case was a commitment to LaRouche's interpretation of Marxist doctrine. Only those who accepted this highly cerebral and pseudo-Leninist version of Marxism were treated as ideal candidates for LaRouche's revolutionary intelligentsia. Although this LaRouchite sect would not develop into a full-blown cult until the early 1970s,

20 Antonio Gramsci, *Prison Notebooks: Volume III*, 277.

21 Lyn Marcus, "The Conceptual History of the Labor Committees," *The Campaigner* 7, no. 10 (October 1974): 14.

22 Ibid., 18.

LaRouche was already establishing himself as a Marxist guru and converting his disciples into arbitrary intellectuals. Other activists in the student movement even started to refer to his followers as "Marcusites." LaRouche had finally found his Leninist boomers.

Since many of the early Marcusites were graduate students at Columbia University, the famous 1968 Columbia protest became a defining event in the mythos of the LaRouche movement. In April 1968, students at Columbia protested the university's contracts with the Pentagon and its plan to construct a new gymnasium in Morningside Park in the working-class, Black neighborhood of Harlem. Demonstrations turned into occupations as students seized several campus buildings. Tony Papert, chairman of the local PL chapter and acolyte of LaRouche, led the occupation of the Low Library, where he roused fellow occupiers with talk of class conflict and revolutionary change. Following the strike, LaRouche lectured on Marxism at a frat house turned Summer Liberation School near the Columbia campus to recruit some of the students who joined Papert's Low Library barricade.

The protest at Columbia quickly became a national media sensation. Although LaRouche planned to use the strike to boost recruitment for the nascent Labor Committees, none of the major news outlets focused on Papert's role in the occupation. The *New York Times* and other newspapers portrayed Mark Rudd—the then-chairman of the Columbia SDS—as the poster boy of the strike. Yet multiple protestors recalled that Rudd fled the Low Library as soon as he heard that the university administrators had called the police.

LaRouche and his supporters were intensely suspicious of Rudd's abrupt rise to revolutionary stardom. A few people even speculated that Marcuse might have had something to do with it. It did not take much digging to unearth connections between Rudd and the German theorist. The *New York Times* mentioned that Mike Neumann, Marcuse's stepson, introduced

Rudd to the leaders of the Columbia SDS chapter. When the reporter asked Rudd about his intellectual development, he replied that he read a lot of Lenin and Marcuse during his first year or so at Columbia. Eventually, Rudd would become a leading member of a violent left-wing faction called the Weathermen (later renamed the Weather Underground) that used guerrilla warfare techniques to protest the Vietnam War and attack institutions associated with American imperialism. The LaRouchites would see Rudd's transformation into a domestic terrorist as incontrovertible proof that Marcuse turned members of the student movement into semi-fascist shock troopers.

In the first few issues of their theoretical journal *The Campaigner*, LaRouche's Labor Committees mocked the politics of the student movement. "New Left, Local Control, and Fascism," co-authored by LaRouche and his then-partner Carol Larrabee, denounced most student radicalism as proto-fascist. LaRouche and Larrabee theorized that fascism always emerges as a populist movement with a pseudo-revolutionary appeal to "community spirit" that splinters the masses into "the local control forms so absolutely indispensable to fascist tyranny by the ruling class."[23] LaRouche and Larrabee's claims were not entirely unfounded. Moderate groups at Columbia accepted Ford Foundation grants to fund a reformist initiative called Students for a Restructured University (SRU); the Ford Foundation also financed a few experiments in community control of schools in New York City. Although Rudd and other SDS members explicitly criticized the SRU's reformist agenda, LaRouche treated this co-optation of student politics as a sign that all New Left radicals were unwitting apologists for or conscious agents of a nascent fascist takeover. Only his disciplined cadre of Marcusite intellectuals was immune to the bribery of wealthy tyrants and the barbarism of the New Left.

23 Carol LaRouche and LynMarcus, "New Left, Local Control, and Fascism," *The Campaigner* 1, no. 4 (September 1968): 30.

LaRouche and his Marcusites' disdain for other student factions compounded their perception that they were the uncorrupted vanguard of an imminent American socialist revolution.

Later that year, LaRouche's New York SDS Labor Committee clashed with Rudd's Columbia SDS chapter over the New York City teachers' strike against community control of schools in Black neighborhoods. Whereas the Marcusites decided to support the United Federation of Teachers, the Columbia SDS perceived the strike as a racist backlash against the Black community's demands for greater control over their children's education. The New York Regional Committee voted to kick the Marcusites out of SDS. News of this expulsion reached the pages of the SDS newspaper *New Left Notes*. LaRouche's New York Labor Committee issued a press statement to claim that this decision violated the anti-exclusionary clause of SDS's constitution and that SDS was "falling into the trap carefully laid by the government in supporting the sabotage of the Ford Foundation . . . against working people, black and white, in the city."[24] Bernardine Dohrn, SDS interorganizational secretary and future member of the Weather Underground, dismissed their statement as "pure and simple trash" and disparaged the Labor Committee for seeing "itself as the intellectual vanguard which will bring ideas to the working class . . . not as a movement which will ally with the working class."[25] Dohrn and others judged that the Marcusite sect represented the wrong kind of pseudo-Leninism. This official expulsion from SDS resulted in a seemingly irreparable cleavage between the Marcusites and the rest of the student movement. In the coming years, LaRouche would successfully rebrand this pariah status as an inevitable consequence of political virtue and theoretical purity.

24 N.Y. Students for a Democratic Society Labor Committee, "Press Release: Issued Dec. 16 by NY Labor Committee," *New Left Notes* 3, no. 38, 4.

25 Bernardine Dohrn, "Labor Committee Statement: Pure and Simple Trash," *New Left Notes* 3, no. 38, 4.

Several months after leaving SDS, the Marcusites became a target of government harassment. From 1956 to 1971, the FBI carried out a vicious counterrevolutionary campaign known as COINTELPRO (Counterintelligence Program) to infiltrate, derail, and neutralize "subversive" organizations, such as the Black Panther Party and Ku Klux Klan. Various FBI field offices used news leaks, anonymous letters, and satirical cartoons to promote factionalism between different groups in the New Left. They understood that aggravating internal conflict would hasten the demise of the student movement. Operatives in the New York field office produced a leaflet called *The Mouse Crap Revolution*—written in what an FBI agent called "the jargon of the New Left"—to discredit Papert and exacerbate the schism between the Labor Committees and the New York student movement.[26] Although other New Left groups were subject to even more severe forms of surveillance and suppression, LaRouche and his followers fell for the COINTELPRO trap and distanced themselves further from the student movement. As the sixties crashed into the seventies, the Labor Committees' sense of isolation fed into their organizational identity.

During the third national NCLC conference in January 1971, LaRouche introduced his "Statement of Founding Principles of the National Caucus of Labor Committees."[27] The twenty-five-point statement represents LaRouche's pseudo-Leninist twist on Lenin's *What Is to Be Done?* Each point intersperses classic Leninist insights—the need for a secret and centralized apparatus of professional revolutionaries who can transmit political consciousness to the working class *from without*—with LaRouche's unique interpretations of Hegel, Feuerbach, and Marx. LaRouche insisted that only those who had attained

26 Special Agent in Charge, New York to Director, FBI, April 10, 1969, Federal Bureau of Investigation, "COINTELPRO—NEW LEFT."

27 National Caucus of Labor Committees, "Statement of Founding Principles of the National Caucus of Labor Committees," *The Campaigner* 4, no. 1 (Winter 1971): 59–60.

a mastery of philosophy, economics, and dialectics could act as the *outside agency* that would transform the working class from a passive class in itself into a revolutionary class for itself. Yet this principle betrays the elitist mentality that pervaded the LaRouche movement. These college-educated Marcusite student intellectuals assumed that the working class could not organize themselves without paternalistic guidance. This attitude reveals an incapacity to wrestle with the limitations of Lenin's proposal for a revolutionary party. They neglected the contradiction between the act of bringing consciousness to the working class and the ideal of proletarian self-emancipation. LaRouche's statement embraced this contradiction and turned his sect into a vehicle for transmitting arbitrary ideology to the presumably clueless masses.

In this statement of principles, LaRouche proposed a pseudo-Leninist organizational model to preserve the purity of his doctrine. NCLC would remain strictly centralized to prevent alien ideas from interfering with LaRouche's ideological vision. The National Committee, which LaRouche chaired, exercised complete executive and policymaking powers over the activity of every local Labor Committee. LaRouche prohibited local committees from forming alliances with other post–New Left organizations, because a "popular front" strategy would deprive him of this executive control. The disciplined centralization of NCLC reflected what Donald Parkinson calls *theoretical centralism*, whereby an organization unites around one "correct" vision of Marxist theory rather than a concrete political program (that could feasibly form the basis of coalition building with other left-wing groups).[28] The statement consolidated and formalized LaRouche's intellectual leadership over the NCLC and excluded members who wanted the organization to adopt a different strategic or theoretical direction.

---

28 Donald Parkinson, "LaRouche: A Warning for Us All," *Cosmonaut*, March 19, 2019.

The statement imposed a boundary between the "Promethean" elite of the NCLC and the "Malthusian" counter-elite of both the post–New Left (which was starting to be known as the "New Communist Movement") and the conspiratorial ruling classes. LaRouche celebrated his Prometheans as the "embryonic representatives of a new human species" that would improve the lives of the American proletariat.[29] He described the Malthusians as the agents of an anti-human force that planned to condemn humanity to an animal-like existence of fear and scarcity. This stark division of the political field would later inform NCLC's portrayals of the Frankfurt School.

During the early 1970s, NCLC centralized itself into an alternative political universe. Members quit their jobs, dropped out of school, and cut ties with family and friends to devote their lives to the task of becoming LaRouche's Promethean elite. They worked twelve-to-sixteen-hour shifts—writing articles for *The Campaigner*, printing and distributing leaflets, inducting new recruits—and lived on paltry stipends that were rarely paid. This level of commitment was relatively common among Marxist-Leninist cadres in the 1960s and 1970s. What was relatively uncommon, however, were LaRouche's methods for exerting complete domination over NCLC's internal culture.

According to former NCLC members, LaRouche launched a program of physical and psychological violence in 1973. He ordered his followers to disrupt the meetings of rival left-wing organizations, such as the Communist Party of the United States of America (CPUSA), with nunchucks, chains, and baseball bats in an aggressive campaign called "Operation Mop-Up." Reportedly, NCLC's combative "mini-phalanxes" assaulted various groups sixty times between April and September in 1973. Operation Mop-Up represents the willingness of certain NCLC members to follow wherever LaRouche led them.

---

29 National Caucus of Labor Committees, "Statement of Founding Principles," 59.

Although Operation Mop-Up demonstrated that NCLCers would sacrifice their physical safety for the cause, LaRouche demanded more. He wanted their psyches. When a follower named Chris White suffered a mental breakdown and proclaimed that the KGB and MI5 had brainwashed him into trying to assassinate the NCLC leader, LaRouche became convinced that he needed to "cleanse" the minds of his supporters. In his 1973 pamphlet *Beyond Psychoanalysis*, LaRouche claimed that he had to cure his followers' political impotence to turn them into effective socialist organizers. He subjected them to long, traumatizing "ego-stripping" sessions, in which he forced them to renounce their petit-bourgeois "little-me" ego ideal, surrender their libidinal investment in their "Mother-image," and embrace LaRouche as their father figure. He assured his disciples that these approaches were "indispensable auxiliary means for directly overcoming the fatal internal flaw of all socialist organizations, Lenin's included, up to this time."[30] LaRouche may have promised to rid his followers of their petit-bourgeois angst, but the former NCLC members Christine Berl and Harry Weinfeld testified that "what was stripped away was their very identities."[31]

LaRouche's psychologization of politics tightened his control over NCLC's collective mentality. The objective of his ego-stripping sessions was the remolding of member's identities according to LaRouche's ideal of the Promethean elite. Many NCLCers acquiesced to, or were complicit in, this treatment simply because they feared that any deviation from LaRouche's demands would hinder the progress of the organization. Furthermore, LaRouche depoliticized any resistance to his methods by suggesting that people who objected to his actions were still clinging onto their "little-me" ego. Disagreement

30 Lyn Marcus, "Beyond Psychoanalysis, *The Campaigner* 7, no. 1 (September–October 1973), 41.

31 Christine Berl and Harry Weinfield, "Letter of Resignation," *LaRouchePlanet*, April 2, 1974.

with LaRouche was a symptom of psychic disorder rather than the expression of a sincere political belief. LaRouche would later build on this claim and insist that anyone who opposed him was a victim of CIA brainwashing. What needed to be explained, however, was the identity of the brainwashers. This is where the Frankfurt School figured in NCLC's increasingly conspiratorial vision of politics.

This early history of the LaRouchites serves as a prelude to their ideological attacks on the Frankfurt School. Hostility to the legacy of the New Left remained a consistent feature of NCLC's narratives. They regarded the other radical factions of the post–New Left as brainwashed collaborators in an elite-engineered project. Left-wing sectarianism was represented as a simple conflict between LaRouchite ideology and "Malthusian" or "petit-bourgeois" ideas. Over the course of the 1970s, LaRouche would reinforce this boundary by arguing that only NCLC's alternative apparatus of knowledge production could expose the brainwashing of the Frankfurt School.

## Rockefeller Fascism: Zombies in America, Brainwashers in Frankfurt

On January 20, 1974, *The New York Times* published an article on the LaRouche movement entitled "How a Radical-Left Group Moved Toward Savagery." Paul Montgomery, the journalist behind this report, had interviewed several former NCLC members who attested that LaRouche's technique of "ego-stripping" was essentially a means of silencing dissent within the organization. Unsurprisingly, LaRouche dismissed these allegations as "wild slanders and libels."[32] He saw Montgomery's article as part of an orchestrated campaign to discredit the only political force with an effective "program

32 Marcus, "The Conceptual History of the Labor Committees," 9.

and strategy for establishing a new age for mankind."[33] And LaRouche claimed to know exactly who was behind this affront to NCLC's public reputation: the Rockefellers.

The Rockefellers are often described as the unofficial royal family of America's ruling class. Their name is virtually synonymous with wealth and power. In the late 1800s, John D. Rockefeller, the patriarch of Standard Oil, established a vast monopoly on the petroleum industry by conspiring against his competitors. His son, John D. Rockefeller Jr., turned to philanthropy to atone for his father's sins. Mighty rivers of money flowed from the Rockefeller Foundation to support various cultural and scientific endeavours, including controversial research on eugenics and population control. Other notable family members include Nelson Rockefeller, who served as the governor of New York (1959–73) and the US vice president (1974–77). Their political and economic activities usually attracted heavy opposition and criticism. In 1965, New Left activists organized anti-apartheid sit-ins at the headquarters of the Rockefeller-owned Chase Manhattan Bank. Several years later, student radicals gathered outside Nelson Rockefeller's office to protest his decision to violently repress the Attica Prison riot. Given this context, it is understandable that LaRouche would choose the Rockefellers as the new villains in his conspiratorial view of history. Yet his writings on the threat of "Rockefeller Fascism" would often lump together unrelated events and phenomena as if they formed a unified global agenda.

From roughly 1974 onwards, LaRouche and his followers were convinced that the Rockefeller family was working to impose a Malthusian "genocidal zero-growth project" on the world's population.[34] In his 1974 *Campaigner* article "The Real CIA: The Rockefeller's Fascist Establishment," LaRouche

33 Ibid.

34 Lyn Marcus, "The Real CIA: The Rockefeller's Fascist Establishment," *The Campaigner* 7, no. 6 (April 1974): 7.

"exposed" the various financial, political, and military operatives who furthered the aims of Rockefeller Fascism. Even the New Left, according to LaRouche, was an instrument of this counterinsurgency apparatus. The agents of Rockefeller Fascism allegedly invented the New Left in the 1960s to prevent the radicalization of college youth. They aimed to divert student organizers from the established socialist parties and funnel these young radicals into the groupuscules of an expanding counterrevolutionary initiative. LaRouche revived PL's rumors about Marcuse to argue that this supposed Father of the New Left had devised a reactionary ideology to convert potential revolutionaries into Rockefeller's fascist goons. There were even a few scraps of evidence to back up this hypothesis. Like many other scholars at American universities, Marcuse solicited Rockefeller Foundation grants to complete work on several of his books, such as his 1958 anti-communist tract *Soviet Marxism* and his 1964 bestseller *One-Dimensional Man*. Additionally, LaRouche pointed out that Rudd's Weathermen faction allegedly received funding from the Ford Foundation through Marcuse's "nephew." (This is a reference to the East Side Service Organization [ESSO], of which Marcuse's stepson Tom Neumann was a member. Apparently, the Ford Foundation money was given to ESSO through the Institute for Policy Studies.) Consequently, LaRouche reframed NCLC's expulsion from SDS and its dispute with Rudd and Dohrn as a major episode in the world-historical clash between his Promethean elite and the Rockefeller-Marcuse-Malthusian counter-elite.

In his anti–Rockefeller Fascism screeds, LaRouche psychoanalyzed his opponents and called them victims of CIA brainwashing. He warned that the CIA could turn people into "programmed zombies."[35] Whereas his closest devotees were immune to CIA psychic manipulation, LaRouche's critics—anyone who doubted his byzantine allegations—suffered from

35 Lyn Marcus, "Will You Eat Shit for Rockefeller's CIA?," *New Solidarity* IV, no. 38 (January 11, 1974): 11.

a neurotic blockage. LaRouche inflated the student movement's critique of the capitalist university to declare that nearly every humanities and social sciences department in the United States was a CIA branch operation. Whenever a tenured historian, sociologist, or philosopher derided conspiracy theorizing, for instance, they were merely concealing their own participation in Rockefeller's counterrevolution. None of these CIA establishment intellectuals wanted the masses to know that global genocide was imminent. Unlike these academic lackeys, LaRouche promised to free people from the CIA's psychic enslavement. To accomplish this mission, NCLC established a counterintelligence division that would report on the institutional networks of Rockefeller Fascism.

The New Solidarity International Press Service, which produced the weekly newsmagazine *Executive Intelligence Review* (*EIR*), operated as an intellectual laboratory for LaRouche's expansive conspiratorial vision of politics. The pages of *EIR* blended genuine reporting—LaRouche's operatives gained White House press accreditations and participated in many presidential press conferences during the Ford and Carter administrations—with wild rumors about the malignancy of Rockefeller Fascism. LaRouche hoped that this publication, as well as such other NCLC periodicals as *New Solidarity* and *The Campaigner*, would demonstrate that his followers were the only activists with enough courage and competence to expose the Malthusian counter-elite.

LaRouche's intense faith in the political impact of the published word may have been another Leninist inheritance. In *What Is to Be Done?*, Lenin recommends a form of propaganda known as "exposure literature" (pamphlets, newspaper articles, and so on) that publicizes all instances of political repression in capitalist society. The revolutionary intelligentsia must disseminate these exposures to develop the workers' economic battle against their employers into a wider counter-hegemonic struggle against the bourgeois state. According to

Lenin, "Political exposures in themselves serve as a powerful instrument for *disintegrating* the system we oppose."[36] Yet NCLC's exposure literature did less to reveal real scandals and injustices and more to articulate LaRouche's disdain for whatever individual or group he saw as part of the Rockefeller-allied elite.

Ironically, other organizations in the post–New Left milieu suspected that this weird and insular cult was itself a CIA-funded agent provocateur. Mike Zagarell, the author of the 1975 article "Phony 'Labor' Party Exposed as CIA Front" in the CPUSA-affiliated newspaper *Daily World*, speculated that the CIA was paying the LaRouchites through secret trust funds to gather intelligence about left-wing radicals.[37] To add to the irony and intrigue, it later turned out that the FBI was secretly feeding false information about NCLC to CPUSA to inflame tensions between the two groups. Although Zagarell's hit piece is likely just another example of FBI-induced sectarianism, it correctly noted that the LaRouchites had assembled a series of counterintelligence reports on the prominent CPUSA leader Angela Davis. In these reports, NCLC expressed deep concerns about Davis's association with two German professors: Marcuse and Adorno.

According to a 1974 *EIR* Special Report, Marcuse and Adorno belonged to an international network of CIA intellectuals that aimed to disrupt communist parties in Europe and America. When Davis was their student, Marcuse and Adorno subjected her to a "CIA zombie brainwash program" to convert her into an agent of "protofascist nihilism."[38] The report adds

36 V. I. Lenin, *Essential Works of Lenin: "What Is to Be Done?" and Other Writings* (New York: Dover, 1987), 120.

37 Mike Zagarell, "Phony 'Labor' Party Exposed as CIA Front," *Daily World*, September 18, 1975, 1.

38 Executive Intelligence Review, "Angela Davis: The Offer the CPUSA Could Not Refuse," *Executive Intelligence Review* 1, no. 17 (August 26, 1974): 31.

that "Marcuse's cronies in the CIA academic social democracy" orchestrated Davis's ban from teaching philosophy at UCLA and her subsequent imprisonment to boost recruitment for the CPUSA, which supposedly diverted young radicals from authentically revolutionary groups like NCLC.[39]

The trope of brainwashing functioned both to discredit opposition to LaRouche and generate commitment to his arbitrary ideology. The rhetorical psychologization of politics divided people into two groups: LaRouche's supporters and Rockefeller's brainwashed victims (and their brainwashers). In turn, NCLCers felt compelled to produce more exposure literature—pamphlets, leaflets, newspapers—to uncover these enemies and enlighten the masses. NCLC needed to spread "consciousness" to the working class to save them from the Frankfurt School's "zombie brainwashing" and Rockefeller's "genocidal policies." None of the other left-wing organizations in the United States, according to LaRouche, were immune to the Frankfurt School's psychological manipulation, because their members had not undergone rigorous "ego-stripping" sessions to inoculate themselves against the CIA's mental warfare. Only LaRouche and his devoted followers were psychologically fit enough to rescue the workers of the world.

The theme of the Frankfurt School as a secret brainwashing operation reappeared in a 1977 *EIR* counterintelligence report entitled "Fascist Wave of 'New Left' Terrorism Under Way." The first half of this report featured an article, penned by LaRouche, that characterized the recent acts of left-wing terrorism—the Red Brigades in Italy, the Red Army Faction in West Germany—as skirmishes in an incipient environmentalist takeover. The second half of the report, which was subtitled "New Left Journals Shape Fascist Debates," claimed that *New German Critique* (*NGC*) and *Radical America* were engaging in an "open debate" about "the creation of a belief structure

39 Ibid., 32.

appropriate to a new fascist movement."[40] The evidence for this assertion is meager. *NGC* had put out a special issue on Ernst Bloch; *Radical America* had printed an article on the New England–based anti-nuclear coalition Clamshell Alliance. Nonetheless, LaRouche declared that the editors of these journals must be fascists because they were influenced by the Frankfurt School. LaRouche's targeting of post–New Left publications reflected the ongoing sectarian tension between NCLC and their former rivals. Although journals like *NGC* were founded to counter the persistent infighting of the American left, LaRouche was less interested in combating factionalism and more concerned about seeking enemies toward whom he could direct his followers' animus.

The report goes on to claim that Anglo-American intelligence agencies established the Frankfurt School in the 1920s. During their exile in the United States, the Frankfurt School conducted "intensive profile studies of the German Nazi and Italian fascist models" to identify techniques for turning teenagers into terrorists.[41] The report may be referring to the Frankfurt School's involvement in the American Jewish Committee's *Studies in Prejudice* series, which resulted in the publication of such groundbreaking texts as *The Authoritarian Personality* and *Prophets of Deceit*. Although the editors of this series—Max Horkheimer and Samuel H. Flowerman—hoped that these studies would help to counter intergroup prejudice, LaRouche and his followers asserted that the Frankfurt School wanted to import European-style fascism to the United States. Consequently, anyone who was even remotely associated with the Frankfurt School—Rudd, Davis, *NGC*, *Radical America*—was nothing more than a fascist in training.

The deliberate reinterpretation of a text's meaning—that a study of protofascist tendencies was in fact a blueprint

40 Counterintelligence, "New Left Journals Shape Fascist Debates," *Executive Intelligence Review* IV, no. 49 (December 6, 1977): 6.

41 Ibid., 6.

for fascism—is common to all LaRouchite accounts of the Frankfurt School. What may appear to be an absurd misunderstanding, however, is the result of a special kind of LaRouchean reading. Whereas the brainwashed reader may simply skim the surface of a text, LaRouchites were allegedly capable of deciphering the hidden meaning that lurked beneath the manifest content. The application of geometrical thinking to historical events, LaRouche averred, allowed the interpreter to "judge which of the apparent facts are real and which represent illusion."[42] The method of LaRouchean analysis may sound impressive, yet it tended to yield the same result: the reinforcement of the boundary between the NCLC elite and their enemies. These special "geometric" readings of the Frankfurt School produced an image of "the enemy" against which the LaRouche movement could continually define itself as an intellectual elite. In the 1970s and 1980s, NCLC would expand this notion of an elite to include their new radical right-wing and conservative allies. These shifting political affiliations would affect the tone and scale of their polemics against the Frankfurt School.

## Aristotle's Secrets: Adorno, Marcuse, and the Rock-Drug-Sex Counterculture

The 1970s was a transformative period for the LaRouchites. As the decade dragged on, the political activity of NCLC shifted away from their original objective of leading a socialist revolution. By the mid-1970s, LaRouche was actively trying to distinguish his movement from the "proto-fascist" rabble of the post–New Left. Yet in their efforts to distance themselves from the left, the LaRouchites strayed into unexpected ideological territory. Increasingly, LaRouche began to fraternize

42 Marcus, "The Real CIA," 6.

with leaders of radical right organizations and mainstream Republican politicians. What were the reasons for NCLC's political turn? How did this cadre of self-professed Leninist radicals rebrand itself as a respectable outfit of right-leaning white-collar professionals?

In his 1979 *National Review* tell-all exposé of the LaRouche movement, a former NCLCer (and FBI informant) Gregory F. Rose recalls a 1975 internal "Security Memorandum" that proposed the idea of working with radical right and Republican groups.[43] Many organizations on the American right, such as the American Conservative Union, opposed the liberal republicanism of then–Vice President Nelson Rockefeller. LaRouchites assumed that these groups might help NCLC to raise more money for their sweeping ideological struggle against Rockefeller Fascism. The plan was partly a success. From 1975, the NCLC enjoyed a range of somewhat productive collaborations with like-minded right-wing allies. For instance, the leader of the neo-Nazi and anti-Rockefeller Liberty Lobby Willis Carto contributed $90,000 to LaRouche's first presidential campaign in 1976. Even if NCLC's move to the right was merely a cynical ploy to grab more funds for LaRouche's campaigns, it also mirrored the political journeys of many Americans in the 1970s who would eventually vote for Ronald Reagan.

To attract potential supporters and financial backers, LaRouche revamped NCLC's organizational identity. After all, no Republican in the 1970s would have wanted to consort with a group of professional socialist revolutionaries. As NCLC members worked to cultivate ties with both mainstream and fringe conservative groups, they started to sanitize their cultic vocabulary. The "revolutionary intelligentsia" became the "Neoplatonist elite;" the "working class" turned into "the sheep." In his keynote address at the first International Caucus of Labor Committees conference in 1979, LaRouche

43 Gregory F. Rose, "The Swarmy Life and Times of the NCLC," *National Review*, March 30, 1979, 409–13.

described his followers as "shepherds of humanity."[44] Instead of bringing revolutionary ideas to the workers, NCLC would guide the masses out of their "pitiful state of sheep-likeness."[45] Although LaRouche and his disciples had abandoned their pseudo-Leninist pretensions, the underlying structure of their arbitrary ideology (and organizational form) remained the same: NCLC was an elite that would save the passive masses and vanquish a sinister counter-elite. And, most importantly, NCLC members could only accomplish these objectives if they embodied LaRouche's Neoplatonic ideal.

In his 1978 essay "The Secrets Known Only to the Inner Elites," LaRouche depicted the history of Western civilization as a titanic struggle between two clandestine forces: the Neoplatonic elite and the Aristotelian counter-elite. Whereas the Neoplatonists wished to advance human civilization and educate the masses, the Aristotelians wanted to subjugate the global population and maintain their status as oligarchical rulers. The members of this counter-elite, which had prevailed for more than two thousand years, included such famous figures as St. Thomas Aquinas, Isaac Newton, T. S. Eliot, and Noam Chomsky. LaRouche argued that these Aristotelians had concealed their role in world history by establishing a "controlled environment" that spread "mythologies" through mass media channels to confuse and deceive humanity.[46] Although they had operated under a variety of guises to suppress human achievement, LaRouche claimed that he could uncover the various nodes of this Aristotelian network to bring an end to this ancient conspiracy.

Why did LaRouche choose to describe NCLC's ideological struggle as a fight of the Neoplatonists against the Aristotelians?

44 Lyndon LaRouche Jr., "What Are the Labor Committees Today?," *The Campaigner* 13, no. 2 (March 1980): 51.

45 Ibid., 51.

46 Lyndon H. LaRouche Jr., "The Secrets Known Only to the Inner Elites," *The Campaigner* 11, no. 3-4 (May–June 1978): 7.

The writer George Johnson speculates that LaRouche may have been drawn to Plato's concept of the "philosopher-kings."[47] To put it quite crudely, Platonists favor the metaphysical over the empirical. They hold that there is a sphere of eternal Ideas or Forms that transcends the material world of ephemeral objects. The concrete and worldly instantiations of beauty and justice—a handsome man, the constitutional documents of a nation-state—are only pale shadows of the pure Absolute Ideas of Beauty and Justice. In *The Republic*, Plato proposes that a group of wise philosopher-kings should govern societies because only they can grasp the true essence of Justice. Something about this blueprint for an ideal society must have appealed to the LaRouchites, who prided themselves on their superior intellectual powers. The method of LaRouchean reading was essentially a technique for revealing the true form of history—a conflict between two elites—that lurked beneath the random drift of historical events. According to LaRouche, this ability to see into the proper essence of things prepared NCLC for the task of creating a New Renaissance.

Aristotelians, however, are known to deal with things in the tangible world rather than Ideas that inhabit some timeless realm. Whereas Plato contemplated the Absolutes, Aristotle gathered and classified specimens. LaRouche held that this favoring of the empirical over the metaphysical was the mark of an anti-human relativism. This charge of relativism introduced strains of cultural racism into LaRouchean ideology. As NCLC gravitated toward the right, LaRouche and his followers started to glorify Western civilization—especially classical German culture—over non-European barbarism. The elitist mentality of NCLC—a vocal celebration of European high culture and the demonization of other, "lower" cultures—aligned in surprising ways with the nascent New Right's

47 George Johnson, *Architects of Fear: Conspiracy Theories and Paranoia in American Politics* (Los Angeles: Jeremy P. Tarcher, 1983), 193.

organized backlash against the 1960s counterculture. Despite its esoteric musings on the history of philosophy and science, LaRouche's overarching narrative about an age-old conflict between two elites offered a useful alternative explanation for the rise of rock music, the increased visibility of LGBTQ+ communities, and the achievements of the women's movement.

In "The Secrets Known Only to the Inner Elites," LaRouche argued the Aristotelian oligarchy spearheaded the "rock-drug-sex counterculture."[48] He alleged that the Frankfurt School participated in this conspiracy to destroy tonal music and erode the distinction between humans and animals. No longer were Adorno and Marcuse perceived as simply a couple of CIA operatives who stage-managed some New Left activists. LaRouche's new version of world history recast these thinkers as the semi-magical practitioners of an Aristotelian secret knowledge and the architects of myths—rock music, free love, drug consumption—that hypnotized the masses. This disdain for popular culture manifested in a kind of LaRouchean cultural criticism that condemned mainstream entertainment as Aristotelian brainwashing.

Various NCLC writers worked to uncover the exact nature of the Frankfurt School's role in the Aristotelian plot. Drawing on the techniques of LaRouchean reading, NCLCers reinterpreted Adorno's writings on music, mass culture, and authoritarianism. Each NCLC piece on Adorno refashioned this masterful critic of the culture industry into the mastermind of the 1960s counterculture. They plucked quotations from Adorno's work and twisted their meaning to match LaRouche's descriptions of the Aristotelian conspiracy. As NCLC authors charted this plot, they displayed what Michael Barkun calls a "fondness for reciprocal citation."[49] Many of the references in these articles

48 LaRouche, "The Secrets Known Only to the Inner Elites," 24.

49 Michael Barkun, *A Culture of Conspiracy: Apocalyptic Visions in Contemporary America* (Berkeley and Los Angeles: University of California Press), 28.

refer the reader to another LaRouchite publication. The overall effect of this insular citational practice was a kind of "pseudo-confirmation" that reinforced the boundaries of NCLC's arbitrary ideology.[50] Over a decade or so, a series of articles in *New Solidarity*, *The Campaigner*, and *Executive Intelligence Review* produced a pseudo-confirmed image of Adorno that dominated LaRouchean conceptions of the Frankfurt School.

In his 1977 *New Solidarity* article "The Frankfurt School's Assault on Music," Peter Wyer described heavy rock as an "open expression of fascist ideology."[51] The distorted guitar riffs and suggestive lyrics of popular rock bands, Wyers explained, represented nothing more than a tasteless outburst of cultural relativism that demolished the distinction between humans and beasts. Wyer insisted that this genre was the product of a conspiratorial operation against music itself. The leaders of this scheme wanted to accomplish two objectives: 1) to subvert musical form, and 2) to convert music into a tool of psychological warfare. The British intelligence–created and Rockefeller-controlled Frankfurt School—that amoral crew of Aristotelian mythmakers—was chosen to fulfil these goals.

The Frankfurt School conspiracy, as Wyer characterized it, infiltrated a broad range of intellectual fields, such as philosophy and musicology, during the twentieth century. As the Frankfurt School was expanding its influence, it promoted "the notion of the inevitable collapse of the individual's potential to determine the course of history through the exercise of the creative faculties of mind, to alter society, to master nature without destroying nature."[52] In this warped portrayal of Critical Theory, Wyer dulls the dialectical edge of Adorno and Horkheimer's theoretical output and misrepresents these thinkers as simple anti-Enlightenment irrationalists. According

50 Ibid., 28.

51 Peter Wyer, "The Frankfurt School's Assault on Music," *New Solidarity* (March 8, 1977): 4.

52 Ibid., 4.

to Wyer, this blunt anti-human philosophy was the theoretical basis for the weaponization of music as an instrument of mass brainwashing.

The responsibility for developing these brainwashing techniques fell to Adorno. Inspired by his mentor Arnold Schoenberg, Adorno turned his piano into an instrument of torture and developed an approach to atonal music that would have devastating psychic consequences. Whereas the real Adorno theorized that Schoenberg's atonal compositions represented a form of truly autonomous art, Wyer's Adorno hypothesized that atonality could help to control the masses psychologically. Wyer contrasted this notion of atonality with LaRouchean beliefs about tonal structure, a harmonious ordering of musical notes that could allegedly stimulate the processes of Neoplatonic reason. Appreciation of tonality, as exemplified by LaRouche's passion for Beethoven, distinguished the Neoplatonic elite from the bestial masses. Those who subjected themselves to the chaos of atonal music—Schoenberg's 1910 song cycle *The Book of the Hanging Gardens* or, say, Led Zeppelin's 1975 album *Physical Graffiti*—suffered a terrible affective response that simulated symptoms of panic, confusion, and anxiety. Adorno and his Frankfurt School co-conspirators hoped that this widespread breakdown of cognitive control—this erosion of the individual—would tame the masses into unthinking sheep.

As Wyer explained, Adorno decided to use the medium of radio to perform this psychological assault. During his exile in the United States, Adorno joined the Rockefeller-funded Princeton Radio Research Project to devise methods for broadcasting atonal music to the listening public. Adorno's classification of different listener types in his 1962 book *Introduction to the Sociology of Music*, which drew on his Princeton Radio Research Project research, served as a blueprint for converting commercial radio stations into transmitters of mass psychic disorder. In Wyer's account, Adorno exercised near total control over the production and dissemination of music in the United States.

Wyer's brief article in *New Solidarity* introduced an image of Adorno that persisted in the pages of LaRouchite publications. Whenever NCLC writers needed to find someone to blame for the popularity of rock music, they often chose Adorno. A year or so later, Wyer speculated in another article in *The Campaigner* that Adorno even invented the concept of an authoritarian personality to discourage parents from limiting their children's radio consumption. *The Authoritarian Personality*, Wyer claimed, argued that strict childrearing practices were tantamount to fascism. As parents worried about being seen as repressive or tyrannical, children were exposed to "the pornographic filth of rock music," which had been "suitably flavored with the drones of Ravi Shankar and the still more primitive degradation of 'Latin music.'"[53] As Wyer put it, Adorno's attack on parental authority eventually reduced the American population to the "cultural status of aboriginal peoples."[54]

Elements of cultural racism pervade Wyer's writings on Adorno and music. He implied that the LaRouchites were the arbiters of a superior Western cultural tradition and that any musical genre or style that deviated from this traditional heritage—jazz, blues, atonal composition—reflected a mental regression in humanity. The creative contributions of Black musicians, which influenced the birth of rock music more than Adorno ever did, were portrayed as "primitive" and "barbaric." Although it is clearly absurd to draw a straight line of causality from Schoenberg to Adorno to George Harrison, the sheer expansiveness of the imagined Aristotelian plot allowed Wyer and others to blame a range of so-called cultural depravities on a unified antagonistic force.

53 Peter Wyer, "Draft Proposal for a Heinrich Schenker Foundation for Musical Science," *The Campaigner* 11, no. 6 (August 1978): 25.

54 Ibid., 25.

For the LaRouchites, Adorno was not just a rock 'n' roller —he was also a drug pusher. In the late 1970s, LaRouche commissioned a 100-member research team to document the involvement of the British royal family—key figures in the Aristotelian elite—in the global drug trade. In 1978, he published the results of their inquiry, *Dope, Inc.: Britain's Opium War against the U.S.*, which identified both Adorno and the Beatles as participants in a shadowy British plot. According to *Dope, Inc.*, the British royal family financed the music of the Beatles to encourage drug consumption in America.[55] Yet the Fab Four would never have succeeded without Adorno's musicological theories. LaRouche and his acolytes distorted a quote from *Introduction to the Sociology of Music* to insinuate Adorno wanted Americans to become hooked on pop music. This fabricated link between Adorno and the Beatles appeared to confirm LaRouche's claim that the Frankfurt School orchestrated the rise of the 1960s counterculture, the increase in the use of narcotics, and the dominance of the mass media.

LaRouchites also claimed to uncover Adorno's influence in another domain of popular culture: television. In 1982, Christina Nelson Huth—then the features editor of *EIR* and a one-time candidate for the Virginia House of Delegates—asserted that Adorno undermined the morale of the American people through the promotion of soap operas.[56] Apparently, Adorno and the Princeton Radio Research Project planned the production of soap operas to get American audiences addicted to watching television. As millions of viewers faithfully tuned in to their favorite shows, they would gradually become passive and accept genocidal policies. The transformation of the

55 US Labor Party, *Dope, Inc.: Britain's Opium War Against the U.S.* (New York: The New Benjamin Franklin Publishing Company, 1978), 373.

56 Christina Nelson Huth, "How Soap Opera Was Designed to Undercut America's Morality," *Executive Intelligence Review* 9, no. 31 (September 7, 1982): 59–61.

American people into a docile mass through the consumption of such Frankfurt School–manufactured "mythologies" as "Hey Jude" and *Dallas* would allow the Aristotelian elite to take over the United States without resistance.

Ironically, the LaRouchites' articles about Adorno's influence on the mass media echoed his own critiques of the culture industry. Adorno argued that the culture industry constituted a "means for fettering consciousness" that impeded "the development of autonomous, independent individuals who judge and decide consciously for themselves."[57] Instead of plotting to dull the critical capacities of the masses, Adorno desired "the emancipation for which human beings are as ripe as the productive forces of the epoch permit."[58] The method of LaRouchean reading dismissed these critiques as irrelevant ephemera. Instead, Adorno's brief—and deeply ambivalent—involvement in the Princeton Radio Research Project proved that the overall goal of his career was to manipulate the masses. The only true reading of Adorno, according to LaRouchite publications, was the one that confirmed his place in an overarching Aristotelian plot. The constant practice of reciprocal citation—a mark of arbitrary intellectual production—elevated this claim to the level of an accepted truth in LaRouchean lore.

What distinguished Adorno's critique of the culture industry from the LaRouchean notion of Aristotelian brainwashing was the question of agency. Adorno observed that "television as ideology is not the result of evil intentions, perhaps not even of the incompetence of those involved, but rather is imposed by demonic objective spirit."[59] The consciousness-numbing effects of commercial television reflected the functioning of a social totality that enforced commodification, standardization, and

57 Theodor W. Adorno, *The Culture Industry* (Abingdon, UK: Routledge, 2001), 106.

58 Ibid., 106.

59 Theodor W. Adorno, *Critical Models: Interventions and Catchwords* (New York: Columbia University Press, 2005), 69.

pseudo-individuality. The tools of Enlightenment rationality, which Adorno and Horkheimer characterized as the domination of nature and the dispelling of traditional myth, had forged a rationalistic order of mass deception. Although it would be possible to temporarily resist the pressure of this objective force, Adorno saw that it could never become the instrument of individual will. Unlike Adorno, the LaRouchites searched for the conscious manipulators behind the culture industry's psychic domination. After all, the notion that a secret elite governs the world implies that a different and more benevolent elite could conceivably gain control of this ruling apparatus. Essentially, LaRouchean cultural criticism worked to reaffirm the belief that NCLC represented a leading organization of philosopher-kings that could rescue humanity from a twisted mass culture.

The most dangerous feature of this new mass culture, according to LaRouche, was casual sex. In the 1987 edition of his autobiography *The Power of Reason*, LaRouche described Marcuse's *One-Dimensional Man* as a blueprint for building the "left-fascist character."[60] The life of the left-fascist, LaRouche argued, revolved around the glorification of the rock-drug-sex counterculture. As soon as these left-fascists were reduced to their bestial urges, they would be recruited into "sensitivity groups" and compelled to participate in "lesbian and male-homosexual practices."[61] In the 1960s, gay liberation activists set up sensitivity groups as a form of consciousness raising to overcome feelings of fear and shame in the LGBTQ+ community. Contrary to LaRouche's homophobic musings, these groups did not have the power to turn people gay. Instead of seeing gay liberation as a movement to obtain acceptance and equality, LaRouche believed that any efforts to destigmatize non-heteronormative sexualities were part of a larger Aristotelian plot to exterminate humanity.

---

60 Lyndon H. LaRouche, Jr., *The Power of Reason: 1988 An Autobiography* (Washington, DC: Executive Intelligence Review, 1987), 115.

61 Ibid., 123.

The outcome of the Frankfurt School's rock-drug-sex counterculture was, in LaRouche's words, "the apocalyptic peril of AIDS."[62] In the early stages of the HIV/AIDS pandemic, people assumed that this disease only affected men who had sex with men. For example, the Center for Disease Control initially referred to AIDs as "gay-related immunodeficiency." Many homophobic conservatives regarded this condition as a kind of divine punishment for homosexuality. Similarly, LaRouche actively stigmatized gay people during the crisis. In 1986 and 1987, LaRouche's organizations sponsored ballot initiatives in California that would have quarantined people with AIDS and sanctioned mandatory HIV testing for the general population. As the HIV/AIDS crisis worsened, LaRouche's writings and campaigns reframed the historic advances of the gay liberation movement as trivial ruses of an oligarchical conspiracy to infect America with disease.

The 1970s and 1980s saw a strategic intellectual convergence between LaRouche's NCLC and the forces of cultural conservatism. The LaRouchites blamed the Frankfurt School (and other supposed members of the Aristotelian elite) for the same cultural trends—rock music, free love, feminism, LGBTQ+ activism, the waning of the patriarchal family—that the New Right lamented in their illiberal jeremiads. Of course, the LaRouchites had always been somewhat hostile to the cultural and political expressions of the 1960s counterculture. By the mid-1980s, this hostility had become almost indistinguishable from the rhetoric of the religious right. Many of these similarities were opportunistic efforts to secure more supporters, donors, and allies during the nation's rightward turn under the presidency of Ronald Reagan. Although the core structure of LaRouche's arbitrary ideology remained the same (an elite versus a counter-elite), the surface level of their arguments increasingly reflected right-wing anxieties. Consequently,

62 Ibid., 182.

criticism of the Frankfurt School in LaRouchite publications became more intelligible to a wider conservative audience. Eventually, this interweaving of LaRouchean "exposure literature" and New Right polemic would give rise to the claim that the Frankfurt School produced "political correctness" to undermine the United States.

## The Authoritarian Personality on Trial: The New Dark Age and Political Correctness

In 1988, LaRouche was taken to trial on charges of mail fraud, conspiracy to commit mail fraud, and tax evasion. During the court proceedings, the Assistant US Attorney Kent Robinson demonstrated that LaRouche and his staff solicited $34 million in loans that they never intended to repay. Although NCLC staff told lenders that their loans would support political campaigns, Robinson proved that most of this money was used to maintain and renovate LaRouche's 172-acre estate in Leesburg, Virginia. LaRouche was sentenced to fifteen years in prison. He was released on parole in 1994.

The first day of LaRouche's trial was full of courtroom drama. In his opening statement, LaRouche's defense lawyer Odin P. Anderson warned the jury that the prosecution would attempt to portray LaRouche as an "authoritarian personality" who forced his followers to participate in a conspiracy to commit mail fraud.[63] The prosecution's case, Anderson seemed to imply, rested on a conspiracy theory that was "formerly called the Authoritarian Personality and was developed in

63 Don McCoy, "Transcript of Opening Statements and Testimony of Elisabeth Sexton on the First Day of Trial," *United States of America v. Lyndon LaRouche, et al*, The United States District Court Eastern District of VA, Alexandria Division, November 21, 1988, Alexandria, Virginia, 82.

Europe during the 1930s by a bunch of disgruntled Marxists."[64] At this point, Robinson objected. The judge responded, "Objection sustained. This is not a proper opening statement. I am not going to go back to the early thirties in opening statement [*sic*] or in the testimony of witnesses."[65]

Three days before Anderson made his opening statement, *EIR* had published the first installment of Michael J. Minnicino's three-part essay "The 'Authoritarian Personality': An Anti-Western Hoax." That issue's editorial warned readers that "the real object of the anti-LaRouche court cases [was to continue] the Marxist-inspired war to destroy what they call 'the authoritarian personality.'"[66] Minnicino's essay added more characters, such as Erich Fromm and Max Horkheimer, to the LaRouchites' anti–Frankfurt School narrative. It claimed that the Soviet Union had founded the Institute for Social Research as a "cultural warfare operation against the West" to "undermine Judeo-Christian culture."[67] Supposedly, this covert Marxist project had targeted LaRouche because he was a significant defender of Western values. For Minnicino, the West needed LaRouche's authoritarian personality to protect itself from the Frankfurt School's "unproven (and unprovable) cult nonsense."[68]

The whole essay is rife with strange mistakes. Minnicino argues that a taken-out-of-context sentence from Georg Lukács's 1962 preface to *The Theory of the Novel*—"Who will save us from Western Civilization?"—served as the semi-official motto of the Frankfurt School. (Ironically, this preface featured Lukács's famous characterization of the Frankfurt

64 Ibid., 82.

65 Ibid.

66 Nora Hamerman, "From the Editor," *Executive Intelligence Review* 15, no. 46 (November 18, 1988): 1.

67 Michael J. Minnicino, "The 'Authoritarian Personality': An Anti-Western Hoax," *Executive Intelligence Review* 15, no. 46 (November 18, 1988): 28–9.

68 Ibid., 29.

Schoolers as the apolitical and detached guests of a "Grand Hotel Abyss"). He defines the authoritarian personality as "anyone who thinks that scientific and technological progress can and should occur under capitalism," even though none of the scales in the 1950 study *The Authoritarian Personality* measured this belief.[69] Despite the well-known fact that Adorno and Horkheimer critiqued mass culture, Minnicino states that the Frankfurt School "manufactured forms of culture—they called their enterprise a 'culture industry'—to undermine Western civilization and the power of reason itself."[70] This LaRouchean reading ignores the actual arguments of these German critical theorists and instead promises to reveal that the Frankfurt School was an anti-Western force that sought to overthrow moral tradition and capitalist enterprise.

The concept of the authoritarian personality, according to Minnicino, was an ideological weapon to dismiss strong-willed and rational leaders like LaRouche. The "vicious Dr. Horkheimer," Minnicino wrote, conceived of the "authoritarian personality hoax" to "discredit republicanism" and "protect Marxism."[71] The Frankfurt School wanted to portray anyone who defended capitalist technological progress as a fascist in disguise to induce "cultural pessimism" in the American population. Horkheimer's hoax managed to trick Americans into becoming pliant liberals who could not resist this Soviet-sponsored threat to Western civilization. Instead of protecting the cultural heritage of the West, these liberals succumbed to Marcuse's *liberating tolerance*: "intolerance against movements from the Right, and tolerance of movements from the Left."[72]

For Minnicino, the Frankfurt School's work presented a road map to the 1960s social revolution. He argued that "almost every concept and catch-phrase of the 1960s" could be

69 Ibid., 28.
70 Ibid., 31.
71 Ibid., 28.
72 Ibid., 30.

found "verbatim" in the school's 1936 research project *Studies on Authority and the Family*.[73] Like LaRouche, Minnicino regarded the sixties ferment as a plot to distance the youth from the heights of Western culture and the goals of capitalism rather than a genuine revolt against social conformity, racial and gender inequality, and American militarism. LaRouche's court case was simply another skirmish in this war against the West.

While he was serving jail time in federal prison in 1989, LaRouche reaffirmed his mission to save the West from a "New Dark Age." According to LaRouche, Lukács devised a plan to replace Western civilization with a World Communist State. Once the forces of this New Dark Age had demoralized the American people, they would impose a Malthusian economic regime to reduce the global population to 1 billion. LaRouche reveals that this counter-elite established the Frankfurt School to eliminate the "immunological factor against Bolshevism from Western European Civilization."[74] To satisfy the wishes of his oligarchical paymasters, Adorno formulated a "Satanic Cultural Paradigm Shift doctrine" that succeeded in creating a rock-drug-sex counterculture from 1964 onwards. Only the virtuous intellectual elite of the LaRouche movement —who at this point saw themselves as protectors of the American republic—could reverse the deleterious effects of this cultural regression.

Until the "culture wars" of the 1990s, these LaRouchean readings of the Frankfurt School remained confined to the boundaries of the NCLC's arbitrary intellectual practice. In 1992, Minnicino took advantage of the polarizing ideological conflict over "political correctness" and revised his LaRouchean (mis)readings of the Frankfurt School for a broader conservative audience. Three best-selling books—Allan Bloom's 1987 *The Closing of the American Mind*, Roger

73 Ibid., 29.

74 Lyndon H. LaRouche Jr., "The Battle to Save Our Civilization," *Executive Intelligence Review* 16, no. 23 (June 2, 1989): 24.

Kimball's 1990 *Tenured Radicals*, and Dinesh D'Souza's 1991 *Illiberal Education*—largely defined the terms of the national debate over campus-based political correctness. Each of these books scorned the apparently high status of "theory" in humanities departments across the country. For instance, Kimball argued that "tenured radicals" used literary theory to inject non-existent political subtexts into the allegedly apolitical works of the Western canon. Minnicino may have felt that the LaRouchean account of the Frankfurt School's legacy was compatible with this generalized hostility toward theory.

In his now-notorious 1992 *Fidelio* article, Minnicino wrote that the Frankfurt School was "the single, most important organizational component of [the] conspiracy" to weaken "the soul of Judeo-Christian civilization."[75] The Frankfurt School, according to Minnicino, had developed an enormous apparatus of "social manipulation," which included radio, television, film, music, and advertising, to spread a sense of cultural pessimism.[76] The ugliness of this modern culture was designed to make Americans feel impotent and disordered. Political correctness, Minnicino averred, was a central part of this manipulative agenda.

At the start of their assault on Western culture, the Frankfurt School supposedly decided to "strip away the belief that art derives from the self-conscious emulation of God the Creator" and thus increase "the alienation of the population."[77] Apparently, Walter Benjamin's friendship with the German playwright Bertolt Brecht resulted in the invention of the Brechtian technique of *Verfremdungseffekt* ("estrangement effect"), which would, in Minnicino's words, "make the audience leave the theater demoralized and aimlessly angry."[78]

75 Michael J. Minnicino, "The New Dark Age: The Frankfurt School and 'Political Correctness,'" *Fidelio* 1, no. 1 (Winter 1992): 5.

76 Ibid., 4.

77 Ibid., 10.

78 Ibid.

In the 1990s, this "Brechtian" alienation pervaded American culture. Cinemas and television sets bombarded audiences with sexual and violent imagery. This constant exposure to shocking stimuli dulled people's capacity to think for themselves, and, in turn, made them vulnerable to genocidal policies. Of course, Minnicino's critique of *Verfremdungseffekt* is completely misguided. The "estrangement effect" worked to provoke critical consciousness rather than trigger irrational responses. This is another instance of a LaRouchean misreading that claims to uncover a secret agenda behind the apparently factual surface.

According to Minnicino, the purpose of Adorno's Princeton Radio Research Project was to test whether mass media could "atomize and increase lability—what people would later call 'brainwashing.'"[79] Public opinion polling, which Adorno critiqued in essays like "Opinion Delusion Society," was a key part of this so-called brainwashing operation. As Minnicino saw it, the "techniques of mass media and advertising developed by the Frankfurt School" had become a cornerstone of contemporary American political campaigns. "Even if they (the people who run the networks, ad agencies, and polling stations) have never heard of Theodor Adorno," Minnicino claims, "they firmly believe in Adorno's theory that the media can and should turn everything into 'football.'"[80] Although Adorno noted capitalism's tendency to reduce politics to consumable entertainment, he never encouraged or endorsed this trend. Instead of faithfully rendering the work of the actual Adorno, Minnicino perpetuated the pseudo-confirmed image of Adorno that belonged almost exclusively to the repertoire of NCLC's arbitrary intellectual output.

Later in his essay, Minnicino turns to the themes of drugs and sex. In Minnicino's account, the Frankfurt School distributed recreational hallucinogens—the Institute's interest in drugs apparently started with Benjamin's writings on hashish—to

79 Ibid., 15.
80 Ibid., 21.

galvanize the libidos of American teenagers. Building on classic PL and NCLC tropes, Minnicino insinuates that Marcuse played a major role in the CIA's notorious Project MKUltra, in which hallucinogens were administered to (both knowing and unwitting) test subjects to experiment with different forms of psychological warfare. Marcuse then used his influence over the New Left to encourage the consumption of psychedelics and thus inspire young radicals to indulge in permissive sexual adventures.

Minnicino's linking of the Frankfurt School to countercultural drug consumption relies heavily on LaRouchean readings. In his misinterpretation of Benjamin's famous essay "The Work of Art in the Age of Its Technological Reproducibility," Minnicino suggests that psychedelic drugs endowed objects with an "aura" and thus "instantaneously achieve[d] a state of mind identical to that prescribed by the Frankfurt School thinkers."[81] However, Benjamin's concept of "the aura," which he described as an artwork's "unique existence at the place where it happens to be," had nothing to do with hallucinogens.[82] In fact, Benjamin even celebrated the rapid increase in mechanical reproductions of art—a phenomenon that diminished the aura of the original—as a potential opening for a new popular and democratic mass culture. Similarly, even though Minnicino assumes that the "Father of the New Left" was pro-hallucinogen, Marcuse's actual writings contradict this interpretation. In his 1969 book *An Essay on Liberation*, Marcuse discussed the use of recreational drugs in the hippie movement and admitted that "awareness of the need for . . . a revolution in perception . . . is perhaps the kernel of truth in the psychedelic search."[83] Nonetheless, he clarified that dropping

81 Ibid., 25.

82 Walter Benjamin, *Illuminations* (New York: Schocken Books, 2007), 220.

83 Herbert Marcuse, *An Essay on Liberation* (Boston: Beacon Press, 2000), 37.

acid did little more than produce temporary "artificial paradises."[84] For Marcuse, taking drugs distracted young people from proper political work. Instead of engaging with historical facts, the interpretive contortions of these LaRouchean readings portrayed the Frankfurt School as culpable for all the cultural ills that American conservatives despised. Although Minnicino was right to lament the sense of spiritual and cultural emptiness that plagued American society in the late twentieth century, he misidentified the Frankfurt School—and political correctness—as the cause of this widespread malaise.

Political correctness, according to Minnicino, dehumanized humanity. Under the influence of the Frankfurt School's cultural pessimism, people lowered themselves to the status of animals. Instead of encouraging people to see themselves as unique and rational beings, political correctness trained them to identify with the accidents of biological circumstance: genders, races, sexualities. As Minnicino puts it, the "importance of the individual as a person gifted with the divine spark of creativity, and capable of acting upon all human civilization, was replaced by the idea that a person is important because he or she is Black, or a woman, or feels homosexual impulses."[85] While Minnicino's article may come across as a classic humanist critique of political tribalism, it trivializes the historical circumstances that made identity politics—Black liberation, women's liberation, gay liberation—necessary in the first place. It ignores real instances of discrimination on college campuses, histories of white supremacy and patriarchy, and the struggle to include previously marginalized perspectives in established institutions. And, moreover, it denies that the social facts of identity—race, gender, sex, sexuality—could ever form a meaningful terrain for political mobilization to contest genuine oppression. For Minnicino and the LaRouchites, these forms of activism were simply instances of Frankfurt

84 Ibid., 37.

85 Minnicino, "A New Dark Age," 27.

School–led Aristotelian subversion. This dualistic mentality, which contrasted the powers of "Western civilization" with conspiratorial "anti-Western" forces, half-rhymed with the American right's portrayal of political correctness as an assault on Judeo-Christian culture.

Minnicino's 1992 article, which rearticulated LaRouchean tropes for the wider debate on political correctness, functioned as a *bridging mechanism* between LaRouchites and cultural conservatives.[86] The main themes of NCLC's attacks on the Frankfurt School—the inauthenticity of the New Left, brainwashing and the psychologization of politics, the rock-drug-sex counterculture, the secret meanings of Frankfurt School theory—are repackaged in Minnicino's essay to converge with the New Right's counteroffensive against political correctness. All the old claims turn up in this Minnicino essay: the PL rumor about Marcuse as a CIA agent, Adorno's control over the culture industry, Horkheimer's motivation for coining the term "authoritarian personality," the endorsement of drug use. Although Minnicino's narrative continued to fulfil the organizational necessities of the LaRouche movement (the preservation of the boundary between two elites), it contained elements that intellectuals in other political forces could extract and rework. In the following years, New Right intellectuals would borrow several ideas from Minnicino to construct their anti–political correctness polemics.

The LaRouchites' writings on the Frankfurt School went on to influence a wide range of authors and activists. Conspiracist writers, such as John Coleman and Daniel Estulin, integrated LaRouchean beliefs into their accounts of the secret global elite. Coleman's conspiracist classic *The Conspirators' Hierarchy: The Committee of 300* argued that Adorno devised "Beatlemusic rock" to promote Satanism. One of Estulin's most well-known books, *Los Secretos Del Club Bilderberg* (*The*

86 Barkun, *A Culture of Conspiracy*, 181.

*Secrets of the Bilderberg Group*), also drew on this LaRouchite "Sgt. Adorno's Lonely Hearts Club Band" theory. Even Fidel Castro once penned an article for the Cuban Communist Party newspaper *Granma* to suggest that American power brokers hired Adorno to compose music for the Beatles. Yet this "Adorno-as-Fifth Beatle" thesis never became as popular as the claim that the Frankfurt School invented political correctness.

How exactly did LaRouchite lies about the Frankfurt School end up becoming so key to the ideology of the mainstream American right? The answer to this pressing question, as far as anyone can tell, lies in a matter of coincidence. Copies of *Fidelio* magazine—the main journal of the LaRouche movement's Schiller Institute—were often sent to various conservative think tanks and institutes to attract new influential supporters and sympathizers. Sometime in the mid-1990s, Raymond V. Raehn, the co-founder of the Washington, DC–based Global Strategy Council, apparently came across an issue of *Fidelio* and read Minnicino's article. The proposition that a group of Marxist émigrés were entirely responsible for the rise of political correctness must have appealed to Raehn, because he decided to do some of his own research on the Frankfurt School. In 1996, he finished an unpublished—and now lost—manuscript entitled "Critical Theory: A Special Research Report." He shared his findings with a friend named William S. Lind, the then-director of the Center for Cultural Conservatism at the Free Congress Foundation, who decided to study the history of the Frankfurt School a little more deeply.

# 2

# Free Congress Foundation: The New Right, Political Correctness, and Family Values

*Having coined the term "Cultural Marxism," the historian William S. Lind should receive royalties every time some conservative pundit repeats it. He would be a rich man.*

—Stephen Baskerville, "The 'Marxism' Narrative Has Gone Too Far"

In a 2020 online discussion for the Charlemagne Institute, William S. Lind—a former director of the Free Congress Foundation's Center for Cultural Conservatism—reflected on the rhetorical effectiveness of calling something "Cultural Marxism."[1] For Lind, all politics is a fight for legitimacy. If one plans to turn people against political correctness or social justice, one must associate it with something they dislike or fear. Lind suggests that the phrase "Cultural Marxism" works as a delegitimizing tool in the United States, because many Americans regard anything even remotely Marxist as illegitimate. There is no need to quibble over definitions of Marxism or prove that political correctness is genuinely Marxist because, as Lind claims, the American public does not generally care about these academic debates. Do not waste your time on research, Lind counsels. Only hard praxis can secure the right's victory over liberalism. Consequently, Lind enjoins conservatives to enter

1 *Chronicles: A Magazine of American Culture*, "Paul Gottfried and Bill Lind discuss 'What Is Cultural Marxism?,'" video, November 24, 2020.

the political battlefield with the weapon of "Cultural Marxism" to delegitimize whatever they perceive as undesirable or unnatural (Black Lives Matter, gender-neutral public washrooms, affirmative action, and so on).

Lind first recoined the term "Cultural Marxism" in the 1990s during the ideological battles over political correctness. Numerous scholars trace the origins of this debate to the efforts of right-wing think tanks and foundations to reclaim the academy in the 1980s. "As early as 1986," Ellen Messer-Davidow writes, "right-wingers had laid out the argument that 'tenured radicals' had embarked on a wholesale demolition of the Western cultural tradition and the US universities charged with preserving it."[2] Conservative authors argued that the dreams of 1960s radicalism had degenerated into a nightmare of 1980s leftist McCarthyism in which progressive academics schemed to restrict their students' freedom of thought and speech. In 1991, *The New York Times* published Richard Bernstein's "The Rising Hegemony of the Politically Correct," which popularized the idea that college campuses were overrun with hypersensitive radicals.[3] According to the NEXIS data, the number of print media articles that mention political correctness surged in the early 1990s:

- 1989: 15
- 1990: 65
- 1991: 1,570
- 1992: 2,835
- 1993: 4,914
- 1994: 6,985

The phrase "political correctness," as Moira Weigel explains, functions as an *exonym*: "A term for another group which

2 Ellen Messer-Davidow, "Manufacturing the Attack on Liberalized Higher Education," *Social Text* no. 36 (Autumn 1993): 41.

3 Richard Bernstein, "The Rising Hegemony of the Politically Correct," *New York Times,* October 28, 1990, 1–4.

signals that the speaker does not belong to it."[4] Those who deploy this label enact a "highly effective form of crypto-politics" that "transforms the political landscape by acting as if it is not political at all."[5] Critics of political correctness accuse left-wingers of injecting politics into inappropriate areas, such as the family, literature, or even casual conversation. These critics portray themselves as defenders of non-political spheres that the left is trying to politicize. Yet many of these claims to "non-politicalness" or "naturalness" are saturated with historical assumptions. In a certain sense, political correctness is an effort to reveal the already-political nature of the things that conservatives like to see as "outside politics."

Whereas the right feared that political correctness would politicize hitherto non-political issues, several left-wing critics argued that speech codes and affirmative action did little to dismantle existing hierarchies. In her critique of the limits of political correctness, Valerie Scatamburlo suggests that these efforts are "intended to avoid offending individuals in particular contexts according to liberal notions of politeness, sensitivity, and tolerance" rather than "pose serious challenges to hegemonic assumptions, material conditions, and structural arrangements."[6] Removing offensive terms and phrases from institutional vocabularies was entirely compatible with preserving the underlying structures of white supremacy, patriarchy, and class oppression. As Scatamburlo quips, "Never hearing a racist or sexist comment . . . does not mean that racism, sexism and the like will cease to exist."[7] In this critique, political correctness is a false cure for the social and historical problems that it claims to remedy.

---

4 Moira Weigel, "Political Correctness: How the Right Invented a Phantom Enemy," *Guardian,* November 30, 2016.

5 Ibid.

6 Valerie Scatamburlo, *Soldiers of Misfortune: The New Right's Culture War and the Politics of Political Correctness* (New York: Peter Lang Publishing, 1998), 102.

7 Ibid.

Frequently, campus-based political correctness exhibits an overreliance on administration-enforced rules. Changing sexist and racist attitudes requires proper persuasion, organizing, and education rather than the imposition of bureaucratic statutes. Political correctness, especially in the forms that it assumes on prestigious college campuses, represents a subsumption of emancipatory discourses into the managerial procedures of university governance. It becomes little more than a set of norms that the capitalist university must instill into students to prepare them for an increasingly integrated and diverse white-collar workplace. In this light, political correctness was simply a mechanism of what Nancy Fraser calls *progressive neoliberalism*: the combination of "an expropriative, plutocratic economic program" with "a liberal-meritocratic politics of recognition."[8] When Lind was starting to complain about the Frankfurt School, the New Democrats of the Bill Clinton era (1993–2001) were paying lip service to the aims of women's empowerment, multiculturalism, and environmentalism insofar as they did not conflict with the demands of an increasingly global financialized capitalism. Right-wing critics often exaggerated the scale and impact of these concessions to social justice. Lind, for instance, regarded affirmative action as tantamount to the forcible seizure of property under a dictatorship. This confusion between progressive neoliberalism and revolutionary communism pervaded most New Right narratives of Cultural Marxism/s.

Lind's attacks on Cultural Marxism must be contextualized within the rise of the New Right as a political force. From the 1970s onwards, the New Right raged against the perceived liberal excesses of the sixties. New Right strategists sought to rejuvenate the conservative movement, defend traditional values, and turn the Republican Party into a vehicle for cultural politics. In their struggle for hegemony, they launched dozens of

8 Nancy Fraser, *The Old Is Dying and the New Cannot Be Born* (London: Verso, 2019), 11–12.

single-issue campaigns—anti-abortion, anti-integration, pro–school prayer—to promote conservative norms. Their end goal was to rebuild what they saw as a non-political mode of American sociality: the normative order of pre-1960s culture.

## The Counter-Politicization of the Social

What was so *new* about the New Right? According to Mike Davis, the New Right marked the arrival of a fresh generation of eager conservative innovators. Whereas the Republican old guard was largely a "network of court-house cliques," the New Rightists were a "cadre of middle-class, mostly college-educated, activists with a transcendental commitment to right-wing ideology."[9] Their political outlook had been shaped by their involvement in one of the right's new youth organizations —Young Americans for Freedom, Intercollegiate Society of Individualists, or the Young Republicans—and their participation in Barry Goldwater's unsuccessful 1964 presidential run. By the 1970s, this new generation of activists suspected that the conservative establishment was not serious about getting into the corridors of power. The chief architects of the New Right —Paul Weyrich, Morton Blackwell, Howard Phillips, Richard Viguerie, Terry Dolan—feared that the existing American right was too aristocratic, pessimistic, and intellectualistic to confront the post-1960s political moment. Weyrich identified four shortcomings of this "blue blood" conservativism: 1) it failed to speak in ordinary, down-to-earth language; 2) it appealed to abstract principles rather than traditional values; 3) it refrained from working with the mass media to amplify its message; and 4) it was more interested in *being right* than

9 Mike Davis, *Prisoners of the American Dream: Politics and Economy in the History of the Working Class* (London: Verso, 1986), 167.

*winning power*.[10] Even if he was exaggerating the extent of the differences between Old and New Rights, Weyrich—and his comrades—clearly had a plan to revitalize the conservative movement.

The 1970s saw an explosion of right-wing political institutions: think tanks, political action committees, magazines and newsletters, training programs, legal centers, and advocacy groups. The New Right courted donations from conservative philanthropists and business magnates to fuel this expanding non-profit infrastructure. While it claimed nonpartisan status, the New Right mostly worked with Republican politicians to push a conservative agenda on a national level. From the early 1970s onward, the New Right looked to dislodge blue collar voters from the Democrat's classic New Deal coalition and persuade them to vote for Republican candidates. They latched onto the diffuse white backlash against civil rights struggles and promoted conservative positions on sensitive issues like abortion, homosexuality, and desegregation. Their strategic use of media technologies helped them to target specific constituencies and build wider support for reactionary policies.

The rise of the New Right took place during America's postwar economic decline. The 1973 oil crisis had delivered a significant blow to the US economy (and its international prestige). The stagflation of the 1970s saw runaway inflation and high unemployment devastate the standards of living for working-class and middle-class households. The decline of the family wage system, as well as the upsurge in divorce rates and the spread of second-wave feminism, compelled many women to enter the paid workforce. Instead of recognizing the pressures of economic uncertainty on the American family, the New Right blamed this crisis on the catch-all cultural sin of *permissiveness*: an infinitely elastic diagnosis that seemed

---

10 Paul Weyrich, "Blue Collar or Blue Blood? The New Right Compared with The Old Right," in *The New Right Papers*, ed. Robert W. Whitaker (New York: St. Martin's Press, 1982), 48–62.

to encompass everything from government welfare spending to homosexuality, from hippies to Hollywood, from single mothers to pornography.

The New Right's ideology, according to the Marxist writer Allen Hunter, rested on a foundational mystification that treated cultural change, rather than structural trends, as the primary driver of social crisis.[11] What was at the heart of this essential mystifying procedure? In brief, the New Right *naturalized* and *eternalized* the postwar cultural order. It clung to a normative image of 1950s America that combined conventional morality with geopolitical strength. The New Rightists believed that desegregation and feminism, as well as the military withdrawal from the Vietnam War and the loss of the Panama Canal, represented a turning away from core American values. As the crises of the 1970s destabilized the conditions of middle-class prosperity and propriety, the New Right put forward an ideological project that sought to defend "the People" from the forces of cultural degradation.

The New Right's *diffuse, petit-bourgeois ideology* suppressed "class distinctions" and highlighted "social distinctions as relevant criteria for excluding and including groups among 'the people.'"[12] It incorporated various strata into a social bloc that Hunter characterized as the so-called *legitimate middle*: small business owners, the full-time employees of the white working class, production-based managers, middle-class suburbanites. It excluded groups that seemed to threaten the naturalized cultural expectations of the People: Black people, immigrants, feminists, unionized workers, queer people, students, single mothers, and so on. It also discounted certain fractions of what the neoconservative thinker Irving Kristol called the *New Class*: the professional middle class of bureaucrats, professors, journalists, and teachers. Neither of the

11 Allen Hunter, "In the Wings: New Right Ideology and Organization," *Radical America* 15, nos. 1 and 2 (Spring 1981): 113–38.

12 Ibid., 128.

so-called extremes—the New Class and the underclass—were viewed as legitimate political rivals but, rather, as symbols of cultural decay. New Class liberals, according to this schema, were heedlessly allocating civil rights and material resources to "the Groups," rather than serving their true purpose and assisting the real American People. This ideological vision was formally articulated in a 1982 essay by the far-right thinker Samuel T. Francis. Building on the research of the sociologist Donald I. Warren, Francis explained that the New Right appealed to those "Middle American Radicals" who were "less an objectively identifiable class than a subjectively distinguished temperament."[13] They possessed "an attitudinal quality" that was defined by a "sense of resentment and exploitation . . . that is directed upward as well as downward."[14] As Francis's diagnosis reveals, the New Right was not that interested in the boring matters of class and inequality. Rather, it was a project to preserve and enforce certain cultural attitudes without altering the underlying capitalist structures that bred alienation and economic hardship.

"Family Values" was the New Right's preferred cure for the social crisis of the 1970s. The liberalizing policies of the New Class, such as the desegregation of schools (pejoratively known as "busing") or the legalization of no-fault divorce, were interpreted as malevolent attacks on the American family. This ideological construction of the traditional family—a male breadwinner, a stay-at-home wife, and children—projected what Anne McClintock calls "hierarchy within unity" as a natural feature of social life.[15] Drawing on McClintock's insight, Patricia Hill Collins observes that families were expected "to socialize

13 Samuel T. Francis, "Message from MARs: The Social Politics of the New Right," in *The New Right Papers*, ed. Robert W. Whitaker (New York: St. Martin's Press, 1982), 66.

14 Ibid., 67.

15 Anne McClintock, *Imperial Leather* (New York: Routledge, 1995), 45.

their members into an appropriate set of 'family values' that simultaneously reinforce[d] the hierarchy within the assumed unity of interests symbolized by the family and [laid] the foundation for many social hierarchies."[16] For the New Right, the nation needed to be reorganized according to this familial logic. Its rhetoric of family values worked to represent a *naturalized hierarchy*—in terms of class, race, gender, and sexuality—as the only acceptable configuration of American society.

It should not be forgotten that the New Right was intervening in a tense and conflictual conjuncture. The 1960s witnessed what Michael Omi and Howard Winant describe as an immense "politicization of the social."[17] The new social movements of the 1960s exposed the links between seemingly personal experiences and wider political issues. The feminist tactic of "consciousness raising" taught thousands of American women that what they had previously experienced as private failings or traumas were effects of a patriarchal system. Black Americans, Latino/as, Asian Americans and Native Americans built vibrant grassroots protest movements to challenge structurally racist institutions and to celebrate their racial identities and heritages. Under the banner of the Gay Liberation Front, many gays and lesbians came out and campaigned to end discrimination against, and the stigmatization of, non-heteronormative sexual orientations. Not only did this politics of identity reveal the hidden violence of the New Right's "moral" cultural order, but it also—to borrow Omi and Winant's phrase—introduced "a new depth to political life."[18]

Whereas the social movements of the 1960s politicized the social, the New Right launched a campaign of "depoliticization" that was nevertheless deeply political. Although the New

16 Patricia Hill Collins, "It's All in the Family: Intersections of Gender, Race, and Nation," *Hypatia* 13, no. 3 (Summer 1998): 64.

17 Michael Omi and Howard Winant, *Racial Formation in the United States*, Third Edition (New York: Routledge, 2015), 185.

18 Ibid., 186.

Right objected to "undue" government intervention into the social fabric, they favored a state-led project of monitoring and regulating society. They hoped for a state that would enforce law and order, impose traditional morality, and defend US geopolitical hegemony. Under the rule of this conservative state, the Groups—and their New Class defenders—would be viewed as an anti-social force that needed to be disciplined, disempowered, and disenfranchised. And so, rather than depoliticizing the social, the New Right *counter-politicized* it.

The New Right needed intellectuals to enact its ambitious program: organizers to weave political alliances, legal experts to draft new legislation, technicians to oversee media output, pundits to promote talking points and narratives. Yet intellectuals do not emerge from nowhere. They are the personifications of longer historical processes. To bring these histories to the surface, we must—in the words of the historian Kim Phillips-Fein—look "at how [the ideas of right-wing intellectuals] contributed to activism and vice versa, at the political and institutional context for conservative ideas, and at conservatives' attempts to build an alternative intellectual infrastructure."[19] Studying this history of the New Right and its intellectuals will help us to better understand the broader context behind the Free Congress Foundation's attacks on Cultural Marxism.

## The Long Histories of the New Right Think-Tank Intellectual

The New Right, as Davis once observed, was more of "a confusing cluster of New Rights" than a single organizational unit.[20] This clustering of various rights was neither coincidental nor predestined. It cannot be reduced to a single essence or origin.

19 Kim Phillips-Fein, "Conservatism: A State of the Field," *The Journal of American History* 98, no. 3 (December 2011): 730.

20 Davis, *Prisoners of the American Dream*, 170.

The New Right's leaders worked diligently to combine different philosophies, technologies, and social strata into an effective political force. They incorporated ideological components from a variety of philosophical and political traditions, such as postwar conservatism, neoconservatism, Southern segregationism, and fundamentalist evangelicalism. They employed techniques like direct mail and the single-issue campaign to mobilize the white suburban family and challenge the hegemony of establishment liberalism. As this clustering took on a more objective form, it gave rise to a subjective figure that I call the *New Right think-tank intellectual*. What made this mode of intellectual practice possible?

Many of the New Right's arguments and ideas stemmed from the intellectual milieu of postwar conservatism. According to George H. Nash, postwar conservatism was a compound of different and occasionally contradictory impulses: *libertarianism*, *traditionalism*, and *anti-communism*.[21] Hostility to twentieth-century liberalism united these tendencies. Libertarians, such as Friedrich Hayek and Frank Chodorov, warned that the post–New Deal federal bureaucracy would inexorably grow into an authoritarian behemoth. Russell Kirk and Richard Weaver, the tenacious defenders of traditionalism, excoriated liberalism as a corrosive philosophy that dissolved the organic roots of Western civilization and produced a secular mass society vulnerable to totalitarianism. The warriors of Cold War anti-communism—Whittaker Chambers, James Burnham, Frank Meyer—preached that liberalism was too rationalistic and semi-socialistic to resist the threat of an expansionist Soviet state. As Nash explains, this notion of a "philosophical continuity of the left" was an enduring theme of postwar conservatism.[22] Whereas Soviet Communism was

21 George H. Nash, *The Conservative Intellectual Movement since 1945*, Thirtieth-Anniversary Edition (Wilmington, DE: ISI Books, 2017), 360.

22 Ibid., 101.

the enemy without, secular liberalism was the enemy within. The McCarthyite Red Scare of the 1950s, for instance, treated many American liberals as essentially Soviets in disguise. This conflation of liberalism and communism has remained a common rhetorical tactic in right-wing discourse to delegitimize progressive changes, such as civil rights and social welfare.

Several conservative thinkers labored to orchestrate a "fusion" between libertarianism and traditionalism. They wished to reconcile free market economics with a concern for traditional cultural norms. The resultant doctrine, known as "fusionism," provided an explicitly moral defense of capitalism to argue that individual freedom and the free market were products of an objective Judeo-Christian tradition. This fusionist thesis permitted conservatives to downplay the inherently alienating effects of capitalism, such as the triumph of monopolies over small enterprise and the dislocation of established living patterns. Whenever the reality of American capitalism did not live up to the fusionist ideal, conservatives simply blamed liberal policies for fostering a materialistic worldview. Although fusionism offered a merely intellectual solution to the contradiction between capitalist license and moral order, it equipped the New Right with a rationalization to deflect the blame for social breakdown onto cultural issues rather than economic instability.

In the late 1960s and early 1970s, a significant number of prominent Cold War liberals—Irving Kristol, Daniel Bell, Nathan Glazer, Jeane Kirkpatrick, and others—shifted their political allegiances from the left to the right. The rightward drift of these *neoconservatives*—a loose grouping of predominantly Jewish ex-Trotskyists, former Kennedy advisors, literary intellectuals, and academic sociologists—started during the turbulent events of the 1960s. Neoconservatives regarded SDS's activism as a nihilistic and misguided assault on American values and institutions. They disagreed with student radicals over the morality of the Vietnam War and, instead, advocated for a vehemently anti-communist and interventionist foreign policy. Additionally, as President Lyndon B. Johnson's Great Society programs failed to meet their goals, the neoconservatives became more skeptical about the ability of sweeping government-led reforms to cure social problems. They publicized their views on the failures of liberalism in journals and magazines like *Commentary* and *The Public Interest* (as well as in William F. Buckley's right-wing publication *National Review*). Neoconservatism eventually became an ideological refuge for those former liberals (or leftists) who, as the famous quip goes, felt "mugged by reality." Its sober realism was touted as a solution to the crisis of the postwar order. Unlike the neoconservatives, the liberal New Class refused to accept the limits of political reality and inflated the expectations of minorities, welfare recipients, and idealistic students by claiming that the bureaucratic state could resolve all national ills. The New Rightists selectively absorbed these neoconservative insights to enrich their own polemics about the dangers of liberal domestic policies and the disintegration of traditional values. Kristol's concept of the New Class, for instance, would be important to Lind's characterization of Cultural Marxism.

The ideology of the New Right did not derive solely from the highfalutin thought of conservative intellectuals. According to Joseph E. Lowndes, the New Right copied their cultural populist rhetoric from the Southern segregationists.[23] Many Southern politicians, such as the Dixiecrat Strom Thurmond and the Alabama Governor George Wallace, argued that the federal government's desegregation efforts were simply an attack on the traditional lifestyles of ordinary white Southerners. Instead of using explicit racial appeals, Wallace and others employed code words—"average citizen" and "the common man"—to conflate the interests and demands of white Southerners with those of

23 Joseph E. Lowndes, *From the New Deal to the New Right: Race and the Southern Origins of Modern Conservatism* (New Haven, CT: Yale University Press, 2008).

the entire American population. As Omi and Winant describe it, the New Right embraced this "new subtextual approach to politics" to rearticulate "white resentment" as the natural grievances of the People or silent majority.[24] "Instead of defending segregation, institutionalized discrimination, and white supremacy," Omi and Winant write, "the new right invoked the code words of 'law and order'; instead of advocating for systemic patriarchy and justifying male chauvinism, it upheld 'family values.'"[25] The use of code words—an ideological inheritance from Southern cultural populism—served to mask the structural racial and gendered exclusions that underpinned the New Right's notion of the People.

Another significant source of the New Right's popular conservatism came from the political mobilization of evangelical Christians. During the 1970s, evangelical churches welcomed thousands of fresh converts into their congregations. Many of these new churchgoers felt unsure about how they should react to the 1960s tumult that had drastically altered the social life of the nation. The Evangelical Church addressed this cultural uncertainty by taking unambiguous positions on controversial moral issues. It equipped people with a clear sense of good and evil that was grounded in a fundamentalist reading of the Bible. Controversial Supreme Court rulings, such as the barring of school prayer from public schools (1962) and the legalization of abortion in *Roe v. Wade* (1973), compelled evangelicals to enter the political sphere and demand a return to traditional values. Church ministers warned that the spread of "secular humanism" would result in a godless society where individuals depended on the state for moral and material support rather than the Christian family. There was extensive institutional and ideological overlap between the New Right and the emerging religious right. For example, Weyrich founded a major conservative organization named Moral Majority with the famous

24 Omi and Winant, *Racial Formation in the United States*, 197.
25 Ibid.

televangelist preacher Jerry Falwell. In the 1970s and 1980s, the leaders of the New Right and the religious right came together to publicly defend "family values" from what they saw as the amoral chaos of modern liberalism.

For the New Right (and the conservative movement as a whole), the opinion makers of the establishment media—*The New York Times*, *NBC*, *The Washington Post*—exhibited a liberal bias that excluded right-wing voices from respectable discourse. The New Right switched to alternative media technologies to counter the hegemony of this monolithic liberal media apparatus. The influential conservative activist Richard Viguerie succeeded in adapting the tool of direct mail—a marketing strategy that targets potential customers and solicits money for products and services—to American politics. His use of direct mail collapsed the distinction between persuasion and advertising. He incorporated techniques from marketing and psychology books to design fundraising letters and figure out which appeals attracted greater financial support.

Direct mail became the New Right's ideological weapon against the left-wing media. The populist premise of direct mail—the posture of speaking directly to the People—implied an immediate and unfiltered mode of expression. The scholar R. Kenneth Godwin explains that the New Right's mail campaigns employed the technique of personalization to create a feeling of unmediated communication. The use of "highly emotive rhetoric" and "appeals to personal efficacy" encouraged the recipient of one of Viguerie's carefully crafted letters to join an ideological battle against an opponent that was portrayed with "strong negative connotations."[26] For instance, an item of direct mail from Senator Steve Symms for the Heritage Foundation warned that the National Education Association was planning to "seize total control" of the American public school system unless "you and I take IMMEDIATE ACTION

26 R. Kenneth Godwin, "The Structure, Content, and Use of Political Direct Mail," *Polity* 20, no. 3 (Spring 1988): 530–8.

on this EMERGENCY situation."[27] The clever use of branding and personalized rhetoric functioned to unify individual Americans into a durable conservative constituency that would consistently donate to New Right initiatives.

Single-issue campaigns were another key technique for mobilizing the New Right's base. The most effective single-issue causes, as Davis observes, were linked to "the defence of the sanctity of white suburban family life."[28] Conservative activists framed the expansion of civil rights as an affront to the natural rights of ordinary Americans. They built on the rhetorical motifs of Southern cultural populism to contrast the "rights" of white families with the "special rights" of the Groups. Ironically, reactionary single-issue campaigners parroted the grammar of the civil rights movement even as they undermined civil rights legislation. They marketed certain ideas about "familial rights" versus "special rights" to organize suburban families against the progressive gains of the 1960s and 1970s. As single-issue campaigns spread from state to state, New Right activists hoped that these separate suburban communities could be fused together into a national conservative voting bloc.

In Miami, Florida, the former pop singer Anita Bryant founded an organization called Save Our Children to challenge the introduction of laws that prevented discrimination based on sexual orientation. Bryant collected signatures to repeal these measures and told voters that gay people were asking to be blessed for their "abnormal" lifestyle choices. Bryant's campaign reframed this legislation as a violation of a child's so-called right to grow up in a decent society rather than a well-meaning effort to guarantee equal treatment for an unfairly maligned minority.

The desegregation of schools, or "busing," was another polarizing issue. In his account of the antibusing movement

27 Quoted in ibid., 527.

28 Davis, *Prisoners of the American Dream*, 170.

in Charlotte, North Carolina, the historian Matthew Lassiter describes a "collective politics of a white, middle-class ideology" that defined freedom of school choice and neighborhood schools as the core privileges of "homeowner rights."[29] Those who opposed desegregation saw busing as a kind of reverse racism. White, middle-class suburban parents did not accept that comprehensive two-way integration was meant to overcome Charlotte's history of displacing and ghettoizing Black families. They felt that the pursuit of racial equality was a form of juridical tyranny that trampled on their own children's rights. As Lassiter points out, these anti-busing activists co-opted "the rhetoric and imitated the tactics of the civil rights movement" to portray their children as victims of a diffuse authoritarianism.[30]

The most notorious and successful single-issue campaign of the 1970s was Phyllis Schlafly's STOP ERA. The Equal Rights Amendment (ERA) was a proposed amendment to the Constitution that would end all legal distinctions between men and women in terms of divorce, property, employment, and other matters. Schlafly led a powerful anti-feminist backlash to oppose the ERA, which she portrayed as an antidemocratic initiative that catered only to the interests of a militant and unrepresentative feminist minority. In a 1972 issue of her newsletter *The Phyllis Schlafly Report*, she blasted the women's liberation movement as a "total assault on the role of the American woman as wife and mother, and on the family as the basic unit of society."[31] Schlafly argued that the ERA undermined the privileges of American women—the so-called security of marriage and motherhood—within a patriarchal society.

---

29 Matthew D. Lassiter, "The Suburban Origin of 'Color-Blind' Conservatism: Middle-Class Consciousness in the Charlotte Busing Crisis," *Journal of Urban History* 30, no. 4 (May 2004): 550.

30 Ibid., 558.

31 Phyllis Schlafly, "What's Wrong with 'Equal Rights' for Women? (February 1972)," in *Debating the American Conservative Movement: 1945 to the Present*, ed. Donald T. Critchlow and Nancy MacLean (Lanham, MD: Rowman & Littlefield, 2009), 200.

Although these campaigns claimed to depoliticize the social, they obscured the deeply political nature of pre-1960s America. They naturalized the form of the white suburban family without examining the historical circumstances that produced it. As Gramsci once noted, that which is experienced as "natural" is often a consequence of "the objective necessity of civil technique."[32] The New Right may have celebrated the white suburban family as a pre-political unit, yet this mode of familial life was a product of postwar federal planning and investment. The Federal Housing Administration channeled loans toward white homebuyers who were moving into segregated suburbs, which helped to unify various European American groups into a "white" population. Such "white unity," as George Lipsitz puts it, "rested on residential segregation and on shared access to housing and life chances largely unavailable to communities of color."[33] The New Right's single-issue campaigning defended this structural arrangement as though it was a fact of human nature rather than a result of racist government policy. Yet these single-issue campaigns were relatively fleeting interventions that required the support of a larger institutional apparatus.

From the early 1970s onwards, the New Right founded several major think tanks that served to bind these single-issue strands into a coherent multi-issue agenda. The historian Jason Stahl defines right-wing think tanks as "research and public relations institutions, populated by conservative intellectuals and policymakers," that are "designed for theorizing and selling conservative public policies and ideologies to both lawmakers and the public at large."[34] In the 1950s and 1960s,

32 Gramsci, *Subaltern Social Groups*, 127.

33 George Lipsitz, "The Possessive Investment in Whiteness: Racialized Social Democracy and the 'White' Problem in American Studies," *American Quarterly* 47, no. 3 (September 1995): 374.

34 Jason Stahl, *Right Moves: The Conservative Think Tank in American Political Culture since 1945* (Chapel Hill: The University of North Carolina Press, 2016), 3.

conservative think tanks and policymakers largely stuck to the boundaries of a post–New Deal liberal consensus that dominated Washington circles. They were committed to an ostensibly objective, scientific, and unbiased approach. Policy was supposedly an area of disinterested planning rather than a battleground for ideological crusades.

The rise of the New Right think tank in the early 1970s disrupted this liberal ideal of technocratic policymaking. Edwin Feulner and Weyrich, who co-founded the Heritage Foundation in 1973, wanted to overturn the political establishment. Instead of striving to present their policy goals and proposals as "objective," these New Right organizations presented their conservative bias as a necessary counterweight to liberal dominance. The populist position of the Heritage Foundation, for instance, implied that the New Right was defending the true conservative interests of the American people from Washington's blind commitment to liberalism. The old technocratic paradigm slowly gave way to a "marketplace of ideas" model that allowed right-wing think tanks to promote explicitly conservative identities and ideologies. The New Right intellectual was a lively combatant in this fray of ideological competition that fought to displace liberal hegemony over the orientation of the American state.

The New Right think tank institutionalized a particular model of knowledge production. This organizational infrastructure formed a whole manufacturing apparatus, in which entrepreneurial intellectuals generated and packaged products —op-eds, books, policy documents, speeches—that could circulate through various channels of distribution and consumption (television, newspapers, conferences, radio interviews, and so on). Messer-Davidow contends that New Right intellectuals blurred the differences between scholarly expertise and think-tank knowledge. New Right think tanks imbued their product with an "academized 'aura' of authority" to compete among different knowledges in policy debates and public discussion.[35] Their job titles—directors, fellows, researchers—served to further confuse the distinction between universities and think tanks. As Messer-Davidow suggests, these competing knowledges were "readily consumed by policy-makers and other publics without much critical analysis to differentiate them."[36] Arguably, what set these New Right intellectuals apart from university academics was their ability to sell their ideas to audiences.[37] The output of the New Right intellectual needed to be effective rather than innovative or verifiable. Winning power, as Weyrich pointed out, was more important than being right. If their ideas managed to shape policy and opinion, then the New Right intellectual did not need to worry about attaining standards of scholarly rigor.

The founding of right-wing think tanks reflected a strategy to redefine the parameters of individual relations and collective life. Think-tank intellectuals engaged in what Messer-Davidow calls "vertical articulatory practices" to construct "institutional nodal points" that leveraged "changes in national and local institutions, which in turn [could] be used to (re)constitute individuals as subjects and agents of a conservative society."[38] They hoped to remake subjectivities to conform to their notion of family values. They wanted to revise school curricula to produce patriotic American citizens, prohibit abortions to shape compliant American women, and dismantle affirmative action to build a "color-blind" (albeit racially unequal) American workforce. Although they positioned themselves as populists, the New Right was a thoroughly elite project. Instead of forming democratic or grassroots organizations,

---

35 Messer-Davidow, "Manufacturing the Attack on Liberalized Higher Education," 54.

36 Ibid.

37 Alex DiBranco, "Conservative News and Movement Infrastructure," in *News on the Right: Studying Conservative News Cultures*, ed. Anthony Nadler and A. J. Bauer (New York: Oxford University Press, 2020), 123–40.

38 Ibid., 68.

the New Right established a range of institutions that were unaccountable to the people that they claimed to represent. This institutional framework fostered a kind of paternalistic attitude to the masses that defined the mentality of the *New Right think-tank intellectual*. How might we describe the main features of this mentality?

The New Right think-tank intellectual performed a *mediating function* between a cross section of American business—primarily single-family foundations—and the spheres of public opinion and government policy. However, they did not advocate for the narrow corporate interests of individual sectors of American capital. Whereas the functionaries of political action committees would lobby for specific legislative changes that might benefit a particular industry, the New Right think-tank intellectual promoted an overarching worldview that emphasized free enterprise and traditional values. As Gramsci points out, the state needs to establish a pervasive worldview to shape "the morality of the broadest popular masses to the necessities of the continuous development of the economic apparatus of production."[39] Consequently, the New Right think-tank intellectual was responsible for envisioning (and, perhaps, even operating) the kind of state that would be most favorable to the expansion of American entrepreneurial capital.

Second, the *oppositional stance* of the New Right think-tank intellectual resulted from their perceived role in intra–New Class conflict. Conservative intellectuals imagined themselves as defectors from the New Class, as though they were class traitors of the intelligentsia. The psychic thrill of betraying the presumed interests of this New Class allowed New Right intellectuals to present themselves as tribunes of the besieged American population. Yet there were no substantial organizational links between these intellectuals and the People. The institutions of the New Right were simply platforms for ideological competition between the intellectuals of established

39 Gramsci, *Selections from the Prison Notebooks*, 242.

political forces rather than a forum for expressing the demands of a true grassroots populist movement. Despite the limitations of the New Right's elite structures, the rhetorical posture of opposing the elite remained key to the messages of the New Right think-tank intellectual.

The third defining characteristic of this mentality was *opportunism*. The New Right's competitive approach to knowledge production prioritized ideas and narratives that could be deployed and circulated quickly. The New Right think-tank intellectual needed to market their messages to intervene in passing debates and single-issue panics. None of their work possessed any lasting philosophical or scholarly significance. They instrumentalized their intellectual skills to develop polemics that were only successful insofar as they shifted the existing dispositions of social forces. They had to secure public and political support for a wider vision of transformation: the reconfiguration of civil society and the state. Effectiveness—winning power rather than being right—was the sole criterion of this intellectual practice.

Lind was a quintessential New Right think-tank intellectual. Drawing on classic conservative tropes, he assumed an essential continuity between the post-Marxist theory of the Frankfurt School and the mildly liberal measures of political correctness. He launched a single-issue campaign against Cultural Marxism to protect the People from the idealism of the New Class and the barbarity of the Groups. As a think-tank researcher, he employed a variety of media technologies—magazines, op-eds, television shows—to market these narratives and promote an agenda of *cultural conservatism*. Not only did he hope to reverse social and legislative progress, but he also wanted to impose a deeply traditionalist vision of society that he called *retroculture*. Today, Lind is remembered as the man who popularized the phrase "Cultural Marxism." However, he would not have accomplished this without the institutional support of Weyrich's Free Congress Foundation.

## Free Congress Foundation and Cultural Conservatism

Weyrich dedicated much of his adult life to the task of building the New Right. From 1973 onward, he helped to establish many influential right-wing organizations, including the American Legislative Exchange Council and the Moral Majority. In 1974, the Colorado beer baron Joseph Coors supplied Weyrich with ample funds to start a political action committee called the Committee for the Survival of a Free Congress (CSFC). CSFC supported the electoral campaigns of Republican congressional candidates who opposed abortion, promoted free market economics, and advocated right-to-work laws. With help from Viguerie, CSFC designed a direct mail campaign to raise $194,000 for thirty-seven congressional candidates. Several years later, Weyrich reorganized the committee into a think tank called the Free Congress Foundation (FCF) for the purposes of formulating a unified cultural agenda for the New Right. With the beer-soaked bucks of the Coors family on tap, FCF eventually became a prominent "inside-the-beltway" hub for traditionalist culture.

In 1986, Weyrich appointed William S. Lind as director of the FCF's Institute for Cultural Conservatism (later renamed the Center for Cultural Conservatism). Lind may have seemed like an unusual candidate for a top position at a think tank devoted to social and cultural issues. At the time, his publication record consisted mainly of writings on military strategy. He had served as president of the Military Reform Institute and advised Senator Robert Taft Jr. and Senator Gary Hart on matters of defense policy. Yet Lind's background in military theory proved to be a transferable skill during the culture wars of the 1980s and 1990s. During his tenure at FCF, Lind devised a campaign of cultural warfare that would supposedly defend the ramparts of American culture from the encroaching forces of post-1960s radicalism.

The Institute's first major publication, a 1987 book entitled *Cultural Conservatism: Toward a New National Agenda*, outlined a strategy for restoring America's traditional values. Lind and his co-author, William H. Marshner, observed that "both parties have had to reach out to activist movements built around values, lifestyles, and other non-economic issues."[40] Whereas most other pundits and policy wonks dismissed these cultural battles as passing fads, Lind and Marshner predicted that these movements were "the vanguards of a profound political change."[41] They interpreted this shift to single-issue campaigning as a sign that twenty-first century politics would focus on culture rather than economics. The New Right needed to move beyond the oppositional campaigns of the 1970s, which only ever mobilized *against* legislative changes, and embrace a broader proactive vision for right-wing politics: cultural conservatism.

When Lind and Marshner's book was published in 1987, the conservative movement was starting to tear itself apart. During the early days of the Reagan presidency, the traditionalists of the New Right assumed that their priorities would drive the agenda of a conservative White House. Yet they soon found out that neoconservatism had outmaneuvered them to become the dominant Reaganite faction. Significantly, the neocons were not as concerned as the New Rightists about restoring traditional culture. For instance, Reagan largely refrained from fighting the New Right's major cultural battles, such as school prayer and abortion. By the mid-1980s, the scholar Paul Gottfried had coined a new ism to give a name to those traditionalists who no longer felt at home in the mainstream American right: *paleoconservatism*. The advocates of this new conservative bloc desired restrictions on immigration and free trade, isolationism

40 William S. Lind and William H. Marshner, *Cultural Conservatism: Toward a New National Agenda* (Washington, DC: Free Congress Research and Education Foundation, 1987), 1.

41 Ibid., 1.

in foreign policy, and a resurrection of cultural tradition. They saw the neocons as opportunistic (and, in some accounts, uniquely Jewish) interlopers who did not respect or even understand the true essence of conservative thought: the conserving of an "organic" culture and civilization.[42] In a 1986 interview, Lind criticized Reaganism as "an enormous disappointment to any conservative interested in anything more than getting rich."[43] Like the paleocons, he believed that Reagan was failing to halt "the decline of the values, ideas, and ways of life that Western civilization has developed over the last 300 years."[44] While *Cultural Conservatism* was not exactly a full-throated paleoconservative polemic, Lind and Marshner's argument placed a similar emphasis on the need to preserve America's cultural norms.

Culture, according to Lind and Marshner, is a "collective conscience" that guides national civic life.[45] It forms the basis for economic growth, political freedom, and personal happiness. The prosperity of Western societies—and America's status as a world superpower—stems from a commitment to Judeo-Christian values. At the heart of this cultural tradition is the patriarchal family. Within this harmonious system, loving parents raise their children to respect the collective superego and, in turn, secure the continuation of traditional culture. If these family values are discarded, the West risks catastrophe.

In a nod to paleoconservatism, Lind and Marshner announced that America was suffering from *cultural drift*: "the gradual emptying of a nation's values of their content."[46] Divorce, abortion, pre-marital sex, and out-of-wedlock pregnancy were symptoms of this spiritual crisis. The waning of family values in

42 Jeffery Bloodworth, "Trumpism's Paleoconservative Roots and Dealignment," *Journal of Right-Wing Studies* 1, no. 1 (2023): 185–205.

43 Paul Taylor, "William S. Lind: Tending to Matters of Hart and Fighting for the Right," *Washington Post*, April 27, 1986.

44 Ibid.

45 Lind and Marshner, *Cultural Conservatism*, 4.

46 Ibid., 5.

the 1980s had given rise to a "'me-first' ethic" that encouraged suicide, hedonism, homosexuality, and rock music.[47]

*Cultural radicalism*—Lind and Marshner's term for a variety of social trends—was accelerating this drift. The major institutions of the United States had fallen into the soft hands of literary critics and legal theorists. Professors in elite universities were using the methods of "deconstruction" and "Critical Studies" to convince their students that the West was a sinkhole of "racism, exploitation, and inhumanity."[48] As more students succumbed to this ideology, they became indoctrinated mercenaries in a prolonged culture war against the traditional family-based order. Environmentalism, campaigns against homophobia and racism, and the establishment of women's studies departments were merely skirmishes in this devastating assault on Western civilization.

In *Cultural Conservatism*, Lind and Marshner outlined their plan for saving the West. They saw education as a crucial mobilizing issue. Their policy proposals assumed that strengthening parental authority would improve national educational outcomes. The reintroduction of discipline to schools, including "reasonable corporate punishment," would help students from "economically disadvantaged communities" to "climb out of poverty."[49] The steady integration of schools and universities into a free market of competition and commodification (broad-based voucher plans, private accrediting agencies, and private funding) would break "the monopoly influence of educational ideologues."[50] Saving Western civilization would mean relegating education to the privatized logics of the family and free market.

Lind and Marshner's proposals rely on a strange kind of fusionism. In his contribution to the 1991 FCF-published

47 Ibid., 6.
48 Ibid., 7.
49 Ibid., 51.
50 Ibid., 52.

*Cultural Conservatism: Theory and Practice*, Lind inverts the Marxist base-superstructure metaphor to assert that culture is the foundation on which any capitalist economy must operate.[51] Certain cultural values are "functional," Lind theorizes, insofar as they produce an efficient workforce that satisfies the needs of capitalism. As Melinda Cooper demonstrates, the New Right's rhetoric of family values usually served to legitimate a neoliberal dismantling of the welfare state and other forms of social provision.[52] It expressed a desire to push social problems back into the private world of the home, where the struggles of workers and minorities would be felt as personal worries rather than political battles. Yet this fusionist approach offers no way to overcome the contradictions of capital that persistently undermine the stability of these cultural units. Family values are no match for the unrelenting fury of exchange value. Without a structural understanding of capitalist crisis, conservatives like Lind need to locate some sort of external cause for social disintegration—cultural radicalism was the perfect scapegoat.

Lind's critique of cultural radicalism remained faithful to New Right ideology. Under this framework, the New Class, or cultural radicals, were answering the demands of the Groups and depriving the People of traditional cultural values. Yet, in his odes to the collective conscience of the West, Lind refused to acknowledge the structural exclusions that operated in pre-1960s US society. Cultural radicals, according to Lind, were simply fabricating the problems of white supremacy and patriarchy with their dubious methods of deconstruction and critical legal theory. Cultural radicalism, in brief, was a doctrine

51 William S. Lind, "Introduction," in *Cultural Conservatism: Theory and Practice*, ed. William S. Lind and William H. Marshner (Washington, DC; Free Congress Research and Education Foundation, 1991), 2–3.

52 Melinda Cooper, *Family Values: Between Neoliberalism and the New Social Conservatism* (Brooklyn: Zone Books, 2017).

of deceit. For Lind, these New Class radicals needed to be removed from positions of power before the American people suffered the consequences of irreversible decline. Several years later, Lind would update this critique to tackle the scourge of what he called "Cultural Marxism."

Lind first used the term "Cultural Marxism" in a 1994 co-authored *Marine Corps Gazette* article entitled "Fourth Generation Warfare: Another Look."[53] Lind and his co-authors wrote that cultural radicals in education, the media, and the entertainment industry were forcing Americans to reject Western values. They suspected that these radicals were hiding a darker agenda behind the bland phrases of "multiculturalism" and "political correctness." When Lind and his co-authors peeled off these deceptive labels, they claimed to find nothing other than "Marxism translated from economic into social and cultural terms."[54] This form of camouflaged Marxism was creeping across the nation and dividing the American people into conflicting racial and sexual groups. It had the potential, Lind and his colleagues speculated, to split the US Marines into a "white Marine corps, black Marine corps, Christian Marine corps, possibly even a gay Marine corps."[55] If no one heeded their warning, then it seemed inevitable that America would degenerate into a state of civil war.

This 1994 essay lacked any detail about *who* translated Marxism from economic into social and cultural terms. A year or so later, Lind would learn about a group of German Marxist thinkers that could function as a plausible scapegoat for the rise of political correctness in the United States. It seems that Lind first heard about the Frankfurt School from his friend Raymond V. Raehn, who allegedly borrowed material from

53 William S. Lind, John F. Schmitt, and Gary I. Wilson, "Fourth Generation Warfare: Another Look," *Marine Corps Gazette* (December 1994): 34–7.

54 Ibid., 36.

55 Ibid., 36.

Minnicino's 1992 *Fidelio* article to produce an unpublished manuscript entitled "Critical Theory: A Special Research Report." In 1997, Lind, Raehn, and other conservative authors contributed to the FCF's journal series *Essays on Our Times* to blame Frankfurt School for political correctness. Lind's own essay "What Is Political Correctness?" featured many of the memorable framings that he would use to characterize "Cultural Marxism" in his later op-eds, speeches, interviews, and television shows.

Political correctness, according to Lind, had transformed America into a totalitarian state. Formerly prestigious Ivy League institutions were now "small, Ivy-covered North Koreas."[56] Although liberals claimed that speech codes existed to spread tolerance and respect, Lind unmasked political correctness as a new form of Marxism. The thinkers of the Frankfurt School, Lind explained, blended Marxism, Freudianism, and linguistics to create a discipline called "Critical Theory" that advocated for a society of "radical egalitarianism."[57] Instead of promoting equality, followers of the Frankfurt School used the power of the state to punish white men and reward the Groups. Lind called on ordinary Americans to defy the rules of Cultural Marxism: "Use the words that it forbids" and "refuse to use the words it mandates."[58] Not only should they use offensive language, but they also should adopt traditional lifestyles: "Ladies should be homemakers and housewives . . . children should not be born out of wedlock, [and] open homosexuals should be shunned."[59] This strategy of defiance, as Lind put it, would rid the United States of Cultural Marxism.

This initial essay contains several of Lind's little quirks. Instead of providing data to prove that political correctness

56 William S. Lind, "What is Political Correctness?," *Essays on Our Times*, Free Congress Foundation, Number 43, March 1997.

57 Ibid.

58 Ibid.

59 Ibid.

was everywhere, Lind uses hyperbole to inspire a sense of dread about "totalitarianism." Instead of discussing the actual theories of the Frankfurt School, he invokes the word "Marxist" to demonize the aims of social justice. And instead of gauging the true impact of social policy, Lind builds on classic New Right rhetorical tactics to reframe moderate reforms—affirmative action, the removal of the n-word from public vocabulary, efforts to increase equality between the genders—as devious mechanisms for disturbing white suburban family life.

It is often unclear whether Lind believes that America's major institutions are salvageable. Would it simply be a matter of replacing progressive (and unionized) educators with cultural conservatives? Does Lind see the need to establish new institutions? In his writings on political correctness, Lind refrains from proposing structural reform and promotes lifestyle changes as the most appropriate mode of political action. These personal choices represent an escape from the incessant politicization of the social that started in the 1960s. For Lind, this kind of individualized activism promises a smooth return to the seemingly non-political sphere of 1950s-era America—before the Frankfurt School ruined everything.

Throughout his work, Lind assumed that merely telling people that political correctness was Cultural Marxism would compel them to accept cultural conservatism. He felt that conservatives needed to engage in educational activism to expose this secret history to their friends, neighbors, and relatives. In that 1997 essay, Lind was testing the field to see whether anyone else would pick up this narrative about the Frankfurt School. In subsequent years, both Weyrich and Lind would work to popularize the narratives of Cultural Marxism/s through different media and in different venues.

## The Letters of St. Paul Weyrich

In February 1999, Weyrich issued his famous "Letter to Conservatives." He lamented that the New Right had lost the culture war. The overwhelming majority of Americans did not appear to share the values of cultural conservatism. Despite the right-wing campaign to impeach President Bill Clinton for lying about his affair with Monica Lewinsky, "Slick Willie" remained in the Oval Office. In his letter, Weyrich mused that "if there really was a moral majority out there, Bill Clinton would have been driven out of office months ago."[60] Weyrich felt that the average American was too distracted by MTV to care about the violation of such old-fashioned taboos as infidelity and perjury. Decades of cultural drift had corroded America's soul.

In a 1997 article for *The New Republic*, the journalist David Grann tested a definition of *Weyrichism*: "the kind of rhetoric that brands one's own people apostates when they make some of the compromises that power inevitably demands."[61] According to this description, "Letter to Conservatives" was the quintessential Weyrichist document. Although the Gingrich revolution of 1994 represented a serious political breakthrough for the Republican Party, Weyrich feared that his conservative allies were not doing enough to regain influence over the culture. If the conservative movement did nothing to prevent this collapse, then it would suffer at the hands of a new barbarism.

Weyrich diagnosed this cultural decline as the consequence of an ongoing assault on American institutions. He wrote that "Cultural Marxism is succeeding in its war against our culture," because the "ideology of political correctness . . . has so grasped the body politic [and our] institutions . . . [and] threatens to

60 Paul M. Weyrich, "Letter to Conservatives," National Center for Policy Research, February 16, 1999.

61 David Grann, "Robespierre of the Right," *New Republic*, October 27, 1997, 22.

control literally every aspect of our lives."[62] He identified the Frankfurt School and Herbert Marcuse as the perpetrators of this totalitarian ideology. These Marxist thinkers had implanted the idea of political correctness into universities to bring about a tyrannical regime.

As Weyrich saw it, the ascendancy of Cultural Marxism proved that the New Right's strategy had failed. The New Right assumed that there was a pre-existing conservative constituency—a moral majority—that could be mobilized to enact social and cultural change through political institutions. Nearly three decades after he had started to build the New Right, Weyrich conceded that conservatives needed a different plan to rescue the remnants of a Moral Minority.

Exodus was apparently the only option left for cultural conservatives. Weyrich reasoned that "a legitimate strategy for us to follow is to look at ways to separate ourselves from the institutions that have been captured by the ideology of Political Correctness."[63] Weyrich modified Timothy O'Leary's countercultural motto—*tune in, turn on, drop out*—into a new slogan for cultural conservatism. He advised families to *turn off* their televisions, video games, and computers to protect their children from propaganda and pornography. They would have to *tune out* of the dominant culture and *drop out* into alternative godly lifestyles. The inversion of O'Leary's acid-trip quip symbolized a strange mimicking of sixties-style rebellion to imply that cultural conservatism had become the new counterculture.

The references to Marcuse and the Frankfurt School in Weyrich's "Letter to Conservatives" continued the New Right's mystifying gesture of blaming social fragmentation on individual deviants rather than structural forces. Although Weyrich intuited the importance of institutions in reproducing cultural norms, he opted for moralizing criticism over institutional critique. Consequently, he resorted to a strategy that stressed

62 Weyrich, "Letter to Conservatives."

63 Ibid.

moral purity over political action. Whereas the New Right once promoted a counter-politicization of the social, Weyrich proposed the gradual shaping of a separate society. He favored the tactic of boycotting over the tired methods of electoral politics. Instead of transforming existing institutions, he encouraged the building of "parallel structures."[64] He urged parents to join the home school movement rather than jockey for position on local school boards. The act of setting oneself apart from a corrupted American culture, Weyrich claimed, would insulate conservatives from impending civilizational ruin. If political correctness continued to be the prevailing ideology of American institutions, then "cultural disintegration" would be inevitable.[65] As Weyrich put it in a 1999 *Washington Post* op-ed, conservatives needed to be ready to "build a new nation among the ruins of the old."[66] Only a truly conservative cultural revival—a strategy of separation—would free the United States from the grip of Cultural Marxism. Yet Weyrich never clarified how the Frankfurt School infiltrated and overpowered American society. He left this explanatory task to Lind.

## Lind and His Single-Factor Explanation of History

In July 1998, Lind was invited to speak at an Accuracy in Academia (AIA) conference. Founded in 1985, AIA was set up to expose instances of political bias on American campuses. Its founder, Reed Irvine, believed that universities were indoctrinating students with progressive ideologies rather than teaching them facts and logic. Although the organization claimed to uphold academic freedom, it instigated several quasi-

64 The Heritage Foundation, "Cultural Renewal," C-SPAN Video, 2:00:09, April 13, 1999.

65 Weyrich, "Letter to Conservatives."

66 Paul M. Weyrich, "Separate and Free," *Washington Post*, March 7, 1999, B07.

McCarthyistic witch hunts against left-leaning professors. They recruited classroom spies, compiled databases of progressive academics, and harassed countless lecturers. Ironically, the ideologues of AIA were bemoaning ideological uniformity as they were actively trying to punish anyone who did not conform to their own conservative standards of correct thinking. At the 1998 conference, Irvine assembled a line-up of anti–political correctness speakers who could share stories about left-wing madness on the modern American campus. Lind's co-panelists included Peter LaBarbera, the leader of the anti-gay lobby group Americans for Truth about Homosexuality, and Christina Hoff Sommers, an American Enterprise Institute fellow whose 1994 book *Who Stole Feminism?* eviscerated contemporary feminist thought and activism.

In his own talk, Lind promised to reveal the Marxist prehistory of political correctness. He outlined five parallels between classical Marxism and Cultural Marxism. First, Lind said, both Marxisms were *totalitarian*. Just as communist bureaucrats censored and imprisoned dissidents, college activists penalized anyone who uttered an insensitive comment. The second similarity was their *single-factor explanation of history*. Whereas classical Marxism insisted that economics determined history, Cultural Marxism held that *power*—defined primarily in racial and sexual terms—was the sole determining force of historical events. Their third shared trait was *an inflexible definition of good and evil*. The villainous bourgeoisie and heroic proletariat of classical Marxism had become the infamous white male—the oppressor—and innocent minority—the oppressed—of political correctness. By comparing affirmative action to Soviet dekulakization, Lind tried to convince his audience that *expropriation* was the fourth link between classical and Cultural Marxism. "Diversity quotas," Lind stated, expropriated college admissions from talented white students and redistributed them to undeserving Black and Hispanic applicants. The fifth and final likeness was a *self-confirming method of analysis*.

Classical Marxists obeyed the laws of Marxist economics; Cultural Marxists brandished the weapons of Derridean theory.

Of course, these parallels relied on caricatures of the practices that Lind associated with political correctness. He even exhibited some of these so-called Marxist qualities—*inflexible definition of good and evil*, *single-factor explanation of history*, *self-confirming method of analysis*—in his own characterizations of Cultural Marxism. Despite the superficiality of Lind's account, his list of comparisons served an implicit rhetorical strategy. He assumed that ordinary Americans would refuse to accept affirmative action or literary theory if they believed that these things were simply new incarnations of the old Marxist claptrap. In this 1998 speech, Lind unfolded a timeline of personalities and events to prove that the Frankfurt School was wholly responsible for importing political correctness to the United States.

According to Lind, Cultural Marxism was born in the aftermath of World War I. Contrary to Marx's predictions, the industrial workers of Western Europe were more willing to don military uniforms and die for their countries than unite with the global proletariat and overthrow their rulers. Several Marxist thinkers felt compelled to figure out why the European working class lacked revolutionary fervor. The theorists Lukács and Gramsci eventually offered a convincing explanation: The workers were too attached to Judeo-Christian values and thus felt no desire to overturn the capitalist system. They urged communists to come up with a strategy that could undermine the West's cultural foundations. Following Lukács and Gramsci's advice, Felix Weil established what Lind calls a "think tank" in Frankfurt, Germany—the Institute for Social Research—to devise a Marxist masterplan for destroying Western civilization.[67]

67 Accuracy in Academia, "Social and Political Issues on College Campuses," C-SPAN video, 4:02:24, July 10, 1998.

Under Max Horkheimer's leadership, the Frankfurt School converted the pseudoscience of Marxist economics into the pseudo-philosophy of political correctness. Horkheimer mixed Marxist and Freudian ingredients to brew a noxious philosophical concoction called Critical Theory, which Lind misconstrues as "the most destructive criticism possible, in every possible way, designed to bring the current order down."[68] Horkheimer's corrosive Critical Theory became the intellectual basis for women's studies, Black studies, and queer studies. Those who taught and researched in these disciplines, Lind suggested, were not producing knowledge but, rather, intensifying cultural drift.

Within the mirror realm of Lind's historical imagination, the Frankfurt School's Cultural Marxism appeared as the evil twin of FCF's cultural conservatism. Critical Theory, Lind implied, was nothing more than a set of left-wing single-issue campaigns. Erich Fromm criticized traditional gender roles to argue that sexual difference was a social construct and thus gave rise to second-wave feminism. Marcuse celebrated "polymorphous perversity" as a mode of sexual expression, which, in turn, inspired the gay liberation movement. Horkheimer, through his writings on materialism and nature, brought about modern environmentalism. Lind's retrospective readings of the Frankfurt School imply that the feminist, LGBTQ+, and environmentalist movements were mere slaves to an ideology rather than rational people with serious complaints about particular social problems.

When young college radicals started to protest the Vietnam War in the 1960s, they fumbled about for some sort of theory to intellectualize their revolt. These sophomoric subversives were not clever enough, Lind judged, to master Marx's *Capital*, so they turned to Marcuse's 1955 *Eros and Civilization* for inspiration. Marcuse urged these quasi-Marxists to indulge their sexual desires, resist the compulsions of the Protestant ethic,

---

68 Ibid.

and refuse to conform to existing society. Not only did Marcuse teach his students to rebel against sexual repression, but he also told them to engage in political persecution. To provide his AIA audience with a scapegoat for political correctness, Lind decided to quote the famous controversial line from Marcuse's 1965 essay "Repressive Tolerance": "intolerance against movements from the Right, and toleration of movement from the Left."[69] According to Lind, Marcuse replaced parental authority with a kind of paternalistic authoritarianism.

Like the rest of the New Right's social critiques, Lind's attack on campus activism was simultaneously and subtextually a defense of "family values." In the 1960s, New Left activists rebelled against the *in loco parentis* rules of the capitalist university. As Melinda Cooper explains, these rules transplanted "the intimate normativity of the Fordist family into a wider institutional context, radiating its discipline well beyond the confines of the family home into the liminal social space of the college campus, where students were considered neither complete adults nor children."[70] The regime of *in loco parentis* empowered administrators and dorm officials not only to regulate behavior, dress codes, and alcohol consumption, but also to monitor and restrict sexual activity. Female students were subject to strict curfews and clothing rules. Students could be expelled for homosexuality. For Southern Black students, *in loco parentis* functioned as a semi–Jim Crow regime to discourage civil rights activism. The discipline of *in loco parentis* was designed to adapt these students to the norms of the new knowledge economy. As noted in the last chapter, graduates were expected to assume professional-managerial roles in industries that supported America's neo-colonial wars around the world. Instead of accepting their place in this system, college radicals resisted the patronizing rules of *in loco*

69 Herbert Marcuse, "Repressive Tolerance," *A Critique of Pure Tolerance* (Boston: Beacon Press, 1965), 109.

70 Cooper, *Family Values*, 230.

*parentis* and protested the hegemonic order that staged military interventions in Southeast Asia. The New Right's reaction to this student revolt was partially an effort to preserve the family-based cultural order that legitimated inequality and oppression in the United States and elsewhere.

Even as a young man, Lind saw the New Left as a threat to this civilizational order. In the late 1960s, he was a baby-faced undergraduate at Dartmouth College. While his contemporaries —including future Secretary of Labor Robert Reich—were getting involved in left-wing causes, Lind was running the Dartmouth Conservative Society and editing its journal, *The Conservative Idea*. In the pages of this student publication, he defended Rhodesia's white-minority government and pilloried the "black power" movement. His most fiery and trenchant articles, however, were leveled at Dartmouth's increasingly radical student body. In a February 1968 essay, "The Real Failure of Dartmouth College," Lind declaimed that "large and growing numbers of students" possessed an "intellectual outlook" that was "totally divorced from reality."[71] Unsurprisingly, Lind's positions did not make him popular on campus. Former acquaintances remember him as arrogant and argumentative. Others recall that Lind tried to organize a rally in support of the Vietnam War on the college green. Fifty people turned up with pro-war signs. They were soon outnumbered by 1,500 counter-protesters. For Lind, Cultural Marxism/s may have provided some sort of post hoc rationalization for why so many of his peers turned against conservative politics in the 1960s. The teachings of the Frankfurt School had imprisoned his classmates in an ideological fantasy world where the well-crafted arguments of *The Conservative Idea* could no longer reach them. Political correctness, according to Lind, was simply the latest phase of this rebellion against the real world rather than a clumsy attempt to relieve the friction of an unequal society.

---

71 William S. Lind, "The Real Failure of Dartmouth College," *The Conservative Idea* 3, no. 2 (February 1968): 15.

In the Q&A session after his talk, Sommers pushed Lind to tone down his inflated rhetoric. Dealing with political correctness, she joked, was not as bad as living in North Korea. In a gruff response, Lind retorted that many Americans were living through a period of "quasi-judicial terror."[72] It was not, in his opinion, a time for moderation. The enemy—Cultural Marxism—needed to be defeated, without delay, before Frankfurt School–inspired tyranny engulfed the American republic.

Unlike other, more well-reasoned critiques of political correctness, Lind's AIA talk offered a dramatic single-factor explanation of history and attributed all-encompassing cultural power to Frankfurt School ideas. As far as Lind was concerned, there were no broader social or material forces that might explain the contested status of free speech on campuses, the heated debates about revising and expanding the canon, and the introduction of new perspectives into certain academic disciplines. The only possible cause of political correctness in the United States was the arrival of the Frankfurt School in the 1930s. This belief—that "bad ideas" are the principal engine of cultural decline—was a key tenet of US conservative thought. The postwar American right, Nash explains, kept to this position, because it felt "easier to resist one's age if 'only' ideas and not 'forces' seem[ed] to be the foe."[73] If bad ideas caused social disorder, then good ideas could presumably re-order society. After all, the production and popularization of so-called good ideas was the whole point of the New Right intellectual. This is what motivated Lind's activity: If he could spread his narrative of Cultural Marxism/s to a large enough audience of ordinary Americans, then they would have no choice but to reject political correctness and embrace cultural conservatism. To accomplish this goal, he reduced the Frankfurt School's

72 Accuracy in Academia, "Social and Political Issues on College Campuses."

73 Nash, *The Conservative Intellectual Movement in America since 1945*, 52.

theories to soundbites, buzzwords, and other compressed forms that circulated more efficiently through the New Right's communicative infrastructure. It may be easy to mock Lind's misunderstandings, but he was merely following Weyrich's wisdom: *Winning power* is more important than *being right*. What Lind's work lacked in depth of research or rigor of analysis was made up for by its sheer communicability. He simply needed to get the message out there. And a year after this AIA talk, Lind would appear on television to transmit his ideas of Cultural Marxism/s into the living rooms of America.

## The Dirty Little Secrets of the Frankfurt School

In 1993, Weyrich launched the Washington, DC–based satellite television network National Empowerment Television (NET, later renamed America's Voice) to broadcast FCF's ideas to American households. He judged that New Right think tanks were failing to capture the minds of the US population, because they had not adapted to televisual culture. Most Americans in the 1990s were receiving their political news from television and talk radio. Yet the printed word was still the preferred medium of the New Right think tank. Unlike his out-of-touch comrades, Weyrich sensed that "alternative media" had the power to reach many more people. NET, which he described as a "network for the movement," would invite viewers to become active members of a conservative majority.[74]

NET, a twenty-four-hour "interactive" television channel, offered a wide variety of programming. Newt Gingrich, the Republican Speaker of the House of Representatives, co-hosted a political talk show called *The Progress Report* to interview politicians and pundits from a conservative perspective. Several right-wing organizations produced their own shows for NET,

74 C-SPAN, "Conservative Leadership Conference," C-SPAN video, 3:35:06, November 12, 1993.

such as the anti–gun control National Rifle Association's *On Target with the NRA*, the anti-abortion group America Life League's *Putting Families First*, and Reed Irvine's anti-liberal media watchdog Accuracy in Media's *The Other Side*. Each show featured a call-in segment, during which viewers could call a toll-free number to speak with the host and voice their own questions and concerns. In a 1993 *Washington Times* article, Weyrich characterized these live telephone calls as "an unfettered link between the American electorate and their representatives in Washington."[75]

Who was NET's audience? An estimated 14 million households—predominantly located in the Sunbelt—subscribed to the network. These viewers, however, were not imagined as passive consumers of NET's programming. In a C-SPAN interview, NET's General Manager Brian Jones promoted the network as a "populist" enterprise that empowered the "American people" to "talk back" to Washington officials.[76] Despite its promise to represent the voice of the People, NET catered to an exclusively conservative public.[77] It offered a mode of participation that was filtered through New Right technologies and discourses. In other words, the opinions of viewers counted—or were perceived as legitimate—only insofar as they matched NET's idealized conception of their audience. This pseudo-populist positioning reflected the New Right's tendency to brand right-wing constituencies as the majority or the People (the silent majority, the moral majority, and so on) and dismiss everyone else as the Groups (special interests, liberals, homosexuals, welfare mothers, Black people, and so on).

75 Paul Weyrich, "Welcome to the Birth of the New Media Age," *Washington Times*, December 15, 1993, 4.

76 C-SPAN, "National Empowerment Television," C-SPAN video, 50:03, December 13, 1994.

77 Anna Williams, "Conservative Media Activism: The Free Congress Foundation and National Empowerment Television," in *Media, Culture, and the Religious Right*, ed. Linda Kintz and Julia Lesage (Minneapolis: University of Minnesota Press, 1998), 288.

Consequently, critiques of political correctness—the so-called Marxist ideology of the New Class and the Groups—helped to bolster NET's definition of itself as a defender of the People. Even *The Next Revolution*, a regular NET program that Lind co-hosted, branded itself as a television show that battled the forces of Cultural Marxism.

In 1999, NET aired a special edition of its call-in news show *American Investigator* called "Political Correctness: The Dirty Little Secret." The episode featured several interviewees, such as *Tenured Radicals* author Roger Kimball, the New-Leftie-turned-neocon David Horowitz, the Hungarian Nazi collaborator Laszlo Pasztor, and the prominent historian of the Frankfurt School Martin Jay. Many years after appearing on this NET program, Jay reflected on his role as Lind's useful idiot: "Interweaving my edited testimony into the larger narrative may have given it an unearned legitimacy."[78] Of course, Lind did not really need the help of a left-leaning historian from Berkeley—a suspiciously New Class profession—to appear trustworthy to NET's audience. Whenever Lind appeared onscreen, he was wearing a smart suit and, sometimes, smoking a wooden pipe. Even these trivial details conveyed a certain faith that the old ways were superior to the new ones. To the typical NET viewer, Lind was the visual epitome of traditionalism —a neat conservative contrast to the slovenly professors and protestors of the 1990s academy.

The episode kicks off with a dramatic and fast-paced montage. As a suspenseful MIDI orchestra score plays in the background, the narrator recites the misdeeds of the politically correct: "Black activists" on an "Ivy League campus" burn "hundreds of copies" of the "conservative newspaper;" Reggie White says that "different races have different talents" and loses "millions in endorsements," and the Boy Scouts of America are sued for

78 Martin Jay, "Dialectic of Counter-Enlightenment: the Frankfurt School as Scapegoat of the Lunatic Fringe," *Salmagundi*, no. 168/169 (Fall 2010/Winter 2011): 34.

"discrimination" for refusing to "appoint an openly homosexual Scoutmaster."[79] The narrator poses a rhetorical question: "Has political correctness taken over America?"[80] Over a black-and-white image of the Institute for Social Research building in Frankfurt, the narrator asks: "And what does it have to do with this small school in 1920s Germany?"[81] The montage combines footage from American college campuses, photographs of Frankfurt School thinkers, and clips from interviews. The result is a jarring patchwork of insinuations. The narrator starts to say, "The agenda of political correctness may not be a secret," which is interrupted by a clip of Horowitz saying, "Attack America," and then continues, "but it didn't start in the 1960s."[82] The formal structure of this montage reinforces the overarching argument of the episode, flattening different temporalities—1920s Germany, 1960s student revolt, 1990s campuses—into a single timeline of straightforward causality. Consequently, it operates as a visual analogue to Lind's claim that the Frankfurt School was entirely responsible for fabricating and transmitting—unimpeded by any obstacles or countervailing forces—the ideology of political correctness. Nothing sums up Lind's argument more clearly than this cheesy line from the narrator: "It may be the 1990s, but the Frankfurt School is still very much in session."

The first segment of this episode explored three anecdotes that allegedly demonstrated the pervasiveness of Cultural Marxism. NET visited Cornell University to interview an editor of the conservative student publication *The Cornell Review*. At the time, the *Review* had published a racist parody of Ebonics to satirize the Africana studies department. According to Lind,

79 National Empowerment Television, "The History of Political Correctness Part 1 of 3," YouTube, 10:37, posted by Theriomachus, November 11, 2009.

80 Ibid.

81 Ibid.

82 Ibid.

a group of Black students protested the article and decided to burn every copy of *The Cornell Review* on campus. They even disrupted an honorary event for the leading civil rights activist Thomas Jones. *The Cornell Review* editor claimed the university administration did nothing to denounce the actions of these Black students and even conceded to their demands.

The second anecdote relayed the story of Reggie White to prove that "being black is no protection against political correctness."[83] White—a former Green Bay Packers defensive end and ordained minister—was invited to speak at the Wisconsin State legislature, where he talked about the sinfulness of homosexuality and the differences between the races. Although White did not apparently say anything offensive, he lost a potential contract as a sports commentator on NBC.

Finally, Lind discussed the case of a gay Scoutmaster who was suing the Boy Scouts of America for discrimination. NET interviewed a longtime Scoutmaster named Lou Doty, who claimed parents would not want their son to spend any time near a gay man. For Doty, this attack on the Boy Scouts was part of a larger agenda: "Society deteriorates" if the "wrong people" destroy "the right institutions."[84] The wrong people, Lind revealed to his audience, were the Cultural Marxists; the Frankfurt School were the architects of this plan to bring down the right institutions.

Each of these stories exemplified what John K. Wilson describes as the conservative technique of "myth-making by anecdote."[85] The reporting in this segment failed to provide a balanced perspective on these incidents. Lind did not interview any Black students or college administrators at Cornell. He did not specify why White's speech was so poorly received or

83 Ibid.

84 Ibid.

85 John K. Wilson, *The Myth of Political Correctness: The Conservative Attack on Higher Education* (Durham, NC: Duke University Press, 1995), 20.

even delve into the actual details of the *Boy Scouts of America v. Dale* case. In fact, Cornell University administrators did denounce the actions of the Black students and affirmed the right to free speech on campus. White was invited to deliver a brief five-minute presentation on his charity work, which devolved into an hour-long diatribe against homosexuality. The Boy Scouts of America expelled—rather than merely "refusing to appoint," in Lind's words—an assistant Scoutmaster in New Jersey when it was revealed that he was gay, even though it violated the state statute prohibiting discrimination based on sexual orientation. NET's framing of these anecdotes reflected a general tendency in American conservative media to replace objectivity and accuracy with ideological integrity. Instead of engaging in standard journalistic practices, NET aimed to counter the presumed dominance of liberal media by affirming and promoting conservative perspectives.

The anecdote is the perfect rhetorical tool for conservative media. Its very form—a brief story of something happening to a specific person—opposes the logic of political correctness. It favors personal experience over structural analysis or contextual explanation. It prioritizes the life of an individual over the structure of the social group and shrinks societal issues down to single incidents. Whereas Cultural Marxism blows everything up into a political conflict, the conservative anecdote shields the individual from politics. Each anecdote in this special edition of *American Investigator* hinted at the intrusion of politics into hitherto protected areas. How can a joke be political? What is so political about the beliefs of an ordained minister? Why would someone dare to politicize the Boy Scouts? Consequently, this realm of the anecdotal becomes a comforting refuge for a conservative worldview that excludes sociological or historical interpretations of events.

Lind's anecdotes follow what Lee Bebout calls the strategy of *weaponized victimhood*. Bebout explains that "assertions of victimhood" in right-wing media tend to "flatten out or invert social hierarchies and make them illegible."[86] For instance, the framing of *The Cornell Review* anecdote obscured the history of discrimination and marginalization that Black people traditionally faced on American college campuses. The true victim of this story, according to Lind, was the conservative student who experienced a backlash for publishing racist stereotypes. Such a "strategic obfuscation" proceeds from the following premise: "The oppressed are not really oppressed, but if they are, the privileged are oppressed in equal or greater ways."[87] Lind's strategy of weaponized victimhood portrayed political correctness as a means to oppress conservatives rather than a relatively unsatisfactory attempt to mitigate historical injustices. Members of NET's public may have identified with the subjects of Lind's anecdotes and felt that they belonged to a larger bloc of conservative victims. In this NET documentary, Lind gave them someone to blame for their perceived sense of victimization: the Frankfurt School.

Building on his earlier arguments, Lind claimed that the Frankfurt School invented political correctness and injected it into the United States. He produced a slanted interpretation of various thinkers to retroactively read elements of political correctness into their work. Erich Fromm pioneered "gender politics," Marcuse kickstarted "gay liberation," and Adorno and Horkheimer inspired "environmentalism." Lind even suggested that the Frankfurt School created "the 'victim groups' that constituted 'the politically correct coalition.'"[88] None of the social movements that emerged in the 1960s, according

86 Lee Bebout, "Weaponizing Victimhood: Discourses of Oppression and the Maintenance of Supremacy on the Right," in *News on the Right: Studying Conservative News Cultures*, ed. Anthony Nadler and A. J. Bauer (New York: Oxford University Press, 2020), 75–6.

87 Ibid., 76.

88 National Empowerment Television, "The History of Political Correctness. Part 3 of 3," YouTube, 7:35, posted by Theriomachus, November 11, 2009.

to Lind, were protesting genuine injustice and inequality. The scholars of Black studies, women's studies, and LGBTQ+ studies were not studying real problems but, rather, inventing victim groups and fabulating stories of oppression. Only the lived experiences of those who matched FCF's agenda of cultural conservatism—*The Cornell Review* editor, Reggie White, Lou Doty—could be trusted. Lind's claim that the Frankfurt School essentially fooled Black Americans, women, and LGBTQ+ people into resisting and researching systems of oppression works to invalidate the collective agency and consciousness of these groups. Not only does Lind deny the existence of these social hierarchies, but he also misrepresents the pursuit of equality as nothing more than a scheme to bully conservatives.

The NET documentary did not propose any concrete solutions or strategies for resisting the spread of Cultural Marxism. At the time, Lind seemed convinced that merely "revealing" the true nature of political correctness would jolt his conservative public into action. However, he would later sketch out a possible method of political change in a handful of fictional texts, where he implied that resorting to violence might be the only way to eliminate Cultural Marxism.

## Lind's Victoria

On April 30, 1995, *The Washington Post* printed a brief piece of speculative fiction called "Understanding Oklahoma." The title alluded to the Oklahoma City Bombing: a devastating attack on the Alfred P. Murrah Federal Building that killed 168 people. The perpetrator of the bombing, former US Army solider Timothy McVeigh, had ties to the far-right, anti-government Patriot Movement. "Understanding Oklahoma" featured an editorial note that described this movement as a loose confederation of militant groups that advocates "armed resistance to the federal government."[89] The note continued: "These apocalyptic visions are not restricted to isolated pockets of rural America, but are also found in Washington."[90] The author of "Understanding Oklahoma" was none other than Lind, who wrote this short story to warn people what would happen if the United States abandoned "our" common culture.

The anonymous narrator of "Understanding Oklahoma" addresses the reader from the "Year of our Lord 2050" in a nation called Victoria that occupies the northeastern regions of what was once the United States (and the Maritime provinces of Canada).[91] He recalls the events of America's Second Civil War to caution future generations. According to the narrator, 1965 marked the end of the American dream and the start of the slow fragmentation of the *E Pluribus Unum* into "blacks, white, Hispanics, womyn, gays, victims, oppressors, left-handed albinos."[92] (Lind's choice of year was possibly a reference to the Immigration Act of 1965 or the Civil Rights Act of 1965.) In the 2000s, the United States suffered from uncontrollable hyperinflation and an uncontainable AIDS epidemic. The New Class could neither overcome these crises nor maintain its control over the apparatus of the federal government. By the end of the decade, various states were seceding from the union to form independent nations.

Each new nation symbolizes a different culture or ideology. "Deep Greeners" founded a totalitarian environmentalist state in Oregon. The Azanian Republic—a coalition of radical feminists, Maoist guerrillas, and militant vegetarians—took over Northern California. The "Reconquista" reclaimed Texas, New Mexico, Arizona, and Southern California. The strongest of these emerging nations, the narrator claims, was the Northern

89 William S. Lind, "Understanding Oklahoma," *Washington Post*, April 30, 1995.

90 Ibid.

91 Ibid.

92 Ibid.

Confederation (later renamed Victoria), which experienced a revival of traditional Victorian culture. The Deep Green regime and the Azanian Republic—those last outposts of New Class smugness and social justice—fell apart within a few years.

Unlike the West Coast's cultural radicals, the Northern Confederation enjoyed the flourishing of something called a "retroculture." The retroculture movement rejected the follies of multiculturalism and embraced the old ways of patriarchy, public religiosity, and parental authority. "The Recovery," as the citizens of Victoria called it, describes this period of rebuilding traditional "Judeo-Christian culture" on "rocky New England soil" and the displacing of "savagery with civilization."[93] As the short story ends, the narrator rejoices that "after so many years of humiliation, the majority had taken back the culture."[94]

"Understanding Oklahoma" dramatized a critique of multiculturalism. No government could rule, according to Lind, without a strong common culture. A multicultural society was always on the brink of civil war. In his fictional writings, Lind blamed the New Class for replacing the enduring tenets of traditional culture with the mumbo-jumbo of 1960s-style cultural relativism. Their incompetence was the primary cause of America's cultural decay. The revival of Western civilization, as outlined in Lind's narrative, would require the violent overthrow of this defunct elite. "Understanding Oklahoma," in other words, synthesized Lind's military theorizing and culture warring. When he adapted this short story into a 585-page novel, *Victoria: A Novel of 4th Generation War* (published in 2014 under the self-aggrandizing pseudonym Thomas Hobbes), Lind pictured America's Second Civil War as a grand conflict between Cultural Marxism and the West.[95]

93 Ibid.

94 Ibid.

95 By 2014, Lind was no longer affiliated with FCF. In a column for *The American Conservative*, he described his 2009 departure as "unexpected."

Within the speculative universe of *Victoria*, Lind could reimagine himself as the West's most prescient thinker. In it, he is proven right about the cause of civilizational decline (Cultural Marxism), the only possible strategy for social change (Fourth Generation Warfare), and the nature of an ideal Western state (retroculture). For instance, the novel's protagonist, Captain John Rumford, learns about Cultural Marxism from a video on TraditionalRight.com. The video is Lind's documentary on the Frankfurt School; the website is Lind's personal blog. In fact, *Victoria* could reasonably be interpreted as Lind's fantasy of what would happen if people simply listened to his warnings about Cultural Marxism. The plot of *Victoria* is the logical culmination of Lind's campaign to end political correctness and establish a right-wing utopia based on the principles of Cultural Conservatism—it is Weyrich's "Letter to Conservatives" brought to life.

*Victoria* was never intended as a work of pure entertainment. A prevailing feature of the novel is the constant discussion of tactics. The planning and execution of military operations, from the reclaiming of Boston from Islamists to the invasion of the radical feminist Azanian Republic, supplies the reader with models that they could emulate in real-life combative scenarios. As the reader progresses through this novel-cum-training manual, they are immersed in the mental attitudes and strategic instincts of Fourth Generation warfare. The text itself is less of an escapist fantasy and more of a literary apparatus for turning people into Fourth Generation Warriors.

What is Fourth Generation warfare? In his writings on military strategy, Lind divides the history of modern war into four generations.[96] The Peace of Westphalia in 1648 marked the birth of First Generation warfare. The treaty established the state's monopoly on war. Before 1648, conflict occurred primarily between various entities—families, tribes, religions,

96 William S. Lind, "Understanding Fourth Generation War," *Military Review*, September–October 2004.

cities, enterprises—rather than formal national armies and navies. The emergence of the modern state resulted in a complete transformation of warfare.

The First and Second Generations represented military cultures of order. Soldiers wore formal uniforms and followed strict instructions. Generals issued grand battle plans that had to be executed diligently and without deviation. The Third Generation—exemplified in the German strategy of blitzkrieg in World War II—introduced a form of maneuver warfare that emphasized speed, surprise, and nonlinearity. This approach to conflict reoriented military culture: self-discipline over imposed discipline, adaptability over obedience, flexibility over procedure. Fourth Generation warfare continues this trend of nonlinear combat. Its defining characteristics are decentralization and initiative. The proliferation of non-state actors (al-Qaeda, Hamas, the Patriot Movement) purportedly shows that the state's monopoly on war has diminished. Lind interprets this decline as a return to the world of cultures—a "return to the way war worked before the rise of the state."[97]

Fourth Generation warfare, according to Lind, liberates the art of war from all the unnecessary elements that encumber modern militaries. It embodies a purer form of conflict that springs from a commitment to cultural bonds that run deeper than mere state allegiances. For Lind, the "universal crisis of legitimacy of the state" presents an opportunity for cultural restoration.[98] He predicts that America, whose "closed political system" is riddled with "multiculturalism," will be one of those states that succumbs to a "homegrown variety of Fourth Generation warfare."[99] Ultimately, *Victoria* sketches out how a Fourth Generation military campaign might operate in the United States to defeat the ideological leviathan of Cultural Marxism.

97 Ibid., 16.
98 Ibid., 14.
99 Ibid.

The plot of *Victoria* charts the decline of a dystopian United States and the subsequent rise of the right-wing Northern Confederation. In the first half of the book, Lind subjects the reader to a blunt critique of contemporary America. Lind's narrator, Rumford, suggests that the New Class, and their ideology of Cultural Marxism, replaced "real life" with a "'virtual reality' devoid of all virtue."[100] He complains that everything during the last days of the American empire was politicized: words, clothes, entertainment. What had disappeared, according to Rumford, were "husband and wife and children, home and household and community, field and farm and village, the age-old lines and limits of our lives."[101] The arrangement of these things into threes (*x* and *y* and *z*) conveys a sense of proportion that frames the true relationship between the personal and the political. He contrasts this harmony with the "collective madness" of New Class America. Elections were futile, because "all the candidates were from the same party, the New Class."[102] The home was no longer a refuge; technology—television and computers—transmitted "Satan's regurgitation into our souls."[103] The economy became a spectacular delusion as the New Class strangled the manufacturing industry and blithely trusted in Wall Street. Those who found "dignity and security by being reduced to commodities" labored fruitlessly in an almost slave-like condition.[104] New Class America, as Rumford describes it, was entirely detached from everything "natural."

Lind's description of American society in *Victoria* feels oddly akin to some left-wing accounts of late capitalism. Under neoliberalism, people are forced into debt payments and precarious contracts. Mainstream politicians rarely offer any radical alternatives to the existing system. Modern technology fosters an

100 Thomas Hobbes, *Victoria: A Novel of 4th Generation War* (Kouvola: Castalia House, 2014), 53.

101 Ibid., 53.

102 Ibid., 54–5.

103 Ibid., 54.

104 Ibid.

individualized and alienated engagement with the world that undermines the building of solidarity and community. Yet, even with these strange affinities, Lind's *Victoria* is nothing more than a pseudo-anti-capitalistic critique that lacks a structural understanding of capitalism. He cannot see the wider economic or geopolitical forces that eroded the conditions for the "traditional culture" that he adores. According to Lind, the abstract and persistent dynamics of global capitalism had nothing to do with the decline of the manufacturing industry or the rise of the service and financial sectors. Only Cultural Marxism is to blame for America's decline.

Central to Lind's portrayal of Cultural Marxism is a specific conception of ideology. For Lind, ideologies force people to adopt a kind of false consciousness that blinds them to the constancy of human nature and the factuality of reality. The ideology of Cultural Marxism, for instance, ignores "differences" between men and women, between whites and other races, and between the West and other cultures. What is so damaging about Cultural Marxism, Lind suggests, is that it teaches women, Black people, and other Groups to overcome these "differences" and demand equality. Whereas Lind regards these "differences" as natural, they are often products of historical processes of patriarchy, white supremacy, and imperialism. Those who protest inequality and discrimination are not rejecting reality but, rather, attempting to transform the manmade conditions that shape their lives. Lind's desire for a pre-1960s reality was always less about free speech or other political liberties, and more about restoring the traditional hierarchies that maintained the proper relations between these racial and sexual "differences."

Retroculture, which Rumford calls "an escape from ideology," realizes the New Right fantasy of depoliticizing the social.[105] The members of the retroculture movement pretend to inhabit various historical periods before 1965. Some

105 Ibid., 369.

households imitate the dress, furniture, and manners of a romanticized Victorian era; others return to the pre-political bliss of 1950s America. The practice of a retroculture cultivates a sort of postmodern moral consumerism that conforms to the New Right's favored social values. The only criterion for selecting a suitably retrocultural period is whether it was "a time when traditional American culture was strong."[106] In other words, these retrocultures must sustain the structures and assumptions of patriarchy and white supremacy.

In *Victoria,* white men occupy positions of power and prestige. Women and Black people are said to renounce their "victimhood" and accept their oppression. For instance, the avid retroculturalist Mrs. Kraft denounces the claim that women were "oppressed and mistreated in the past" as a "modern lie."[107] Through the voice of Rumford, Lind distinguishes between "Responsible Negros" and "bad blacks," and praises the former for abandoning their "professional victim hokum."[108] He sees these "responsible" Black people as grateful for the histories of slavery, dislocation, and discrimination in the United States: "I'm thankful for that slave ship that brought my ancestors over here, cause otherwise I'd be livin' in Africa, and I don't think there's a worst place on Earth."[109] Later in the book, the Northern Confederation experiences what can only be described as a voluntary revival of segregation, where "Black and white . . . mostly keep to themselves socially, as is only natural."[110] This vision of retroculture naturalizes historical patterns of gendered and racial discrimination, as though they were not outcomes of political histories. In *Victoria*, the subordination of women and the segregation of races is simply human nature.

106 Ibid., 61.
107 Ibid., 62.
108 Ibid., 238–47.
109 Ibid., 238.
110 Ibid., 247.

Like the rest of Lind's work, *Victoria* lacks any genuine explanation of why someone might be drawn to Cultural Marxism. Everything that the reader is told about Cultural Marxism comes from the mouths of favored characters: Rumford, Professor Gottfried Sanft, the Northern Confederation Governor Bill Kraft. None of the Cultural Marxists in the novel—the New Class of Washington, the Deep Greeners, the radical feminists of the Azanian Republic, the last few politically correct professors—are permitted to defend their beliefs in direct speech. Even when a character is said to "offer a stirring defense of Cultural Marxism," Lind does not bother to share any details about it with the reader.[111] These omissions reveal the utter narrow-mindedness of Lind's writings on Cultural Marxism. Although *Victoria* is a work of fiction, Lind seems entirely incapable of imagining why someone would believe in what he sees as the noxious ideas of political correctness. Cultural Marxists are an unfathomable enemy, whose concern for minorities masks a base craving for power and status. They cannot be understood. They can only be eliminated.

The most openly violent scene in *Victoria* is the Dartmouth College Massacre. Rumford explains that the hyperinflation of New Class America decimated college budgets and forced the closure of all higher education institutions. Soon after the founding of the Northern Confederation, a Zurich-based group called the Foundation for Higher Learning swooped in and offered to reopen Harvard, Dartmouth, and Yale. These universities rehired all their Cultural Marxist professors and relaunched their project of spreading political correctness in America. Halfway through the novel, Rumford learns that Dartmouth College—Lind's alma mater—is arranging a faculty workshop on Columbus Day to "discover the means for reversing Eurocentrism and white male domination over the North American continent."[112] In response, the leaders of

111 Ibid., 258.
112 Ibid., 283.

the Northern Confederation hatch a plan to eliminate these Cultural Marxists.

Governor Kraft and his troops interrupt the workshop to expose the true nature of political correctness. Television crews are present to capture Kraft's speech, which largely regurgitates Lind's writings on Cultural Marxism. He accuses the left-wing professors of betraying "every man and woman who for three thousand years has labored and fought and died for Western culture, the culture you sought to sacrifice to your own pathetic egos."[113] The punishment for this crime is public execution.

Lind's description of this scene is thick with heavy-handed references. Kraft's troops wear a "white surplice with the red Crusader cross emblazoned on a shield over the heart" and wield a "Roman gladius."[114] A choir of monks accompanies the troops and starts to sing *Dies Irae* to commence the massacre. In less than five minutes, 162 professors are murdered. The ancient Roman and Crusader imagery implies that these troops are slaughtering barbarians and infidels. *Dies Irae*, or "The Day of Wrath," is a medieval Latin poem and Gregorian chant that depicts the Last Judgement, in which sinners are condemned to hell. These symbols are meant to signify a lasting, coherent, and unified Western tradition. In this climatic scene, the bloody and gruesome slaughter of Cultural Marxists represents the triumphant revenge of the West against political correctness.

The Dartmouth College Massacre proposes violence as a strategy of depoliticization. Like all Fourth Generation warfare, it blurs the distinction between culture war and military conflict. It implies that simply killing all Cultural Marxists would bring an end to Cultural Marxism. The Groups would no longer protest social inequality, because no one would be telling them that they were oppressed. Women and "good blacks" would accept their places in the natural hierarchy of retro-

113 Ibid., 292.

114 Ibid.

culture. The restoration of traditional culture, as Lind suggests, requires violence, otherwise the corrosive influence of Cultural Marxism will linger.

The belief that lethal force will eliminate Cultural Marxism is not confined to the pages of *Victoria*. On July 22, 2011, the Norwegian white supremacist Anders Behring Breivik killed seventy-seven men, women, and children in a spree of mass shooting and bombing. Breivik targeted teenagers at a summer camp held by the center-left Arbeiderpartiet's youth wing, as well as government officials in Oslo. Before he commenced the attacks, he released a 1,500-page manifesto-cum-compendium, *2083: A European Declaration of Independence*, that blamed Cultural Marxism for the "Islamification" of Europe. Nearly the entire text was copied and pasted from other sources with small amendments and erasures to adapt them to Breivik's European context. One of Breivik's major sources was an online FCF pamphlet that compiled writings on political correctness and the Frankfurt School by Lind, Raehn, and others. It is striking that Breivik's solution to the problem of Cultural Marxism was essentially identical to what Lind imagines in *Victoria*. Breivik even embodies the ideal Fourth Generation Warrior as he combines cultural and military warfare and assaults a "defunct" state on behalf of an imagined white Western Christian culture. It would be wrong to say that Lind "inspired" Breivik's rampage. However, it is undeniable that Lind's conception of Cultural Marxism legitimates political violence. Cultural Marxists, according to this understanding, cannot be redeemed or accommodated. Unless they—the living human beings that Lind and Breivik identify as Cultural Marxists—are eradicated, Western culture will fall apart. Violence becomes the only method for establishing the right-wing utopia. What matters, of course, is how Lind, Breivik, and others decide *who* deserves to be executed for "betraying" the West.

## That 2002 Conference: Cultural Marxism/s as Coded Antisemitism

During his talk at *The Barnes Review*'s Third International Conference in 2002, Lind made a peculiar admission: "I do want to make it clear for the foundation and myself that we are not among those who question whether the Holocaust occurred."[115] Later in his talk, Lind mentioned that the Frankfurt School thinkers were all "Jewish."[116] Why do these remarks matter? *The Barnes Review* was founded by the prominent neo-Nazi—and onetime LaRouche ally—Willis Carto to serve as an outlet for Holocaust revisionism. Even more disturbingly, the notorious antisemite E. Michael Jones was speaking on the same panel as Lind. It is difficult to ignore the implications of these facts. Although Lind claims that he was simply following FCF's policy of working with other groups on an issue-by-issue basis, his appearance at this conference exemplified the growing ideological convergence between ex–New Right paleocons and "respectable" white nationalists. Take the example of a 1997 episode of NET's *The Next Revolution*, where Lind and his co-host favorably interviewed Jared Taylor, the editor of the white nationalist magazine *American Renaissance*. Of course, it is debatable whether Lind is personally an antisemite. What is undebatable, however, is the influence of Lind's concept of Cultural Marxism/s on the uses of coded (and explicit) antisemitism in contemporary far-right discourse.

Since 1945, open antisemitism has been considered unacceptable in mainstream American political debate. The legacy of World War II and the memory of the Holocaust cemented the association between antisemitic beliefs and German Nazism. In the postwar period, far-right groups in the United States

115 Intelligence Report, "Ally of Christian Right Heavyweight Paul Weyrich Addresses Holocaust Denial Conference," *Intelligence Report*, September 30, 2002.

116 Ibid.

developed allusive rhetorical strategies to blame Jewish people for social and economic problems without explicitly referring to them as "Jewish." In response to the successes of the civil rights movements, the far right drew on the code words of the New Right to defend "white" identity and demonize other racial groups without deploying racist rhetoric. This form of coded racism was an adaptation to a political and legal climate that discouraged explicit bigotry. When the far right encountered Lind's ideas about the Frankfurt School, for instance, they adopted the term "Cultural Marxism" as a coded critique of "the Jews."

Why were the ideas of a paleoconservative like Lind so attractive to the far right? There were some clear ideological affinities between the causes of white nationalism and paleoconservatism. They agreed that non-white immigrants were incapable of assimilating into the culture of Western nations and that multiculturalism represented a civilizational threat to white people.[117] They remained critical of free trade and foreign intervention, arguing that the American people should be protected from the ravages of globalization. Their shared disdain for neoconservatism stemmed from the belief that these new conservative elites had neglected the true task of any meaningful political right: the preservation of the organic national community (or race). In the 1990s and 2000s, paleoconservatives started to work with white nationalist institutions and individuals, such as Carto's Holocaust-denying Institute for Historical Review. Several of these purged paleos, such as *National Review* writer Joseph Sobran, had been subject to accusations of antisemitism. Paleoconservatism, it must be said, is not inherently antisemitic. (After all, Gottfried—the leading paleoconservative thinker and originator of the term *paleoconservatism*—is ethnically Jewish). However, the marginalization

117 Jean-François Drolet and Michael C. William, "America First: Paleoconservatism and the Ideological Struggle for the American Right," *Journal of Political Ideologies* 25, no. 1 (2020): 28–50.

of paleoconservatives within the mainstream conservative movement pushed them to seek new allies and audiences who would be more receptive to their message. The organizational links between paleoconservatism and the far right would facilitate the transformation of Lind's narratives about the Frankfurt School into a tool of coded antisemitism.

In 2002, Lind contributed to an *American Free Press* pamphlet —another Carto publication—entitled *Cultural Communism: The Vivisection of America*. The pamphlet featured coded and overt antisemitic messages. F. C. Blahut, a supporter of Carto, accused the Frankfurt School of burdening the German people with "eternal guilt" for the Holocaust, which, he claimed, "is evidenced most clearly in the 'anti-hate' laws of that benighted country."[118] Carto's brief essay attributed the successes of Western civilization to the accomplishments of the "Aryan Races" and branded "Cultural Communists" as "Neanderthals" who inhabited a "sick intellectual ghetto of sex-obsessed and parasitic Freudian Talmudist[s]."[119] The use of multiple antisemitic allusions—Jewish people inhabit a ghetto, Jewish people are sexual deviants, Jewish people are parasitical on the productive Aryan race—was meant to demonstrate the link between so-called cultural subversion and Jewishness. In 2020, Blahut republished an updated version of his original 2002 essay that replaced the coded term "Cultural Communism" with its openly Nazi equivalent "Cultural Bolshevism."

Lind was not the only paleoconservative to promote Cultural Marxism narratives to white nationalist audiences. In 2002, the paleoconservative Patrick J. Buchanan—former Nixon and Reagan advisor and perennial political campaigner—published

118 F. C. Blahut, "Communism Isn't Dead, It's Just Been Renamed," in *Cultural Communism: The Vivisection of America*, ed. F. C. Blahut (American Free Press: 2002), 4–5.

119 Willis A. Carto, "The Significance of Cultural Communism," in *Cultural Communism: The Vivisection of America*, ed. F. C. Blahut (America Free Press: 2002), 6–7.

a book called *The Death of the West: How Dying Populations and Immigrant Invasions Imperil Our Country and Civilization*. Building on Lind's arguments, Buchanan speculated that the Frankfurt School was largely responsible for the decline of white birth rates in the United States and Europe.[120] Adorno's critique of the family in *The Authoritarian Personality* apparently stigmatized parenthood; Marcuse's concept of polymorphous perversity allegedly compelled women to abandon their wifely duties and indulge in sexual adventures. Although his book is not explicitly antisemitic, Buchanan had a reputation for blurring the lines between conservatism and antisemitism.[121] Buchanan was one of the paleoconservatives that William F. Buckley chastised in his long 1991 essay "In Search of Anti-Semitism." During his 1992 run for the Republican presidential nomination, Buchanan campaigned on issues of immigration and multiculturalism to win over the supporters of David Duke (a former Ku Klux Klansman who was also seeking the Republican nomination). Several far-right leaders, such as the director of Aryan Resistance, Tom Metzger, backed Buchanan. And, intriguingly, a handful of Buchanan's campaign staffers were also associates of Carto. Given this history of flirting with the far right, it is hardly surprising to find out that some of Buchanan's readers have drawn on *The Death of the West* to develop their own antisemitic critiques of multiculturalism.

In the 2000s, the term "Cultural Marxism" became a useful tool of coded antisemitism in white supremacist online spaces. During the research for his 2010 *Salmagundi* essay, Martin Jay came across a startling comment in the neo-Nazi forum Stormfront:

---

120 Patrick J. Buchanan, *The Death of the West: How Dying Populations and Immigrant Invasions Imperil Our Country and Civilization* (New York: St Martin's Press, 2002).

121 Bloodworth, "Trumpism's Paleoconservative Roots and Dealignment," 195–6.

> Talking about the Frankfurt School is ideal for not naming the *Jews as a group* (which often leads to a panicky rejection, a stubborn refusal to listening anymore and even a "shut up") but naming the *Jew by proper names*. People will make their generalizations by themselves—in the privacy of their own minds. At least it worked like that with me. It was my lightbulb moment, when confusing pieces of an alarming puzzle suddenly grouped to a visible picture. Learn by heart the most important proper names of the Frankfurt Schoolers—they are (except for a handful of minor members and female "groupies") ALL Jews. One can even quite innocently mention that the Frankfurt Schoolers had to leave Germany in 1933 because "*they were to a man, Jewish*," as William S. Lind does.[122]

Other far-right websites appropriated Lind's notion of "Cultural Marxism" to inform antisemitic propaganda. The Swedish fascist online encyclopedia *Metapedia* maintained an entry that presented "Cultural Marxism" as synonymous with "Cultural Bolshevism." (This reference to "Cultural Bolshevism" was removed in 2015). The webpage also listed Lind and Buchanan as credible authorities on the history of the Frankfurt School.

However, the *Metapedia* article on "Cultural Marxism" mainly relied on the work of a far-right evolutionary psychologist named Kevin MacDonald. In 1998, MacDonald published a tome entitled *The Culture of Critique: An Evolutionary Analysis of Jewish Involvement in Twentieth-Century Intellectual and Political Movements*. According to MacDonald, Jewish people have tended to organize intellectual and political movements as part of a "group evolutionary strategy" to "neutralize" antisemitism and deconstruct Gentile cultures.[123] For MacDonald, the Frankfurt School's theories of antisemitism

122 Jay, "Dialectic of Counter-Enlightenment," 35.

123 Kevin MacDonald, *The Culture of Critique: An Evolutionary Analysis of Jewish Involvement in Twentieth-Century Intellectual and Political Movements* (Westport, CT: Praeger, 1998).

were mere expressions of their own fanatical Jewishness rather than attempts to analyze the complex psychosocial relationships between capitalism and fascism. Regardless of its well-documented flaws, MacDonald's *The Critique of Culture* became something of an antisemitic bible for the online far right. In 2007, he founded the online magazine *The Occidental Observer*, where contributors drew on MacDonald's theories to complain about the Frankfurt School's so-called assault on Gentile civilization. By the 2010s, Lind's claims about Cultural Marxism had been fully absorbed into this vast antisemitic discourse on murky Internet forums and in obscure digital publications.

Despite his influence on what we now call "the alt-right," Lind cannot be isolated from the longer histories of the New Right. His narratives of Cultural Marxism/s remained tied to the practices and priorities of the New Right as a political force. He blamed "Cultural Marxists" and "the Groups" for American decline without considering more structural or economic factors. Instead of considering whether women and Black people continued to face discrimination, Lind asserted that "Cultural Marxists" were tricking "the Groups" into believing that they were oppressed. The strategy of *weaponized victimhood*—the claim that white people are the most maligned group in the United States—allowed his ideas to resonate with the fears and worries of his conservative audiences. His gift for marketing ideas meant that his narratives of Cultural Marxism/s circulated more easily than the LaRouche movement's esoteric tracts on the Frankfurt School. Lind may never have intended for his message to be picked up by white supremacist terrorists and keyboard antisemites. Yet his work carries many of the same racial assumptions that drive the agendas of other more virulently reactionary political forces. They are all, in some way, seeking their own "pure" retroculture.

On December 18, 2008, Weyrich died. Lee Edwards, a distinguished fellow at the Heritage Foundation, eulogized him as a "major architect of the modern conservative movement."[124] Yet, in the winter of 2008, that movement was facing a crisis. A month before Weyrich's death, Barack Obama had surged to victory in the presidential election. In symbolic terms, Obama's triumph represented a refutation of everything that the New Right stood for. The American electorate had voted overwhelmingly for someone who belonged to the New Class (a law professor) and who came from the Groups (the Black child of an interracial marriage that ended abruptly in divorce). As he reflected on this political situation in his final column for the FCF website, Weyrich observed that "conservatives appear lost and without a serious agenda or a means of explaining such an agenda to the public."[125] At that moment, it may have looked like the Cultural Marxists were finally going to conquer the United States. Without a visionary leader like Weyrich, the American right simply did not know what to do next.

124 Lee Edwards, "Paul Weyrich Made a Difference," *National Review*, December 18, 2008.

125 Paul Weyrich, "The Next Conservatism, A Serious Agenda for the Future," *Free Congress Foundation*, December 18, 2008.

# 3

# The Tea Party Movement: Red Smoke, Blue Donkey

*9. Dependency on the state or state benefits*
*10. Control and dumbing down of media*
*11. Encouraging the breakdown of the family*

—"The 11 Aims of the Frankfurt School," an online hoax document originally shared on the blog politicallyincorrect.me.uk

Following Barack Obama's inauguration in January 2009, sales of Ayn Rand's 1957 novel *Atlas Shrugged* shot up. Fans of Rand's work reinterpreted the book as a prophetic cautionary tale about the incoming administration's "collectivist" policies. Sarah Palin, the former governor of Alaska and 2008 Republican vice presidential candidate, claimed that Obama's proposed healthcare reforms would establish "death panels" to decide whether elderly and disabled patients deserved to receive medical care. The National Rifle Association warned their members that Obama was planning to confiscate everyone's guns. As the imaginary specter of Obama socialism loomed on the horizon, the Wisconsin State Representative Paul Ryan pronounced that "we are right now living in an Ayn Rand novel."[1]

*Atlas Shrugged* is set in a dystopian America where the prodding fingers of government bureaucrats meddle incessantly with the affairs of private business. As the plot drags on, the upper classes—the millionaires, the manufacturers, the

1 "Paul Ryan on Ayn Rand," YouTube, 1:09, posted by gallicho1, April 26, 2012.

magnates—start to realize that they are the wronged victims of a rigged political and economic system. In a startling reversal of the Marxist worldview, it turns out that the pols and proles have been sucking value from the ingenuity and perseverance of moneyed producers. Eventually, these tycoons retreat into a mountain fortress built by the enigmatic inventor John Galt. The withdrawal of their entrepreneurial might causes civilization to unravel. In a climactic radio address to the nation, Galt issues a dire warning: "If you desire ever again to live in an industrial society, it will be on *our* moral terms."[2]

In the aftermath of the Financial Crisis of 2007–8, many conservatives found comfort in the simplistic moral terms of *Atlas Shrugged*. The novel features stilted and unconvincing dialogue between flat characters that often devolves into didactic monologues about the virtue of selfishness and the cravenness of government intervention. The protagonists are virtuous heroes; the bad guys are unrepentant villains. It was the perfect read for Americans who felt that Obama epitomized all evil.

When Tea Party rallies started in 2009, observers noticed that protestors were brandishing Rand-themed placards: "Ayn Rand was Right," "Who is John Galt?," "Atlas is Shrugging." The Tea Partiers drew parallels between the scenes of *Atlas Shrugged* and their own plight to imply that a tyrannical government was squeezing the productive middle classes. They saw Obama's bank bailouts and healthcare legislation as precursors to a socialist takeover of the United States. Those who drew on this mythos saw Tea Partiers as heroes of a new American Revolution and demonized Obama as a mascot of terror (the Antichrist, Hitler, the Joker, and an assortment of racist stereotypes). Although it would be silly to describe the Tea Party as little more than an Ayn Rand book club run amok, many Tea Partiers clung to this Randian conception of politics: a clear conflict between individualism

2 Ayn Rand, *Atlas Shrugged* (New York: Signet, 1996), 937.

and collectivism, between objectivism and irrationalism, and between the producers and the parasites. Various segments of the Tea Party movement—patriot groups, Christian ideologues, media entrepreneurs—rearticulated existing right-wing claims about the Frankfurt School to identify an ultimate culprit for what they saw as the Obama administration's social engineering experiments. According to these new narratives, the Tea Partiers needed to develop alternative forms of media to contest Cultural Marxism's dominance over the major institutions of knowledge production: universities, the film and music industries, newspapers, television networks.

Although the Tea Party movement no longer exists as a political force, it continues to shape the ideological debates and discourses of the Republican Party. Several Republican representatives, who once campaigned on Tea Party–approved platforms, have recently regurgitated the movement's rhetoric about Cultural Marxism. In a 2021 Fox News interview, the Republican Senator Marco Rubio—his 2010 campaign was Tea Party–endorsed—described the University of Central Florida's (UCF) Graduate Certificate in Social Justice in Public Service as "Cultural Marxism." Without referring to the actual content of the program, Rubio proclaimed that UCF was teaching students to hate America. Similarly, Florida Governor Ron DeSantis, whose 2012 congressional campaign received the Tea Party's blessing, has repeatedly condemned "wokeness" as a form of "Cultural Marxism." In his 2024 book *Unwoke: How to Defeat Cultural Marxism in America*, the Texas Senator Ted Cruz—another former Tea Party darling—names Gramsci and Marcuse as key architects of the left's supposedly successful "long march through the institutions." If one wants to understand how Cultural Marxism/s became such a potent ideological tool in contemporary American politics, one must first figure out why the Tea Party hated the Frankfurt School.

## All You Capitalists Out There: The Structure and Ideology of the Tea Party Movement

According to its founding myth, the Tea Party emerged in 2009 from an impromptu speech by the CNBC reporter Rick Santelli on the floor of the Chicago Mercantile Exchange. Instead of blaming the financial crisis on market deregulation or reckless trading, Santelli alleged that "your neighbors," especially those lazy ones who own a fancy house and refuse to repay their debts, caused the recession. Obama's bank bailout, as Santelli portrayed it, was simply subsidizing "the losers' mortgages."[3] He exclaimed that prudent Americans should not be forced to bear the cost of their neighbors' irresponsibility. As he bantered with his co-hosts on-air, Santelli issued an invitation to "all you capitalists out there" to attend a "Chicago Tea Party" on the shores of Lake Michigan.[4] A handful of leading conservative organizations latched onto this throwaway comment and scrambled to organize the first Tea Party rally in Washington, DC. The sociologist Clarence Y. H. Lo describes this Washington gathering on February 27, 2009, as a "test marketing phase" during which conservative leaders tried to figure out whether the concept of an anti-Obama Tea Party would take hold in a variety of locales.[5]

Nearly every scholarly account of the Tea Party indulges in a circular debate about whether it was a top-down "astroturfed" operation or a genuinely grassroots social movement. The political scientists Theda Skocpol and Vanessa Williamson suggest that this framing is reductive, since it assumes

---

3 The Heritage Foundation, "CNBC's Rick Santelli's Chicago Tea Party," YouTube, 4:36, posted by the Heritage Foundation, February 19, 2009.

4 Ibid.

5 Clarence Y. H. Lo, "Astroturf versus Grass Roots: Scenes from Early Tea Party Mobilization," in *Steep: The Precipitous Rise of the Tea Party*, ed. Lawrence Rosenthal and Christine Trost (Berkeley and Los Angeles: University of California Press, 2012), 100.

that the Tea Party was a homogenous bloc. Contrary to this assumption, Skocpol and Williamson argue that the Tea Party consisted of three interweaving forces: local grassroots activists, well-funded think tanks and political organizations, and right-wing media purveyors.[6] Each of these forces worked in tandem, on various institutional and interpersonal levels, to direct Tea Party activity. The average Tea Party supporter was older, whiter, wealthier, and more conservative than most Americans. They formed a network of smaller regional groups that met regularly in church halls and other community venues. Local organizations received support, guidance, and leadership from various national funders and free market advocates, such as FreedomWorks, the Tea Party Patriots, and the Tea Party Express. The decentralized nature of the Tea Party allowed smaller groups to exercise varying degrees of what Lo calls *marginal autonomy* from these professionalized entities.[7] Major establishment organizations acted to channel the energy of the initial Tea Party gatherings into a project of remaking the Republican Party and lobbying for libertarian policies on taxation, healthcare, and government regulation. The third force—a rabble of conservative media hosts from Fox News television anchors to right-wing radio jocks and bloggers—attempted to forge a common political identity for these scattered groups. For example, the chalkboard-assisted rants of Glenn Beck and the online pranksterism of Andrew Breitbart helped to portray the Tea Party as a popular rebellion against the so-called socialism of Obama's Democratic Party machine.

During this period of mobilization, the Tea Party became a pole of attraction on the American right. Other political groups adopted a kind of "entryist" strategy to gain a foothold in the Tea Party. The far-right John Birch Society ("the

---

6 Theda Skocpol and Vanessa Williamson, *The Tea Party and the Remaking of Republican Conservativism* (New York: Oxford University Press, 2012), 12–13.

7 Lo, "Astroturf versus Grass Roots," 99.

Birchers"), which had been established by the candyman-turned-conspiracist Robert W. Welch Jr. in 1958, experienced something of a revival as Tea Partiers searched for a way to understand America's transformation into a socialist dystopia. The books of prominent Birchers, such as G. Edward Griffin's *The Creature from Jekyll Island* and W. Cleon Skousen's *The Naked Communist*, became required reading for many Tea Party activists. To take another example, a right-wing extremist paramilitary organization called the Oath Keepers would turn up to Tea Party rallies to express their solidarity. In 2012, the Oath Keepers even funded a billboard advertisement that declared "The Tea Party is not the Enemy." Like the Tea Partiers, they opposed gun control legislation and portrayed Obama as a far-left tyrant. Although these groups did not fall under the official Tea Party banner, they played an active and significant role in the life of the movement.

The Tea Party, which might be more appropriately called the Tea Parties, never properly settled on a unified and coherent ideological message. The three main threads of Tea Party ideology—social conservatism, economic libertarianism, constitutional originalism—were rarely tied together neatly. Disagreements between traditionalist conservatives and free market libertarians would sometimes cause local groups to fracture. Those who wanted the Tea Party to focus exclusively on economic matters, such as taxation, believed that social and cultural issues distracted the movement from its core agenda. But other Tea Partiers felt that the subprime mortgage crisis stemmed from an underlying national moral decay. Neither of these competing tendencies ever succeeded in gaining complete control over the direction of the movement. Even when conservative activists Ryan Hecker and Dick Armey tried to unite Tea Partiers with their libertarian manifesto "Contract from America," the Tea Party remained an awkward ideological Frankenstein.

Constitutional originalism often served as a bridge between cultural conservatives and free market libertarians (and thus generated a vague kind of Fusionism 2.0). Within the moral universe of the Tea Party, the Constitution was less a legal document to be interpreted and more a sacred text to be memorized and revered. Its twenty-seven amendments acquired the same hallowed status as the Ten Commandments. Skousen's 1981 book *The Five Thousand Year Leap*, which speculated that the Founding Fathers transplanted certain beliefs from the Bible directly into the Constitution, became a best-selling hit in Tea Party circles. Tea Partiers drew on Skousen's arguments to suggest that Obama's "unconstitutional" healthcare reforms were an affront to God and the American republic. Any elected politician who exhibited a lack of familiarity with the Constitution immediately became a target of the Tea Party's scorn.

Invocations of the Constitution managed to satisfy the social conservative's traditionalist sentiments and the libertarian's desire for unconstrained freedom. Right-wing intellectuals learned that references to the Founding Fathers, as well as encomiums to the free market and the family, played well with Tea Party audiences around the United States. Unlike the LaRouchites or FCF, these Tea Party intellectuals did not promote a rigid doctrine (LaRouche's arbitrary ideology) or offer a clearly formulated vision (cultural conservatism). On the contrary, these ideologues fashioned a brand of cultural politics that mirrored the contradictory demands of the movement.

The term *conjunctural intellectual*, coined by the theorist Robert F. Carley, describes intellectuals that are semi-attached to political movements and opportunistic in their designs.[8] Conjunctural intellectuals emerge from sudden realignments of socio-political life. They treat the initial stages of popular mobilizations as timely opportunities to boost their own reputations. The rumbling aftershocks of the financial crisis, as well

8 Robert F. Carley, *Cultural Studies Methodology and Political Strategy: Metaconjuncture* (Cham, Switzerland: Palgrave MacMillan, 2021), 64.

as dissatisfaction with the Bush-era Republican Party and the polarizing election of the first African American president, formed a political terrain on which a variety of conjunctural intellectuals could insert themselves into the temporary quasi-institutional forms of the Tea Party. During the first few months of Tea Party organizing, conservative bloggers and local talk hosts latched onto the notion of a grassroots insurgency to promote their own platforms and programs.

The lack of centralization in the Tea Party movement favored a proliferation of conjunctural intellectuals. These semi-professional and self-professed right-wing philosophes flourished in the emerging online ecosystem of conservative content creation. The Tea Party Patriots website claimed that there were over two hundred Tea Party–affiliated blogs. The wide availability of technological devices (affordable camera phones, microphones, editing equipment), as well as the popularization of user-friendly social media platforms (Facebook and Twitter) and content sharing websites (WordPress, YouTube, Blogger), helped to spawn a new generation of minor right-wing culture warriors.

The media practices of the Tea Party were dispersed throughout the movement. Someone could record a heated exchange between Tea Partiers and their Democratic representative at a tense town hall meeting on their smartphone, upload the footage to the Internet, and share a link to the video on various conservative forums and mailing lists. Someone else might embed that clip in a blog post, along with commentary about a Tea Party insurgency. Local talk radio hosts might play audio from the clip on-air; a Fox News anchor might discuss the video in a segment on popular opposition to the Obama administration. Skocpol and Williamson observe that this "active relaying" of ideas and stories was a common Tea Party practice.[9] The Tea Partiers were never mere passive receivers of

9 Skocpol and Williamson, *The Tea Party and the Remaking of Republican Conservatism*, 128.

media content but, rather, semi-active participants who used their computers to spread (mis)information to others. The emergence of opportunistic right-wing conjunctural intellectuals, as well as the Tea Partiers' dependence on online media, contributed to what I term the Tea Party's *media populism*.

Many Tea Partiers felt that the mainstream media favored liberal perspectives and disparaged conservative values. The Tea Party's conjunctural intellectuals portrayed such outlets as CNN and *The New York Times* as a hostile force that sought to stifle free expression. Various bloggers, freelance journalists, and amateur filmmakers marketed themselves as right-wing rebels who exposed the lies of these media institutions. As Skocpol and Williamson observe, "Both the constant refrain of 'us versus them' and the everyday flow of political information and misinformation reinforce[d] the sense of an embattled community of conservatives—whose latest effort to fight back valiantly [was] embodied in the Tea Party."[10] Even Fox News, a prominent and well-funded television network, reiterated this self-perception of the Tea Party as the victim of a media elite. The Fox host Bill O'Reilly, for instance, once commented that the "American media will never embrace the Tea Party [because] they look down on the folks . . . they think you are dumb."[11] Just as LaRouche's *EIR* and FCF's NET branded themselves as truthful alternatives to a lying elite, the Tea Party's network expressed an intensely felt need to develop sources of information that countered the perceived dominance of left-wing ideology.

The Tea Party's media populism suited the more localized character of the smaller groups. Tea Party organizers discovered that they needed to arrange regular programming, such as an entertaining speaker or visual presentation, to increase donations and recruitment. The Tea Party Patriots urged

10 Ibid., 137.

11 Quoted in Skocpol and Williamson, *The Tea Party and the Remaking of Republican Conservatism*, 137.

local activists to host "Patriots and Popcorn" nights to screen documentaries that would introduce prospective members to the movement's beliefs. Other Tea Partiers, especially those in remote areas, were encouraged to invite their friends and relatives into their homes for "House Party" events. According to the Tea Party Patriots' website, "House Parties" were an opportunity to "show a film that expresses our values in an easy to understand, easy to digest format."[12] Once the film was over, Tea Partiers could "explain what the Tea Party movement is all about, our core values, and why we exist."[13] The ongoing demand for political documentaries benefitted those conjunctural intellectuals, such as Steve Bannon and James Jaeger, who were already producing right-wing films. Certain documentaries, especially Jaeger's *Cultural Marxism: The Corruption of America*, recycled paleoconservative polemics about the Frankfurt School (usually Buchanan's *The Death of the West*) to assert that American conservatives were fighting a hidden Marxist network. While LaRouchites used narratives about the Frankfurt School to identify the ranks of NCLC as an elite, the conjunctural intellectuals of the right drew on the enduring right-wing folklore of Cultural Marxism/s to define the Tea Party as a movement for the deserving American majority.

The image of the "deserving" American citizen was central to the Tea Party's conception of the United States. According to Skocpol and Williamson, this image derives from a long-standing dichotomy between "deservingness" and "dependency."[14] Yet this distinction between workers and nonworkers—between the producers and the freeloaders—has a surprising lineage in American politics. "Deservingness" is a residual popular belief that stems from the legislative and

12 "House Party DVD Request," *Tea Party Patriots Action*.

13 "Patriots and Popcorn," *Tea Party Patriots Action*.

14 Skocpol and Williamson, *The Tea Party and the Remaking of Republican Conservatism*, 74.

material infrastructure of the New Deal. The Social Security Act of 1935 excluded agricultural laborers and domestics—who at the time were predominantly Black—from its definition of the "deserving" worker and thus invested "whiteness" with a social standing that was invisible as racial privilege. Similarly, Federal Housing Administration mortgages were disproportionately approved for white borrowers and structured to encourage purchases in redlined suburbs. Although their official propaganda impugned the "collectivism" of the New Deal, Tea Partiers defended interests and identifications that they had inherited from Roosevelt's policies. Older white Americans were so accustomed to the benefits of social security that these advantages had become imperceptible and naturalized. As the political scientist Lisa Disch explains, this *white citizenship* was "constituted by an independence that seems to have been personally earned when it [was], in fact, publicly subsidized."[15] She notes that the spirit of this white citizenship was epitomized in the famous Tea Partier rant at a town hall meeting in South Carolina: "Keep your government hands off my Medicare!"[16] Liberal commentators mocked this slip as a sign of the Tea Party's ignorance about the workings of the government they claimed to protest. However, this misstatement reveals the contradictory ideological prism through which Tea Partiers understood social reality.

In *The Eighteenth Brumaire of Louis Bonaparte*, Marx writes that "as in private life one distinguishes between what a man thinks and says of himself and what he really is and does, still more in historical struggles must one distinguish the phrases and fancies of the parties from their real organism and their real interests, their conception of themselves

15 Lisa Disch, "The Tea Party: A 'White Citizenship' Movement?," in *Steep: The Precipitous Rise of the Tea Party*, ed. Lawrence Rosenthal and Christine Trost (Berkeley and Los Angeles: University of California Press, 2012), 140.

16 Quoted in Disch, "The Tea Party," 133.

from their reality."[17] Although ordinary Tea Partiers may have conceived of themselves as steely Randian individualists, their so-called independence depended historically on a government-mandated organization of resources and recognition. The symbolic difference between "deservingness" and "dependency," which may seem like a color-blind distinction, became a material force that maintained a firm hierarchical division between racial groups (white people as deserving recipients of invisible government support, Black people as visible dependents on the state). The deeply felt sense of "deservingness" that animated Tea Party resentment sprang from seemingly neutral benefits that perpetuated racial inequality (and that continued to exert racializing effects). It represented a racialized politics that claimed to speak in the language of universality. It was not the result of top-down "astroturfed" manipulation in the twenty-first century but, rather, a residue of the historical processes that shaped the practices and environments of the white American middle class.

Deservingness, even though its liberal heritage may seem to contradict its conservative uses, proved to be a potent tool for constructing a supposedly non-racial Tea Party identity. Conjunctural intellectuals promoted certain phrases and fancies about "taxpayers" and "producers" that—to finish the Marxian paraphrase—merely echoed the white American middle class's conception of itself. Several right-wing media-makers—James Jaeger, Curtis Bowers, Andrew Breitbart—would draw on this ideological theme of deservingness to produce new Cultural Marxism narratives for Tea Party audiences. They revisited Buchanan's paleocon lamentations, where they encountered the New Right's claims about Cultural Marxism. They characterized the Frankfurt School as the architects of a left-wing media monopoly that denigrated the values

17 Karl Marx, "The Eighteenth Brumaire of Louis Bonaparte," in *Karl Marx: Selected Works in Two Volumes, Vol.* 2, ed. Vladimir Adoratsky (London: Lawrence and Wishart Limited, 1943), 344–5.

and experiences of the deserving American family. Additionally, they urged Tea Partiers to embrace alternative media to counter the mainstream elite's Cultural Marxist propaganda. Ultimately, the interventions of these conjunctural intellectuals portrayed the Tea Party as a counterrevolutionary force that would defend the meaning of the Constitution and restore the status of a downwardly mobile middle class.

## Cultural Marxism: The Corruption of America

In 2010, the filmmaker and head of the Matrix Entertainment Corporation (MEC) James Jaeger released *Cultural Marxism: The Corruption of America*. Between 2006 and 2015, Jaeger wrote, directed, and produced a series of documentaries in collaboration with the libertarian lawyer Edwin Vieira to promote Christian traditionalism, constitutional originalism, and market fundamentalism. *Cultural Marxism* was an abridged version of Jaeger's tedious 2008 three-hour-and-fifteen-minute-long *Original Intent*. According to a 2013 interview with Jaeger, the *Cultural Marxism* cut was marketed primarily to conservatives who were dissatisfied with the mainstream Republican Party. Its debut screening took place at an Oath Keepers meeting in Bozeman, Montana. It went on to become one of his most popular documentaries.

Jaeger and his coterie of right-wing interviewees—Buchanan, the libertarian zealot and Republican congressman Ron Paul, the anti–Federal Reserve Bircher G. Edward Griffin, the Christian media critic Ted Baehr, and Vieira—allege that the Frankfurt School's Cultural Marxism and the Federal Reserve's "Corporate Fascism" have undermined the Constitution. Whereas the Frankfurt School encouraged cultural pessimism to attack the conventional family unit, the Federal Reserve imposed unfair taxes on the productive middle class to fund collectivist policies. As Griffin remarks, the Frankfurt School aimed to eradicate the family and thus force people to depend on government support. If Americans wanted to retake their country from this regime, then they would have to sign up for a project of nationalistic restoration.

Jaeger assumed that his documentaries would attract new citizens to this political project. The online version of *Cultural Marxism* entreats viewers to buy a DVD copy of the film and recommend it to friends, relatives, and acquaintances. The final credits warn the viewer that the "mainstream media" will ignore this documentary because they do not want the public to know about the Frankfurt School's influence on the television and film industries. To educate others about Cultural Marxism, the audience is urged to host public screenings of Jaeger's work and recommend his documentaries for programming at public-access television stations. Jaeger's repeated appeals to his audience taps into the Tea Party's reactionary media populism, which contrasts the decadence of the mainstream media and Hollywood with the authenticity of word-of-mouth recommendations to friends and family members (and "Patriots and Popcorn" and "House Party" events).

Anyone who watches *Cultural Marxism* will quickly realize that Jaeger is not a talented filmmaker. Various titles are misspelled (Critical Theory is rendered as "critcal theory"); the sound design is sloppy and disorienting. Yet Jodi Dean theorizes that this lack of technical polish adds to the allure of these kinds of documentaries. The absence of *slickness*, as Dean calls it, is a visual manifestation of Jaeger's "rejection of the mainstream," because the *slick* denotes a "mindset and aesthetic overattuned to the deceptions of the mainstream."[18] Counterintuitively, the sheer amateurishness of *Cultural Marxism* may function as a mark of its reliability for an audience that distrusts the mainstream media.

18 Jodi Dean, *Democracy and other Neoliberal Fantasies: Communicative Capitalism and Left Politics* (Durham, NC: Duke University Press, 2009), 155.

Throughout the documentary, Jaeger uses the technique of superimposition to underscore his argument about the Frankfurt School's infiltration of America. Superimposition places one image over another in the same frame to create a layering effect. Often, filmmakers will use superimposition to combine or contrast different scenes and visual metaphors in the same shot. The main motif of Jaeger's superimposed shots, for instance, is an animated cloud of red smoke. In the opening montage of the documentary, Jaeger superimposes a sequence of images—a stock photo of a divorce decree, a portrait of the Supreme Court justices, the US Capitol building—over a gently drifting, albeit menacing, wisp of red smoke. The scene implies that these institutions of American political and private life have fallen under the shadow of a malevolent force. Just as the powers of Old Europe wished to exorcize the specter of communism, Jaeger hoped that this documentary would expose the red smoke of Cultural Marxism that hovers over America like a foul smog.

Visual representations of conspiracy exhibit an "associative logic" that communicates intuitively to viewers.[19] Whereas the written word or verbal testimony attempts to convince the reader or listener with a linear and rational-argumentative model, the dream-like logic of the conspiracy image bombards the audience with a series of impressionistic allusions and cultural associations. The imagery of the red smoke evokes an array of pseudo-Gothic tropes, such as ghosts, hellfire, and Satan. To take this image literally, smoke is a collection of airborne particles and gases that can change form, seep into various spaces through cracks and gaps, and suffocate people in the middle of the night. It seems that Jaeger exploits these implications to instill a sense of dread about the elusive and shape-shifting presence of Cultural Marxism.

19 Ute Caumanns and Andreas Önnerfors, "Conspiracy Theory and Visual Culture," in *Routledge Handbook of Conspiracy Theories*, ed. Michael Butter and Peter Knight (London: Routledge, 2020), 447.

The red smoke symbolizes the suffusion of the Frankfurt School's ideology into every area of American life. As black-and-white footage of a college graduation ceremony is overlayed with the image of red smoke, the narrator tells us that the Frankfurt School infiltrated American universities in the 1960s to indoctrinate impressionable students with something called critical theory: a so-called doctrine that challenges "all previously accepted standards in every aspect from a Marxist perspective."[20] Critical Theory, as portrayed in the documentary, becomes little more than a puerile anti-Americanism that tarnishes the legacy of the Founding Fathers. The narrator reports that these "consciousness-challenged baby boomers" absorbed and "internalized the criticism" that "the Establishment" was a "bunch of racist, overly religious, and sexually deprived sexists, who were xenophobic Indian killers and antisemites."[21] This deeply unserious parody of the New Left glosses over why student activists objected to the politics of the American establishment. For Jaeger, the social revolt of the 1960s is only understandable as a symptom of foreign and anti-American influence. College radicals, according to Jaeger's narrative, were merely passive instruments of the Frankfurt School.

When these students graduated and entered the professional sphere, they started to inject the doctrine of Critical Theory into the messages of the mass media. Hollywood—a major villain of Jaeger's tale—inserted the Frankfurt School's critique of the patriarchal family into screenplays to portray nuclear families as dysfunctional and repressive. Various films, such as *The Graduate* and *Harold and Maude*, taught youngsters to disrespect their parents and dismiss the Christian institution of marriage as an outdated relic. Jaeger claims that the "invalidation" of traditional parental roles—the man and his wife, the father and the mother—in Hollywood movies directly caused

20 MEC Films, "Cultural Marxism: The Corruption of America," YouTube, 1:38:38, posted by OriginalIntentDoc, August 30, 2011.

21 Ibid.

a rise in divorce rates.[22] Divorce split families into separate households that had to file separate tax forms, which, in turn, financed the Federal Reserve's corporate fascism. Children struggled to cope with the stress of their parents' divorce and thus required therapy sessions and medications that gradually drained their sense of individuality. This is what Jaeger sees as the denouement of the Frankfurt School's cultural subversion: the total dependence of atomized victims on the government.

Jaeger represents this disintegration of the family unit in a sequence that blends sped-up footage of network news, the motif of red smoke, and a scene from a sadomasochistic porno of a blonde dominatrix in a red leather bodysuit whipping a man in a black gimp costume. The layering of images produces a nauseating impression of causality. The Frankfurt School (red smoke) constructed the media (news footage) to destroy the sacred marital bond and break apart the family (pornographic scene). The average television viewer can no longer see the degradation of the patriarchal family that serves as the subtext of twenty-first-century mainstream media. The Father has become a cowering and effeminate submissive; the Mother, a sadistic and domineering nymphomaniac. For Jaeger, America has lost the masculine ideal that organized the national project. The white working male is held up as a paradigm of independence, even though his affluence depended on the unwaged labor of his wife and the naturalized support of the state. Like other figures in the Tea Party movement, Jaeger mystifies the genuine social conditions that underpinned the ideology of white citizenship that he promulgates.

Building on the New Right's legacy of coded racism, Jaeger conceives of the American people in implicitly racial terms. He contrasts the white citizenship of the United States with the "Jewishness" of the Frankfurt School. During one sequence, the narrator says that the audience will "hear from some of

---

22 Ibid.

the Frankfurt School graduates themselves."[23] This scene features grotesque impersonations of Horkheimer, Marcuse, and Gramsci with heavy, stereotypically antisemitic Jewish accents. The script appears to attribute "quotations" to these thinkers that are actually taken from Buchanan's *The Death of the West*. The device of stereotypical accents permits Jaeger to associate Cultural Marxism with Jewishness without explicitly naming the Frankfurt School thinkers as Jews. The use of coded antisemitism can result in two separate interpretations of the film. As one scrolls through the YouTube comments for *Cultural Marxism*, one can find jokes about the "Jewish voiceovers" as well as remarks about how Marcuse sounds like Oscar the Grouch. Whereas some naïve viewers may interpret the documentary as a straightforward critique of un-American dependency, "in-the-know" watchers may recognize it as a call to cleanse the American body politic from decidedly Jewish others. The racial subtext of Jaeger's films becomes more explicit on the MEC website, where he promotes a range of antisemitic tropes and arguments (such as Holocaust denial, and the notion that Jewish people "run" Hollywood).

*Cultural Marxism* concludes with a vision of American restoration. The narrator urges "citizens" to "get familiar with the original intent of the Founders" and learn more about how the "forces of Cultural Marxism have been raping and pillaging the United States for decades."[24] Echoing Weyrich's "Letter to Conservatives," Jaeger tells his audience to "disconnect from all sources of Cultural Marxist propaganda, media, and lifestyles." Just as Weyrich encouraged conservatives to separate themselves from politically correct institutions, Jaeger wants Americans to "disconnect" from Cultural Marxism and revive a brand of right-wing populism grounded in Constitutional originalism. For Jaeger and the Tea Partiers, faithful adherence to the Constitution is the only answer to the crisis of American life.

23 Ibid.
24 Ibid.

How should we interpret Jaeger's promise of restoration? When Gramsci searched for a criterion to distinguish between progressive change and counterrevolution, he sensed that "the problem is to see whether in the dialectic 'revolution/restoration' which predominates."[25] He added, "In the movement of history there is never any turning back, and that restorations *in toto* do not exist."[26] Those who support reactionary movements are looking to revive the circumstances that secured their ascendency and supremacy. Yet it often turns out that the material forces that underpinned this period of national glory have dissipated. As Marx observed in *The Eighteenth Brumaire*, the Bonapartist coup d'état wished to resurrect the Napoleonic era even though the conditions for it no longer pertained. Consequently, the *idées napoléoniennes*—those "ideas of the undeveloped small hold in the freshness of its youth"—became "hallucinations of its death struggle, words reduced to phrases, spirits reduced to ghosts."[27]

The dreams and ideals of the Founding Fathers, as Jaeger articulates them, had withered into the delusions and fancies of the Tea Party. The scattered and commercialized Tea Party protests were parodies of the American Revolution. Balding and bloated businessmen donned tricorne hats and embarrassed themselves by adopting faux-colonial accents and parading down the street with antique muskets. They may have borrowed the poetry of the War of Independence, yet they represented the hallucinations of a white American middle class in distress. Mike Davis, the sardonic analyst of American crisis and class, was right to diagnose the Tea Party as little more than "the gangrene of imperial decline."[28] The imagery and rhetoric of Jaeger's documentary were an effort to repackage the downward mobility of the white middle class—who

25 Gramsci, *Selections from the Prison Notebooks*, 219.

26 Ibid., 219–20.

27 Marx, "The Eighteenth Brumaire of Louis Bonaparte," 422.

28 Mike Davis, "The Last White Election?," *New Left Review*, no. 79 (January-February 2013): 52.

received their racial privilege and economic security from the fading legacy of the New Deal—as an epochal revolutionary moment. It was a reactionary vision with revolutionary pretensions, a restoration of exhausted cultural norms paired with a revolution of aggressive financial deregulation.

*Cultural Marxism* offers a particular theory of cultural hegemony, in which cinema and television become the most powerful tools for transforming society. Instead of identifying the structural trends behind the decline of traditional American life (the unraveling of the family-wage system, for instance), Jaeger accuses Frankfurt School–dominated Hollywood of producing too many damning portraits of family life. For Jaeger, conservative movies would almost automatically organize patriotic Americans into a potent political movement that could expel "the wrong sort of people" (Jewish people) from positions of power. Of course, the Tea Party did not underestimate the mobilizing force of these right-wing documentaries. The purpose of films like *Cultural Marxism* was not merely informational but also inspirational. These documentaries reinforced a certain way of looking at American history that eschewed systematic explanations and motivated Tea Partiers (or prospective recruits) to defend the naturalized privilege of white citizenship. As we shall see, the other conjunctural intellectuals of the Tea Party argued that the only way to restore this traditional cultural hegemony was through media activism.

## Agenda: Grinding America Down

"This story really begins for me in the summer of 1992," remarks the right-wing filmmaker Curtis Bowers in one of the introductory scenes of his 2010 documentary *Agenda: Grinding America Down*.[29] According to Bowers, an old friend asked

29 Curtis Bowers (dir.), *Agenda: Grinding America Down*, Black Hat Films, 2010.

him to attend a meeting of the Committees of Correspondence (CoC)—an organization of former CPUSA members—in the early 1990s to find out what these communists were planning to do after the collapse of the Berlin Wall and the much-publicized defeat of world communism. Bowers expected to enter a lecture hall full of rowdy, long-haired college idealists, yet he was surprised to discover that most of the attendees were well-dressed, well-spoken, and well into their fifties and sixties. He listened attentively to their discussion. Allegedly, the CoC wanted to take over the feminist, environmentalist, and "homosexual" movements to destroy the family, the free market, and the Christian faith. At the time, Bowers dismissed these aims as unrealistic. Yet, when he was appointed as a representative in the Idaho state legislature in 2008, he recalled that meeting and decided that the CoC had accomplished their objectives. He penned a letter to the *Idaho Press* entitled "Communist Agenda Makes its Way to Our Mainstream," in which he claims that many prominent "politicians and activist judges [share] the same agenda that just sixteen years ago was that of communist strategists."[30] Bowers ends his letter with a plea for "patriotic Americans to wake up and get involved."[31]

Two years later, he turned this letter into a full-length documentary that won the Jubilee Prize at San Antonio Christian Film Festival—*Agenda: Grinding America Down*. The film continues Bowers's effort to alert American citizens to the slow socialist takeover of the United States. Drawing on W. Cleon Skousen's 1958 *The Naked Communist*, Bowers claims that twenty-first-century America is the victim of a decades-long socialist agenda. Bowers and his impressive roster of conservative celebrities—David Noebel, Phyllis Schlafy, Trevor Loudon, Edwin Meese—argue that Barack Obama's "microwaved communism" is the result of a vast coordinated effort, which

30 Curtis Bowers, "Communist Agenda Makes Its Way to Our Mainstream," *Idaho Press*, January 14, 2008.

31 Ibid.

includes the Frankfurt School and Gramsci, to conquer capitalism.[32] Bowers's quilt-like conspiratorial narrative stitches together patches of rumour and allegation from the various anti-leftist polemics of the Old Right, the New Right, and the religious right. Like the Tea Party itself, Bowers's film represents an effort to unify the contradictory impulses of American conservatism.

Bowers casts himself as *Agenda*'s heroic protagonist. The arc of the documentary follows his personal mission to discover what happened to America. He portrays himself as a clean-shirted patriot who wants to defend the nation from government tyranny. Various scenes capture Bowers at notable monuments in Washington, DC, to demonstrate his respect for the Founding Fathers and the fallen soldiers of the Vietnam War. Other scenes show Bowers at home with his family to represent his commitment to marriage and parenthood. He tells the audience that he enjoys spending time with his family over footage of his children waving American flags as they run across a green field. Although Bowers's love for his family and country may seem irrelevant to the topic of the documentary, these scenes work to subtly convince his conservative Christian audience that his testimony is reliable.

Throughout *Agenda*, Bowers uses direct address to establish rapport with the viewer. At the start of the documentary, Bowers states, "The left wants *you* [my emphasis] to think that the cultural changes that have taken place in America since the 1960s have done nothing but progress us forward toward a brave new world."[33] This ironic statement—already the audience knows that what "the left" wants is *wrong*—foreshadows the main themes and arguments of the film. According to Bowers, "the left" wants to delude and confuse *you* about what has happened in *your* country since the 1960s. Whereas "the left" wants *you* to believe that these cultural changes were a

32 Bowers, *Agenda: Grinding America Down.*

33 Ibid.

series of happy accidents, Bowers wishes to demonstrate that they have been part of an agenda to promote the decline of *your* America. The phatic address of this statement establishes Bowers's role as the trustworthy guide who will reveal the truth behind the left's veil of deception. Bowers's posture of steadfast certainty implies that he will not waste his audience's time with any counterarguments or differing interpretations. No representative of "the left" will be consulted. As Bowers establishes in the first scene, "the left" would only want to deceive *you* and fill *your* mind with uncertainty. On the contrary, Bowers—that pleasant Christian fellow who loves his country and cares for his family—promises to provide absolute clarity about what is really going on.

Whereas Jaeger uses the motif of red smoke to symbolize the Frankfurt School's infiltration of American life, Bowers constructs a gigantic chart of left-wing intellectuals, politicians, and organizations to convey the scale and complexity of the communist plot. At the base of this chart is a large red box labeled "Karl Marx" with arrows that branch out to other boxes that refer to the "Frankfurt School," the "Fabian Society," "Antonio Gramsci," and the "Communist Party of the United States." Countless arrows shoot out from these four boxes to form a sprawling and convoluted web of relationships. Bowers assures his viewers that "you will find connections to about every left-leaning person and organization in America."[34]

The main effect of this chart lies in what Ute Caumanns and Andreas Önnerfors would describe as its "pseudo-informative impact."[35] Like the motif of red smoke in *Cultural Marxism*, Bowers's chart expresses an associative logic that has more to do with "connecting the dots" than explaining the exact links between these groups. Although Bowers relies on his interviewees to supply more information, their knowledge is often

34 Ibid.

35 Caumanns and Önnerfors, "Conspiracy Theory and Visual Culture," 448.

shallow and erroneous. Many of these connections are simple untruths. For instance, Bowers repeats the false claim that Bill Ayers—a former member of the Weather Underground—was the ghostwriter for Barack Obama's memoir *Dreams from My Father.* One of his interviewees even quotes the hoax document "The 11 Aims of the Frankfurt School," as though it were a credible source for understanding the work of the Institute for Social Research. ("The 11 Aims of the Frankfurt School" was a copy-and-paste-able online list that purported to expose the Frankfurt School's secret agenda. It included such items as "Huge immigration to destroy identity" and "The promotion of excessive drinking.")

The chart is little more than a device for signifying influence without demonstrating it. Even Bowers's criterion of what counts as "influence" is simplistic and ahistorical. The logic of his chart forces him to believe that as soon as two people or organizations are discovered to be linked in some vague way (and most of his links are pure fabrications), these figures must be agents of a unified agenda. The ultimate purpose of this chart is to incriminate the modern-day Democratic Party. Each arrow flows inexorably from Karl Marx (at the bottom) to Barack Obama (at the top). Consequently, Bowers supplies the Tea Partiers with a fraudulent genealogy that rationalizes their perception of Obama as a left-wing dictator.

Yet Bowers does not limit himself to suggesting that Obama is a communist. He continues the New Right's project of sixties bashing to suggest that 1960s radicals have snuck into the ruling institutions to manipulate the American public. Bowers suggests that these radicals have followed a Gramscian blueprint to overwhelm the main centers of power. These former rabble-rousers have settled down into lucrative careers of subverting the American popular mind in the spheres of Hollywood, media, education, and government. As he describes the impact of this "long march," new arrows sprout from countless boxes on the chart to form additional layers of association.

For Bowers, this is where influence becomes infection, where the communist virus inserts itself into the body politic of the United States. It is almost impossible for the viewer to grasp the increasingly elaborate and confusing connections of influence that supposedly confirm Bowers's claims. The pseudo-informative impact of the chart intensifies into a kind of pseudo-information overload that frazzles the viewer's capacity for critical interrogation.

Nonetheless, there is something affectively compelling about Bowers's chart. As Johannes von Moltke observes, these kinds of semi-conspiratorial images adopt a "fundamental critical posture: things are not as they seem."[36] What may appear to the average American as the twenty-first-century Democratic Party is—*gasp*—the culmination of a deep and persistent conspiracy that stretches back to Karl Marx himself. One cannot underestimate the pleasure and gratification of this secret knowledge. It may be laughably untrue, but it is somewhat *exciting* to hear Loudon claim that "Obama is all the things that Gramsci wanted to use for social change."[37] The hunt for these hidden connections is ultimately a search for meaning in an unstable conjuncture. The discovery of these so-called links provokes an emotional experience that can bind people together into an epistemological community. Not only do Tea Partiers require the ideological category of deservingness to assure their status, but they also seek this enjoyment of "being in the know" (in contrast to those other indoctrinated Americans who cannot penetrate the deceptive forcefield of the mainstream media).

Just as *Cultural Marxism* encouraged viewers to become familiar with the Constitution and participate in patriotic social movements, *Agenda* tries to turn its audience into a

36 Johannes von Moltke, "The Meme is the Message: Alt-Right/ Neue Rechte and the Political Affordances of Social Media," (lecture, John F. Kennedy Institute at Freie Universität Berlin, Berlin, Germany, July 4, 2019), Youtube.

37 Bowers, *Agenda: Grinding America Down.*

new cohort of conservative activists. Near the end of the documentary, each of Bowers's interviewees offers some advice about how ordinary citizens can stem the Red tide. Like Jaeger, Bowers urges his viewers to "arrange a monthly movie night with family and friends" to "watch one of the great documentaries out there about what is going on in our country."[38] The interviewees also encourage viewers to spread information on social media platforms. Noebel recommends starting a blog; Loudon tells viewers to exploit "the power of YouTube."[39] If, as Bowers argues, 1960s radicals dominate the media networks, then conservatives must construct their own platforms.

In this way, *Agenda* articulates an alternative media literacy. Instead of urging viewers to verify claims or deconstruct arguments, Bowers invites them to participate in the creation of staunchly conservative media. He builds on the populist branding of social media companies—the injunction to create your own content—to suggest that these platforms can become useful venues for such right-wing political forces as the Tea Party. The only relevant criteria for judging the reliability of these documentaries, blogs, and YouTube videos is no longer "objectivity," but, rather, fidelity to conservative ideology. After all, "the left" would only want to lie to *you*.

## Righteous Indignation: Excuse Me While I Save the World!

In his 2020 essay "Pioneering Countercultural Conservatism," the scholar Anthony Nadler identifies the emotional dynamic that pervades contemporary right-wing media. He argues that most conservative media platforms exhibit a countercultural affective style "that promotes loyalty and identification through hailing audiences as members of an embattled cultural

38 Ibid.
39 Ibid.

identity."[40] Countercultural conservatives package conservativism as a personal brand that must be protected from an increasingly liberal media and government elite. Those who employ this style, such as Rush Limbaugh and Matt Drudge, invert the "cultural hierarchy of hipness" and reframe the American right as a lively and punk-like subculture that prizes authenticity, rebellion, and swagger.[41] The stylized posturing of countercultural conservatism is arguably a symptom of a wider media landscape in which ideological values have become indistinguishable from entertainment values. To engage their audiences, countercultural conservative media hosts must play the role of a trickster figure who dares to embarrass and offend the traditional establishment. And no one embodied this spirit of right-wing trickery with as much panache and arrogance as Andrew Breitbart.

Breitbart's 2011 autobiography-cum-manifesto *Righteous Indignation: Excuse Me While I Save the World!* chronicles his career-long rampage against what he dubs the "Democrat-Media Complex."[42] According to Breitbart, the networks and newspapers of the mainstream media serve the Democrats and demonize Republicans. CNN, *The New York Times*, and the *Huffington Post* control "the narrative" and force ordinary Americans to imbibe the discredited ideas of the left. The Prodigal Son–esque narrative of *Righteous Indignation* follows Breitbart as he strays from the traditional middle-class values of his parents in his teenage years. In his early twenties, he wanders around New Orleans and Los Angeles as a hedonistic liberal before he finally returns to his true conservative self after listening to Rush Limbaugh's radio show.

---

40 Anthony Nadler, "Pioneering Countercultural Conservatism: Limbaugh, Drudge, Breitbart," in *Affective Politics of Digital Media: Propaganda by Other Means*, ed. Megan Boler and Elizabeth Davis (Abingdon, UK: Routledge, 2020), 154.

41 Ibid., 154.

42 Andrew Breitbart, *Righteous Indignation: Excuse Me While I Save the World!* (New York: Grand Central Publishing, 2011), 4.

Inspired by Limbaugh's shock jock tantrums, Breitbart reinvented himself as a right-wing culture warrior. Following stints of working at *The Drudge Report* and *The Huffington Post*, he founded his eponymous media platform *Breitbart.com* in 2007 to offer a conservative spin on the daily events of government, journalism, and Hollywood. He characterized *Breitbart.com* as part of the rise of right-wing New Media—the "constellation of AM talk radio, the Internet (Drudge Report, plus countless bloggers), and Fox News"—that threatened the Democrat-Media Complex.[43] In an inversion of the New Left counterculture, Breitbart claimed that these platforms represented a resurgence of investigative journalism and participatory democracy. Whereas the Democrat-Media Complex stood for censorship and repression, Breitbart's countercultural conservatism promised joyful rebellion, free expression, and authentic living. Unlike the 1960s counterculture (where young people expressed themselves against a puritanical society), this Breitbartian cultural revolt hoped to restore the primacy of traditional conservative values.

Breitbart built his persona by following the Rush Limbaugh School of Right-Wing Gramscianism. What became known as the Breitbart Doctrine—*politics is downstream from culture*—is essentially a pithier rendition of Limbaugh's interpretation of Gramsci. In his 1993 book *See, I Told You So*, Limbaugh claims that Gramsci proposed a strategy of cultural warfare to change people's values and beliefs. According to Limbaugh, student radicals swallowed Gramsci's ideas in the sixties and regurgitated them as Clintonism in the nineties. He urged his conservative readers to learn from the example of the Democratic Party's Gramscianism to launch their own "fight to reclaim and redeem our cultural institutions with all the intensity and enthusiasm we use to redeem our political institutions."[44] For Limbaugh and Breitbart, the right needed

43 Ibid., 5.

44 Rush Limbaugh, *See, I Told You So* (New York: Pocket Books, 1993), 88.

to imitate this strawman effigy of Gramsci if they wanted to change the opinions of the American electorate.

Whereas Limbaugh blames Gramsci for the excesses of Clinton-era liberalism, Breitbart traces the origins of the present-day Democrat-Media Complex to the arrival of the Frankfurt School in America. He brands mainstream journalists as "partisan critical theory hacks" who pose as "objective observers of reality."[45] Breitbart may pretend to abhor the hypocrisy of liberal media, yet he remained conveniently blind to his own hypocritical behavior. As Andreas Huyssen points out, the American right's "over-the-top attack on the Frankfurt School points to the fact that they themselves are doing what they falsely accuse their opponents of doing."[46] Breitbart is not offering a proper critique of the ideological framing of objectivity in American journalism but, rather, mirroring his portrait of the enemy and dressing up his partisanship as objective reporting. Like Jaeger and Bowers, Breitbart believes that a right-wing ideological vantage point offers a transparent and authentic view of social reality. This attitude of countercultural conservatism—and its intertwining with media populism—is key to understanding Breitbart's rendition of Cultural Marxism/s.

The Democrat-Media Complex, as Breitbart portrays it, is the love child of American progressivism and the Frankfurt School. Whereas the Founding Fathers drew on the wisdom of Western civilization to compose the Constitution, American progressives (Franklin Roosevelt and Woodrow Wilson) and the Frankfurt School adopted a warped notion of human nature from Jean-Jacques Rousseau, Hegel, and Marx. This Washington-Frankfurt alliance rejected the transcendent authority of the Constitution and laid the foundations for the Democratic-Media Complex.

According to Breitbart, the Institute for Social Research received a warm welcome at Columbia University during its

45 Breitbart, *Righteous Indignation*, 58.

46 Andreas Huyssen, "Behemoth Rises Again," *n+1*, July 29, 2019.

period of exile. As soon as the members of the Frankfurt School arrived in the United States, they started to creep "into every crevice of American culture."[47] Horkheimer implanted his deranged brand of Critical Theory—an "adolescent rebellion against all established rules and norms"—into the curricula of philosophy, history, and English departments across the country.[48] Drawing on the psychoanalytic theory of Wilhelm Reich, Fromm told American parents never to discipline their children to avoid bruising their offspring's egos. Adorno disparaged popular cultural forms and called for a true art that reflected the barbarity of an exploitative American system of capitalism. In his 1955 *Eros and Civilization*, Marcuse encouraged young people to be sexually promiscuous and transgress the repressive sexual norms of marriage and family. For Breitbart, the Frankfurt School worked to slowly erode the sexual, social, and artistic customs of their new home country to prepare it for the ideological assault of the nascent Democrat-Media Complex.

The thinkers of the Frankfurt School, Breitbart contends, orchestrated America's descent into "permissiveness." In the 1970s, the moralists of the New Right grouped together a range of unspeakable sins—abortion, homosexuality, promiscuity, pornography, drug abuse, godlessness, feminism—into the catch-all crime of permissiveness. The moral universe of the American right dictated that the permissive attitude of the liberal elite—the willingness to set up and support a functioning welfare state, for example—contributed directly to the lawlessness of the poor. Breitbart's narrative adapts this New Right truism, which would have been familiar to Tea Party audiences, and rearticulates it as the notion of a broad and coordinated Marxist offensive against traditionalism. Yet Breitbart's pro-business leanings prevent him from admitting that the most significant source of so-called permissiveness in American culture is consumerism. The waning of traditional

47 Breitbart, *Righteous Indignation*, 117.

48 Ibid., 113.

values had less to do with the Frankfurt School and more to do the marketed desire to consume (and to pay for it on credit). Although Breitbart's Tea Party readers may not identify the right cause for this spread of permissiveness, they still experience this crisis as a threat to their white citizenship. In his rendition of Cultural Marxism/s, Breitbart manages (or tries) to persuade Tea Partiers that anything they feel as an assault on their sense of status results from the plots of the Frankfurt School rather than the dynamics of contemporary capitalism.

Breitbart suggests that the Frankfurt School needed a popularizer to translate their abstruse philosophical ideas into a clear American vernacular. Apparently, the community organizer Saul Alinsky engaged in an act of "trickledown intellectualism" to transmit the ideas of Marcuse to the American public in his accessible and riveting 1971 handbook *Rules for Radicals*.[49] As Breitbart puts it, Alinsky turned the Frankfurt School's drab academicism into a strategy of cultural warfare and used "the methodologies of political correctness . . . to frighten people into submission and create an informal anti–First Amendment regime."[50] For instance, the Democrat-Media Complex exhibits its fidelity to Alinsky's rules whenever it brands the Tea Party as a "racist" organization.

Breitbart's leap from Marcuse to Alinsky is puzzling. Why not focus on Angela Davis or Abbie Hoffman, two famous American left-wing activists who studied under Marcuse? However, Alinsky was the radical that the Tea Party loved to hate (and imitate). For instance, the Tea Party organization FreedomWorks published a right-wing adaptation of Alinsky's ideas called *Rules for Patriots* that was disseminated through its network of activists. Breitbart's linking of the Frankfurt School with Alinsky justifies the use of the same methods for countercultural conservatives. Breitbart even applies Alinsky's thirteenth rule—pick the target, frame it, personalize and

49 Ibid., 124.
50 Ibid.

polarize it—to single out Obama as the new tyrant of Cultural Marxism. He characterizes Obama as a "Frankfurt School scholar" and a "community organizer in the Alinsky mold" who wants to "turn America into a Frankfurt School dystopia."[51] Whereas the Tea Party is faithful to the Constitution, Obama is a conscious agent of an anti-American conspiracy to implement socialism. Yet the pro-Obama propaganda of the Democrat-Media Complex hides this reality from the American public. To expose the truth of Obama Socialism, Breitbart argues, the Tea Party needs to double down on its media strategy.

The rise of the Tea Party symbolizes what Breitbart calls the "counterrevolution" of the "American bourgeois."[52] Just as Jaeger and Bowers borrow the poetry of the American Revolution to dramatize their visions of restoration, Breitbart invokes the imagery of the Founding Fathers to praise the Tea Party's counterrevolutionary media practices. Whereas the beleaguered American colonists fired muskets to free themselves from the British Crown, Breitbart and his fellow Tea Partiers wield their digital recorders and Blackberrys to resist the Democrat-Media Complex. He sees the emergence of this countercultural conservative movement as a special opportunity to retake the public discourse of the United States. The use of New Media, according to Breitbart, was the only way to restore the American bourgeoisie to their former status of white citizenship.

In 2007, Breitbart leapt into this struggle against the complex by launching his eponymous far-right news platform *Breitbart*. Like other countercultural conservative news sites, *Breitbart* championed an alternative journalistic paradigm that threatened to displace the professional norms of mainstream media. Instead of adopting the conventional practice of "balance" (the quoting and counter-quoting of multiple sources and so on), *Breitbart* advanced an antagonistic discourse with clear distinctions between the "legitimate self" and the "dangerous

51 Ibid., 139.
52 Ibid., 215.

other."[53] Most Breitbart articles use this *strategy of vilification* to portray "the left" as an unfathomable and immoral political enemy.[54] For instance, Gerald Warner's 2015 *Breitbart* article "For the First Time in History, 'Conservatives' Are at the Forefront of Cultural Revolution" condemned the "evil" and "destructive" plans of the Frankfurt School, especially Adorno's apparent promotion of "degenerate atonal music to induce mental illness, including necrophilia, on a large scale."[55] Not only does this vilifying rhetoric establish firm boundaries between "us" and "them," but it also acts out the affective difference between "our media" and "their media." *We*—Breitbart and other countercultural conservatives—are honest enough to tell you what we truly think; *they* hide their ideological agenda behind a mask of false balance. Breitbart predicted—and hoped—that this alternative paradigm would supplant the Democrat-Media Complex and eventually became the new mainstream. In this vision of the future, *Breitbart*—with its incendiary articles about immigrants and liberals—would replace *The New York Times* as the newspaper of record.

When Breitbart died in March 2012, he was canonized as one of the great saints of the American right. Conservatives quoted the Breitbart Doctrine as if it were a Bible verse or Confucian saying. Several *Breitbart* writers even picked up on his anti-Democrat version of Cultural Marxism/s. In 2015, Michael Walsh—who wrote for Breitbart's *Big Journalism* (a subsidiary of *Breitbart*)—published *The Devil's Pleasure*

---

53 Mark Davis, "A New, Online Culture War? The Communication World of Breitbart.com," *Communication Research and Practice* 5, no. 3 (2019): 241–54.

54 Jason Roberts and Karin Wahl-Jorgensen, "Strategies of Alternative Right-Wing Media: The Case of Breitbart News," in *The Routledge Companion to Political Journalism*, ed. James Morrison, Jen Birks, and Mike Berry (Abington: Routledge, 2022), 170.

55 Gerald Warner, "For the First Time in History, 'Conservatives' Are at the Forefront of the Cultural Revolution," *Breitbart*, February 4, 2015.

*Palace: The Cult of Critical Theory and the Subversion of the West*, in which he described the Frankfurt School's ideas as "satanic."[56] What was most striking, however, was Breitbart's influence on the rise of a new political movement called *the alt-right* (which, in several ways, led to Donald Trump's 2016 presidential victory).

The term "alt-right" (or "alternative right") was originally coined in 2008 by Richard Spencer, an editor for *The American Conservative*—which Buchanan helped to set up—and a former mentee of Paul Gottfried. Those who belonged to this alternative right believed that the "white race," or "Anglo-Saxon culture," was under attack from multiculturalism. Like the Tea Party, the members of the American alt-right sought to distinguish themselves from establishment conservatism, because they felt that mainstream Republicans were not willing to restrict immigration or limit the social freedoms of minorities. During the 2010s, the alt-right existed predominantly as an "edgy" Internet subculture that used offensive memes to flout the rules of political correctness and "own the libs." To understand how Breitbart and the Tea Party led to Trump, we need to focus on a pivotal moment in the history of the online alt-right: Gamergate.

In the summer of 2014, the hashtag #Gamergate started trending on social media. The hashtag referred to an online harassment campaign against a video games developer, Zoë Quinn, who had allegedly been trading sexual favors with gaming journalists to receive positive reviews. At the heart of Gamergate was the belief that feminist "social justice warriors" had infiltrated the video game industry. To "re-masculinize" the world of gaming, the Gamergate community—a swarm of Internet users on Twitter, Reddit, and 4chan—coordinated a series of hateful and misogynistic attacks on female game

56 Michael Walsh, *The Devil's Pleasure Palace: The Cult of Critical Theory and The Subversion of the West* (New York: Encounter Books, 2015), 23.

developers and critics (sending them death threats, posting their personal details online, and so on). In September 2014, a young *Breitbart* reporter named Milo Yiannopoulos latched onto the Gamergate controversy and wrote articles that characterized Gamergaters as innocent victims of a vast progressive media elite. As Yiannopoulos gained a larger audience for his sympathetic reporting, the Gamergaters became more immersed in the worldview of *Breitbart*.

Gamergate was the teenage Tea Party—it was media populism on Adderall. The Gamergaters portrayed themselves as a maligned and marginalized group—gamers—who were up against an entrenched anti-male media elite. They embraced alternative digital platforms, such as 4chan, and developed new political tactics like "trolling." For the thinkers of the alt-right, Gamergate was a potent example of what they called *metapolitics*. In simple terms, the concept of metapolitics supposes that cultural and ideological production is the primary driver of political change. If a movement can shift how people think about an issue, then they will succeed in pushing their agenda. Although the term *metapolitics* comes from the work of the French New Right thinker Alain de Benoist, its meaning is essentially identical to the Breitbart Doctrine: *Politics is downstream from culture*. When viewed metapolitically, Gamergate—and the online alt-right movement it promoted—altered the cultural landscape of the Internet and promoted far-right positions through the tactics of memeing, trolling, and online harassment. A major example of this metapolitical activism was the Gamergaters' hijacking of the Wikipedia page on "Cultural Marxism."

In December 2014, Wikipedia editors debated whether the page "Cultural Marxism" should be merged with another page called "Frankfurt School Conspiracy Theory." Several editors pointed out that the term "Cultural Marxism" was a valid descriptor for post-Marxist thought, as evidenced in the titles of books like Dennis L. Dworkin's *Cultural Marxism in Postwar Britain: History, the New Left, and the Origin of Cultural Studies*. Others argued that the pages for "Western Marxism" and "Critical Theory" already discussed the work of the Frankfurt School in detail, so it was pointless to maintain a separate page on "Cultural Marxism" (especially when most uses of the term—by Lind, Buchanan, and others—were intended to spread an inaccurate political narrative). After some heated discussion, Wikipedia decided to delete its page on "Cultural Marxism."

The online trolls of r/KotakuInAction, a Reddit community at the center of Gamergate, were outraged. They perceived the deletion of this Wikipedia page as an act of deliberate censorship to conceal the fact that Anita Sarkeesian—a feminist media blogger targeted in Gamergate—was a Frankfurt School–inspired critical theorist. The Gamergaters pestered Jimmy Wales, Wikipedia's founder, until he restored the page on "Cultural Marxism." Wales intervened and opened a second debate over the fate of the page. To sway the discussion, the Gamergaters created dozens of single-purpose or "IP" accounts (newly registered or unregistered Wikipedia accounts) to insist that the page should be kept and cleansed of "left-wing bias." At the end of the debate, three experienced Wikipedia administrators adjudicated the case and concluded that the original "Cultural Marxism" page should be deleted. Its contents would be merged with a recently created page on the "Frankfurt School Conspiracy." Although they failed to reinstate the page, the Gamergaters had demonstrated their ability to mobilize their community around contentious issues. Their online metapolitical activism, especially through r/KotakuInAction, would go on to shape the outlook and activity of the notorious pro-Trump subreddit r/The_Donald.

In the 2016 presidential race, Donald Trump was the anti–Cultural Marxism candidate. The chief executive of his campaign, Steve Bannon, had been *Breitbart*'s executive chairman and a key Tea Party ally. As the new face of the Republican

Party, Trump seemed to attract all the political constituencies that blamed the Frankfurt School for America's problems: the Gamergaters, the neo-Nazis, the Tea Partiers, the paleoconservatives, a handful of the last surviving LaRouchites. Even an elderly William S. Lind made an appearance on Trump's campaign trail to take a picture with the presidential hopeful and gift him a copy of a book that he had co-authored with Weyrich. When Trump won in November 2016, former Tea Partiers may have felt that they had finally toppled the Democrat-Media Complex. Yet, as it turned out, their campaign against Cultural Marxism was still incomplete.

# 4

# Contemporary Permutations: Critical Race Theory, Wokeness, and Gender Ideology

*I would insist that we currently live mostly in Herbert Marcuse's world.*

—James Lindsay, *Race Marxism*

What is the relationship between Cultural Marxism/s and the right's more recent ideological campaigns against "Critical Race Theory," "gender ideology," and "wokeness"? Have these new buzzwords entirely replaced the older stories and labels? Has Cultural Marxism lost out to its competitors in the marketplace of right-wing ideas? Although talk of "wokeness" and "Critical Race Theory" has become more prevalent, the narratives of Cultural Marxism/s have not dropped out of circulation. The history of Cultural Marxism/s has always been a story of revisions, borrowings, and recontextualizations. Conservative activists and authors have built on existing anti–Frankfurt School discourses to craft arguments about emerging civilizational threats. Consequently, the classic tales of Cultural Marxism/s have been inserted into a fresh discursive constellation that fuels the right's attacks on social and political equality.

According to the right, their new ideological foes—Critical Race Theory, wokeness, gender ideology—are the descendants of Cultural Marxism. Conservative intellectuals construct elaborate genealogies to trace the bloodline of left-wing thought to the Frankfurt School. These "experts" are invited to speak at transnational conservative gatherings, such as the National

Conservatism Conference or the Conservative Political Action Conference. Social media platforms and right-wing institutions sustain the activity of a whole anti-theory knowledge economy, where entrepreneurial ideologues and influencers perform "deep dives" on the history of woke ideology. These new buzzwords function as what Ico Maly calls "deglobalized" discursive units that circulate online to be appropriated and adapted to different situations and events.[1] The widespread diffusion of these terms mirrors the transnational right's understanding of itself as an alliance of different nationalist movements that represent the People's organic interests against elite "globalist" ideologies. In a peculiar inversion of decolonial rhetoric, the transnational right declares that they are reversing a process of ideological colonization and recultivating the "natural" state of their national cultures.

What are the discursive histories of these new additions to the right's anti-theory vocabulary? How did these terms end up on the right's ideological hitlist? What are their meanings and implications? The origins of "woke" can be traced back to pre-war Black American vernacular. Its use reminded Black people to be aware, or "woke," about racist structures that oppressed African American communities. In a 1938 recording of his song "Scottsboro Boys," the blues musician Lead Belly advised his listeners to "stay woke" about racial discrimination and violence against Black people in the American South. During the 2014 Black Lives Matter protests over the police killing of Michael Brown, the phrase "stay woke" experienced a revival. Since then, the notion of "wokeness" has been expanded to include awareness about other forms of prejudice, such as misogyny and transphobia. In the late 2010s, right-wing commentators twisted this term into an insult. Nowadays, woke usually refers to a performative or superficial belief in

1 Ico Maly, *Metapolitics, Algorithms and Violence: New Right Activism and Terrorism in the Attention Economy* (Abingdon, UK: Routledge, 2024), 34.

the values of social justice. To call someone woke means that they support progressive causes merely to signal their own virtue or goodness. "Woke-washing," or the deployment of the markers of equity and diversity as an advertising strategy, has become prevalent in the corporate world. This "woke capitalism," as the theorists Akane Kanai and Rosalind Gill point out, "exploits the historical politicization of identity, reaffirm[s] the centrality of capital, and reinscrib[es] movements of resistance without dismantling the hierarchies to which they refer."[2] Frequently, the right's anti-woke diatribes focus on this contradictory incorporation of progressive values to deny the necessity and urgency of serious political struggles, such as anti-racism and anti-sexism. Their arguments express a desire for a return to a purer form of capitalism that does not make these shallow concessions to the causes of social and environmental justice.

Wokeness is not the only term that the right has weaponized. Before 2020, Critical Race Theory (CRT) referred to a field of scholarship that studied the relationship between race, racism, and power in law and legal institutions. The concept of "intersectionality," coined by Kimberlé Crenshaw, originated in this field and became a popular way of talking about how different forms of oppression and discrimination can overlap. In 2020, a young conservative activist named Christopher F. Rufo turned the label of "Critical Race Theory" into a potent ideological tool by using a simple rhetorical technique called *linguistic framing*. This technique plays on the connotations of certain words to shape the vocabulary for discussing a subject or an event. For instance, organizers and activists use the term "grassroots" to characterize a political movement as something natural, organic, and grounded. When other people accept and affirm this framing, they legitimize a certain way of talking

2 Akane Kanai and Rosalind Gill, "Woke? Affect, Neoliberalism, Marginalised Identities and Consumer Culture," *New Formations: A Journal of Culture/TheoryPolitics* 102 (December 2020, 24).

about an issue. In a consummate display of political storytelling, Rufo used linguistic framing to explain the rise of what he saw as a "left-wing racial ideology." When he came across CRT, he felt that he had found the right villain for his narrative. The connotations of Critical Race Theory, Rufo judged, were "all negative to most middle-class Americans, including racial minorities, who see the world as 'creative' rather than 'critical,' 'individual' rather than 'racial,' 'practical' rather than 'theoretical.'"[3] Rufo and other conservative intellectuals would later provide a prehistory of CRT to argue that the Frankfurt School inspired radical Black activists to engineer the collapse of the United States.

Whereas "CRT" mobilizes the right over issues of race, "gender ideology" addresses notions of sex, sexuality, and gender. The concept of "gender ideology" has its roots in the teachings of the Catholic Church.[4] As early as 1984, Cardinal Joseph Ratzinger expressed concerns about the belief that gender roles were cultural and historical constructs rather than God-given biological realities. Ratzinger blamed feminism for making people think that sexuality could be separated from procreation or that one could undergo surgery to change sex. The Catholic doctrine of complementarity decreed that men and women possessed clear physical and psychological differences. Although the notion of complementarity granted both sexes equal dignity, it also perpetuated limiting and rigid stereotypes about the nature of femininity. Several lay Catholic authors, such as Dale O'Leary, helped to popularize these criticisms of gender ideology and portrayed feminist and pro-LGBTQ+ initiatives as part of a United Nations–led

3 Benjamin Wallace-Wells, "How A Conservative Activist Invented the Conflict over Critical Race Theory," *The New Yorker*, June 18, 2021.

4 Mary Anne Case, "Trans Formations in the Vatican's War on 'Gender Ideology,'" *Signs: Journal of Women in Culture and Society* 44, no. 3 (2019): 639–64.

conspiracy to impose sexual deviance on the world population. Opposition to gender ideology has extended beyond the Catholic Church and intersected with the campaigns of trans-exclusionary radical feminists, evangelical Christians, far-right political parties, and social conservatives. The elasticity of this signifier means that it can be presented as the conspiratorial enemy behind a range of social changes and political issues: HIV prevention, sex education, discussions of gender identity, same-sex marriage, decriminalization of sex work, abortion. The attack on gender ideology has escalated into a global phenomenon as activists have formed transnational links to share arguments, tactics, and slogans. Various influential theorists, such as Marcuse and Judith Butler, have been branded as the nefarious progenitors of this ideology, as though their theories created—in a foul parody of God's creation—the very realities they were attempting to elucidate.

In this chapter, I investigate how older anti–Frankfurt School narratives informed and inspired recent attacks on CRT, gender ideology, and wokeness. While it would be preferable to examine a broader range of national contexts (and to see into the future), I limit myself to the United States, the United Kingdom, and Brazil (and confine my analysis to events that took place roughly between 2018 and 2024). Each section of this chapter will attempt to address a series of pressing questions. How do right-wing intellectuals in these countries draw on the existing ideas and narratives of Cultural Marxism/s? Which political forces are engaged in these anti-woke struggles? How do they use different forms of media to intervene culturally, ideologically, and politically? What kind of legislative and institutional changes are proposed or implemented to deal with these cultural threats? In the United States, the anti-CRT movement demonized efforts to remedy gender and racial inequality in the post–George Floyd conjuncture. In the United Kingdom, conservatives engaged in a War on Woke to delegitimize social movements and progressive beliefs. In

Brazil, the New Right scapegoated minorities and activists for political and economic crises and proposed the renewal of a traditional social order. In each of these contexts, the forces of the political right sought to disempower left-wing activism (and even liberal reform) and introduce new legislation for the control of public life.

## The United States: A Cultural Counterrevolution

In September 2020, President Donald Trump established an advisory committee called the 1776 Commission (the name was chosen to contrast with *The New York Times*'s 1619 Project). According to Trump, the George Floyd Uprising resulted from decades of "left-wing indoctrination." The eighteen-member commission, which featured an array of conservative politicians and activists, was responsible for developing a pedagogical cure for the Marxism-infected school system. When *The 1776 Report* was released on January 18, 2021 (less than two weeks after the US Capitol attack), it faced scathing criticism. None of the commission members were scholars of American history; many of the report's claims were inaccurate. For instance, it asserts that Martin Luther King Jr. was a critic of affirmative action, even though he supported these kinds of reparative policies. Of course, official historical narratives are rarely neutral or objective. They often reflect the political anxieties and agendas of the present. In the case of the 1776 Commission, their report promoted a version of American history that was intended to delegitimize the Black Lives Matter movement (BLM) and deny the persistence of racism in the present-day United States.

Tucked away in Appendix III of *The 1776 Report* was an odd argument about the origins of identity politics (which the authors compared to the racial hierarchies of the antebellum South). In the report's account of modern intellectual history,

Gramsci urged Marxist revolutionaries to foster a counterculture that could undermine Western cultural hegemony. The Frankfurt School enthusiastically adopted this Gramscian strategy and elaborated a set of revolutionary ideas called Critical Theory. When Marcuse imported this doctrine to the United States, he inspired the inception of Critical Race Theory. Since the 1960s, Critical Race Theorists have rewritten American history as a formulaic "oppressor-victim narrative."[5] Various radical movements started to "invent" grievances to agitate for more power. Feminists reimagined the West as a patriarchal system; Black power revolutionaries reimagined America as a white supremacist regime. Other activists constructed new artificial categories, such as "Asian-American," to demand more economic advantages and benefits. The 1776 Commission argued that the principles of patriotic education would help to combat all this fraudulent talk of oppression and restore America's faith in the nation's school system.

This argument in Appendix III comes from commission member Mike Gonzalez's 2020 book *The Plot to Change America: How Identity Politics is Dividing the Land of the Free*. Like the other participants in the commission, Gonzalez was not a historian. After working in journalism for around twenty years and getting an MBA from Columbia Business School, Gonzalez joined President George W. Bush's administration as a speechwriter for the Securities and Exchange Commission and the State Department. At the end of the Bush presidency, he followed the traditional career path of many other out-of-office Republicans and became a fellow at the Heritage Foundation. In his role as the Angeles T. Arredondo *E Pluribus Unum* Senior Fellow, Gonzalez churns out op-ed after op-ed for the *New York Post* and *Fox News* to condemn the worldwide spread of wokeness.

5 The President's Advisory 1776 Commission, *The 1776 Report*, January 2021, 30.

In the 2020s, the Heritage Foundation operated as a major institutional hub of the war on wokeness. It produced thousands of op-eds, YouTube videos, podcast episodes, Instagram posts, and tweets. Heritage's staff published books and reports with such titles as *The Critical Classroom: How Critical Race Theory Undermines Academic Excellence and Individual Agency in Education* and *How Cultural Marxism Threatens the United States—And How Americans Can Fight It*. In April 2023, Heritage launched an initiative called *Project 2025* to provide a blueprint for a future Trump administration, including proposals to "defang and defund the woke cultural warriors" in America's governing institutions. The development of *Project 2025*'s anti-woke agenda can be traced back to some of the discussions that were taking place in the Heritage Foundation during the George Floyd protests. In July 2020, Heritage hosted an online panel called "Wokeism at Work: How 'Critical Theory' and Anti-Racism Training Divide America."[6] The panelists —Gonzalez, Rufo, and James Lindsay—shared their concerns and criticisms about the spread of "Conflict Theory" in the United States. All three speakers ignored the social and political problems that triggered the George Floyd Uprising and implied that theory itself was responsible for fostering the unrest.

In September 2020, Rufo appeared on *Tucker Carlson Tonight*. In this interview, Rufo declared that CRT had become "the default ideology" of America's institutions and called on Trump to issue an executive order that would end "CRT trainings" in the federal government. Within a few weeks, Trump signed Executive Order 13950 to prohibit federal contractors from providing training that involved "divisive concepts" about race, sex, and gender. On his first day in office, President Joe Biden rescinded Trump's executive order. During the first half of the Biden administration, Rufo became the public face

6 "Wokeism at Work: How 'Critical Theory' and Anti-Racism Training Divide America," YouTube, 1:14:49, posted by the Heritage Foundation, July 27, 2020.

of a nationwide campaign against CRT. By the end of 2022, 241 anti-CRT measures had been enacted or adopted at the federal, state, and local level.

The charge of the anti-CRT brigade was hardly a surprise attack. Rufo was simply the latest culture warrior in the American right's long-running assault on education, civil rights, and social progress. Like the New Right, this anti-CRT movement hoped to reverse the *politicization of the social* and convert the public issues of racism, sexism, and homophobia back into private troubles. It planned to restrict the terrain on which progressive groups could gather momentum and issue demands for greater equality and inclusion. Not only did this anti-CRT project build on the New Right's legacy, but it also drew on the ideas of other ideological movements that emerged in the 2010s: the alt-right, the so-called Classical Liberalism of the Intellectual Dark Web (IDW), and Trumpism.

Although it had roots in the earlier waves of the American far right, the alt-right conceived of itself as a reaction to the "identity politics" of the Obama era. Influenced by the thought of the French New Right, alt-right intellectuals rearticulated discourses of diversity to promote a hierarchical and essentialist conception of race known as *human biodiversity*. The principle of biodiversity reduced race to a matter of genetic difference and assumed that different races must be kept separate to preserve cultural purity. The alt-right vanguard weaponized this identitarian rhetoric to portray white people as victims of a globalist agenda. Political correctness, according to the alt-right, had corrupted the American education system. They argued that, instead of teaching ethnic studies or gender theory, schools and universities should prioritize white interests and Western traditions.

The leading figures of the so-called IDW tended to be journalists or professors who were "canceled" for advancing arguments against progressive forms of social justice. Although they supposedly abhorred alt-right racism, these IDW liberals shared many of its preoccupations: worship of Western civilization, hostility to political correctness or "postmodern neo-Marxism," and free speech absolutism. Instead of praising human biodiversity, they were committed to the purely formal principles of individuality and equality that the sociologist Eduardo Bonilla-Silva calls "abstract liberalism."[7] They claimed that attempts to remedy institutional racism, such as affirmative action or changes in curricula, represented a form of reverse racism or discrimination.

Although Trumpism was never really a coherent ideology, Trump was fluent in the discourses of racial animosity and anxiety. His campaign was endorsed by the Klan, the American Nazi Party, Stormfront, Aryan Nations, and many other far-right elements. Throughout his presidency, Trump pushed for the construction of a Mexican border wall to keep out immigrants from Mexico (whom he characterized as criminals and rapists). In January 2017, he signed an executive order to ban travel from seven Muslim countries and suspend the US Refugee Admissions Program. During a speech at the foot of Mount Rushmore on July 4, 2020, he declared that George Floyd protestors wanted to "wipe out our history, defame our heroes, erase our values, and indoctrinate our children."[8] Like the alt-right and the IDW, Trump tapped into a feeling that various Others—immigrants and refugees, anti-fascist and anti-racist protestors, politically correct educators and woke elites—were destroying Western culture.

Echoing these existing themes and arguments, Rufo claimed that the George Floyd Uprising was the consequence of a widespread "cultural revolution." He branded CRT as an elite-driven

---

7 Eduardo Bonilla-Silva, *Racism without Racists: Color-Blind Racism and the Persistence of Racial Inequality in the United States* (New York: Rowman & Littlefield, 2014), 76.

8 "Remarks by President Trump at South Dakota's 2020 Mount Rushmore Fireworks Celebration, Keystone, South Dakota," Donald Trump White House, July 4, 2020.

and quasi-Marxist movement that demonized white people. He rearticulated a critique of racial essentialism to suggest that even acknowledging the persistence of racial inequality was itself racist. In collaboration with activists, pundits, and lawmakers, he worked to alter the conceptions of race that circulated within schools, workplaces, and universities.

Rufo's attack on CRT channeled a neoliberal logic of reactionary color blindness. If, in the post–civil rights era, racial inequality was no longer an effect of sociohistorical processes, then state institutions would not need to host programs or initiatives to address the ongoing effects of racism. If racism was not occurring on an institutional or structural scale, then all racial issues would be displaced onto individuals. If any reference to race was a violation of color blindness, then fields of study that concentrated on race must themselves be racist. These neoliberal arguments could be applied to other issues, such as misogyny and transphobia, to prevent any action or discussion over systematic inequality and discrimination ("the concept of patriarchy is sexist as it claims that men are inherently bad" or "to call people 'cisgender' is a slur," for example). Like many others in the American right, Rufo planned to dismantle anything that obstructed his vision of a conservative United States.

Rufo is a product of the right-wing think-tank system. In 2017, he joined the Lincoln Fellowship Program for "patriotic young professionals" at the Claremont Institute (a "thought resort" for West Coast Straussians). Since then, he has held positions at various conservative institutions: a visiting fellow at the Heritage Foundation, the director of the Center on Wealth & Poverty at the creationist Discovery Institute, a senior fellow at the libertarian Manhattan Institute (as well as a contributing editor of its in-house publication *City Journal*). Like the New Right think-tank intellectuals that preceded him, he must perform a specific function: to produce polemics that contest liberal policies or left-wing ideas and promote right-wing alternatives. Unlike academics or journalists, Rufo does not need to fret about peer review, fact-checking, and balance. He is more interested in winning power than being right.

From mid-2020 onwards, Rufo threw himself into a war against CRT. He produced many articles for *City Journal* to document the alleged dominance of CRT in America. Each article stays within the realm of the anecdotal: a training session for a certain company, a lesson plan at a particular school. In these exposés, he apes the procedures of investigative journalism and solicits shocking whistleblower documents. Yet, as several researchers point out, Rufo's sensationalist reporting misrepresents his evidence. For example, one of his articles claims that an elementary school teacher encouraged a fifth-grade class to define "communist" in "favorable terms," even though the class materials instructed students to "use a dictionary." In another article, Rufo asserts a training document at the San Diego Unified School District told teachers that "you are racist," even though the training was merely asking them to reflect on how they would feel if someone called them racist. Nonetheless, the scandal-hungry right-wing mediasphere devoured Rufo's opportunistic framings and empowered him to establish the terms of the debate on CRT.

In 2021, Rufo released a short YouTube video essay that apparently revealed CRT's intellectual origins.[9] He argued that Marcuse, Adorno, and other German thinkers imported a new theory of Marxist revolution to the United States. Instead of sticking to the old economic dialectic between bourgeois and proletariat, the Frankfurt School proposed a new racial dialectic of white and Black. A handful of radical movements—CPUSA, the Black Panther Party, the Weather Underground—absorbed the Frankfurt School's arguments and tried to use racial unrest to overthrow the American government. When these efforts

9 Christopher F. Rufo, "Critical Race Theory," YouTube, 17:57, posted by Christopher F. Rufo, June 14, 2021.

failed, far-left radicals fused Critical Theory with identity politics to produce CRT. Rufo warns his audience that CRT operates under a series of benign euphemisms, such as equity, diversity, and social justice. Critical Race Theorists, according to Rufo, deploy these labels to conceal their secret neo-Marxist agenda and trick the American public into accepting their ideas. This historical narrative justifies Rufo's preferred strategy of scandal-making. If, as Rufo claims, CRT hides behind a series of aliases and disguises, then anything—an insipid training session, a book in a high school library, a company's workplace policies—could feasibly be "exposed" as a so-called Marxist front. In his 2023 book *America's Cultural Revolution: How the Radical Left Conquered Everything*, Rufo elaborated on this original story to suggest that every public institution in the United States has succumbed to CRT.

Rufo presents his book as a "genealogy of darkness."[10] In it, he names the Four Horsemen of the Woke Apocalypse—Herbert Marcuse, Angela Davis, Paulo Freire, Derrick Bell—whose ideas ignited a rebellion against the American republic. Their respective doctrines—Critical Theory, Critical Praxis, Critical Pedagogy, Critical Race Theory—inspired the chaos that plagues contemporary America: riots on the streets of Portland, DEI training sessions, BLM protests, ethnic studies curricula, the Capitol Hill Autonomous Zone. The left, as the subtitle of Rufo's book insinuates, has become ubiquitous in American culture.

How did this cultural revolution happen? Since the end of the 1960s, Rufo explains, former New Left activists have successfully carried out a "long march through the institutions" and infiltrated the university, the media, the state, and the corporation. Although Rufo acknowledges that America's official political structures may have not changed, he insists that

10 Christopher F. Rufo, *America's Cultural Revolution: How the Radical Left Conquered Everything* (New York: Broadside Books, 2023), xi.

"the entire intellectual substructure has shifted."[11] The public bureaucracy—now staffed by older 1960s radicals—has allegedly formalized the ideas of Critical Theory into new federal regulations. The lingo of the revolutionary left (liberation, white privilege, racism) has been translated into the jargon of DEI training (equity, implicit bias, racial disparity). Building on Claremont Institute fellow John Marini's concept of the *administrative state*, Rufo theorizes that this "ideological regime" uses woke beliefs to regulate the social, political, and economic life of the nation.[12] Over the course of the book, Rufo tries to demonstrate that these alleged changes constitute a full-blown structural revolution.

Rufo distorts evidence to exaggerate the scale of this so-called structural revolution. For instance, he cites a 2014 Thomas B. Fordham Institute report, *The Hidden Half: School Employees Who Don't Teach*, to claim that the number of school administrators has increased by 130 percent since 1970.[13] According to Rufo, this statistic proves that woke graduates have swamped the educational bureaucracy to impose diversity, equality, and inclusion.[14] Yet the report states that this rise in non-teaching personnel stems from legislation, such as the Education for All Handicapped Children Act (1975), that required schools to deliver free and appropriate education to all students. As the report plainly reveals, the main cause for the 130 percent growth was the hiring of new instructional aides (who work one-on-one with special-needs youngsters). Misused statistics like these severely weaken the credibility of Rufo's argument. The rest of Rufo's evidence for the left's "structural revolution"

11 Ibid., 4.

12 Ibid., 54; John Marini, *Unmasking the Administrative State: The Crisis of American Politics in the Twenty-First Century* (New York: Encounter Books, 2019).

13 Matthew Richmond, *The Hidden Half: School Employees Who Don't Teach* (Washington, DC: Thomas Fordham Institute, 2014).

14 Rufo, *America's Cultural Revolution*, 166–7.

largely comes from his own reporting (which, as multiple journalists point out, is deeply misleading). Although Rufo repeatedly misreads data and confuses the anecdotal for the structural, he remains convinced that the left, defined in the broadest terms, dominates America's institutional order.

Whereas Weyrich and Lind counseled a retreat into a retroculture, Rufo demands counterrevolution. Inspired by Richard Nixon's 1968 presidential run, Rufo proposes a strategy of "laying siege to the institutions" to dismantle the left's bureaucratic apparatus.[15] Instead of seizing these institutions, he hopes to replace the administrative state with a more decentralized system that serves the needs of ordinary citizens. As of early 2024, Rufo's so-called counterrevolution has already begun. Under the gubernatorial rule of Ron DeSantis, Florida has become a laboratory for Rufo's social experimentation. In the summer of 2022, DeSantis approved of the Stop WOKE Act, or "Stop Wrongs to Our Kids and Employees Act," to prevent schools and employers from using theoretical concepts that might cause people to "feel guilt, anguish or any form of psychological distress" due to their race, color, sex, or nationality. He also signed the "Don't Say Gay" bill, or Parental Rights in Education Act, to prohibit any educational discussion of sexual orientation or gender identity in classrooms. In 2023, DeSantis appointed Rufo to the Board of Trustees at New College of Florida to turn the school into a haven of conservative pedagogy. As a board member, Rufo helped to terminate the gender studies program and introduce affirmative action policies for underqualified male applicants.

In his work, Rufo claims to speak on behalf of the "common citizen."[16] He points out—truthfully—that elites rarely address the real needs and interests of the American people. The life of the common citizen has deteriorated into a "revolving

15 Ibid., 271.
16 Ibid., 281.

nightmare of addiction, violence, and incarceration."[17] Rates of "deaths of despair" have risen sharply over the past two decades, especially among white, Black, and Native Americans. Although America's public institutions and private corporations have absorbed the language of "equity" and "inclusion," class continues to be a major dividing line in the United States. In fact, Rufo's critique touches on the greatest contradiction of woke capitalism. Woke corporations will tolerate a concession to the causes of social justice insofar as it does not interfere with their ability to exploit workers and extract value. For instance, Amazon's pristine diversity, equity, and inclusion statement has never stopped Jeff Bezos from repressing unionization efforts in his warehouses (and vilifying Black union leaders, such as Chris Smalls). Evidently, any analysis of inequality in the United States must reckon with the role of class.

Nonetheless, Rufo promotes a pseudo–class politics that frames the plight of the American working class in conspiratorial terms. His book never mentions the 1973 recession or the 2007–8 financial recession that devastated working-class communities. According to Rufo, the common citizen is a victim of elite wokeness rather than market forces or systemic shifts. As the historian Gabriel Winant puts it, this vision of contemporary America assumes that there "is no historical logic to class inequality and exploitation, only inexplicable and unique acts of cruelty that bear no useful comparison to anything that has happened to others."[18] For all his wishy-washy talk of the structural, Rufo cannot conceive of social crisis as anything but the actions of malicious individual agents.

Instead of recommending higher wages or universal healthcare, Rufo argues that simply getting rid of wokeness will improve the lives of ordinary citizens. Yet his counterrevolution represents nothing but the replacement of a woke ruling

17 Ibid., 273.

18 Gabriel Winant, "J. D. Vance Changes the Subject," *n +1*, no. 45 (Spring 2023).

class with a conservative one. Despite his criticism of patronizing elites, Rufo's proposals substitute one paternalism for another. Whereas the woke restricted free speech to protect the "feelings" of the "snowflake left," Rufo's counterrevolution prohibits any speech that induces "guilt" or "distress" in white America. He pays lip service to meritocracy and excellence but hands out undeserved advantages to those who fit his desired demographic and political aims. Ultimately, Rufo reveals that the true function of the New Right think-tank intellectual is not to deconstruct the administrative state but, rather, to maneuver it toward conservative ends.

*America's Cultural Revolution* was hardly the first anti-woke text to be published in the post–George Floyd era. As Moira Weigel puts it, Rufo's book belongs to a popular genre in American conservative publishing: the *adversarial intellectual history*.[19] These books present themselves as explainers that identify the intellectual culprits for America's decline. Many of them, such as Mark Levin's *American Marxism* and David Horowitz's *The Enemy Within*, cast the Frankfurt School thinkers as a major source of this social and cultural rot. Yet none of these texts are quite as bewildering as James Lindsay's 2022 *Race Marxism*.

Lindsay rose to prominence during the grievance studies affair in 2018. According to media coverage of this scandal, Lindsay and his fellow pranksters—Helen Pluckrose and Peter Boghossian—successfully published bogus papers in a range of academic journals. In a piece for *Aero Magazine*, Lindsay and his collaborators explained that the target of their prank was grievance studies: a so-called field of ideologically motivated scholarship on issues of race, gender, and inequality.[20] Over the course of the

19 Moira Weigel, "Christopher Rufo's Troubling Path to Power," *The New Republic*, November 13, 2023.

20 James A. Lindsay, Peter Boghossian, and Helen Pluckrose, "Academic Grievance Studies and the Corruption of Scholarship," *Aero Magazine*, October 2, 2018.

project, they wrote twenty fraudulent papers—seven of which were published—that definitively "exposed" the epistemological and ethical faults of this "critical constructivism."

Most journalists accepted Lindsay and company's claims at face value. Closer scrutiny of the grievance studies affair, however, shows that the authors overstated their achievements. For instance, they purported to submit a "feminist rewrite" of a chapter from Adolf Hitler's *Mein Kampf*, yet their article bore no significant resemblance to the original text (which somewhat ruined the joke that feminist journals would approve of Nazi ideology if it only promoted the right groups). Despite the flawed nature of this social experiment, Lindsay took advantage of the publicity and worked to establish his reputation as a "world-level expert" of Critical Theory and progressive ideology.

Following the grievance studies affair, Lindsay became a "terminally online" anti-woke crusader. He set up a website called *New Discourses*, where he posts long, rambling podcast episodes about Hegel, Gnosticism, and the American Library Association. His Twitter/X account has turned into an endless stream of conspiratorial aspersions, puerile insults, and self-aggrandizing pronouncements. He is regularly invited onto various media platforms, such as *The Rubin Report* and *The Daily Signal*, to share his knowledge about the true nature of woke ideology. In 2022, Lindsay published a book entitled *Race Marxism*, in which he "revealed" CRT's secret Marxist (and Hegelian) lineage. The term "Race Marxism," as well as Lindsay's other coinages ("Identity Marxism" and "Woke Marxism"), performs a similar function to Lind's "Cultural Marxism" as it riffs on popular anti-communist tropes to delegitimize minor cultural changes and progressive policies. Just as Lind felt that affirmative action was equivalent to dekulakization, Lindsay insists that there is no difference between a Maoist struggle session and a corporate diversity workshop. Like Lind, Lindsay believes that his work on CRT will help to protect "the free people of the world and humanity" from a "civilization-threatening" danger.[21]

In *Race Marxism*, Lindsay refers to CRT as "the tip of a 'one-hundred-year-long spear that is being thrust into the side of Western Civilization' [that] has well over two hundred years of intellectual muscle behind it."[22] The immediate influences of CRT—the metaphorical spear—are all Cultural and Neo-Marxists: Lukács, Gramsci, Horkheimer, and Marcuse. The great-grandfathers of CRT—the intellectual muscle—are Rousseau, Hegel, and Marx. Lindsay even throws a few French postmodernists—Jacques Derrida, Michel Foucault, Jean François Lyotard, Jean Baudrillard—into this CRT genealogy.

Methodologically, *Race Marxism* is a work of intellectual determinism. Theory itself is cast as the central antagonist of Lindsay's narrative. Theorists, severed from their own historical contexts and cultural milieus, are portrayed as mere servants of the "dialectical faith of Leftism."[23] According to Lindsay, Crenshaw did not coin the term "intersectionality" to address shortcomings in anti-discrimination law but, rather, to channel the dialectical synthesis of "post-modernism" and "neo-Marxism."[24] Lindsay implies that all critical theorists operate in this kind of separate "theory-time," in which they behave as conduits for the further development of the dialectic. Theory possesses its own intentionality and seeks an overarching teleological goal: to "seize as much institutional authority as possible to raise enough 'racial consciousness' to establish a Dictatorship of the Antiracist that will enforce Critical Race Theory on everybody."[25] Overall, *Race Marxism* offers a master narrative for "Theory" that treats it as a unitary agent rather

---

21 James Lindsay, *Race Marxism: The Truth about Critical Race Theory and Praxis* (Orlando: New Discourses, 2022), vii–viii.

22 Ibid., 17.

23 Ibid., 166.

24 Ibid., 139.

25 Ibid., 254.

than a somewhat broad and clunky umbrella term for distinct theoretical tendencies and philosophical movements.

Many of Lindsay's claims follow a bizarre associational logic. They form, as Adorno would put it, "an organized flight of ideas," where the "relation between premises and inferences is replaced by a linking-up of ideas resting on mere similarity."[26] For instance, Lindsay tries to prove that Critical Race Theory has Marcusean roots by showing that both Marcuse and Crenshaw use the word "sensibility" in their work.[27] This desperate linking up of ideas almost resembles a surreal mathematical equation: Crenshaw cited Angela Davis—in a footnote that mentions dozens of other authors—in her 1991 essay "Mapping the Margins" + Davis was Marcuse's doctoral student = the lens of intersectionality is the same as what Marcuse calls a "new sensibility."[28] Similarly, Lindsay latches onto Cheryl I. Harris's 1993 paper "Whiteness as Property" to conclude that Critical Race Theory wants to fulfil Marx and Engels's demand for the abolition of private property. He connects this to the corporate diversity training materials of Robin DiAngelo, which tell people to be "less white," without ever demonstrating the link between *The Communist Manifesto*, Harris's essay, and DiAngelo's training programs.[29] Lindsay's approach to texts seems to mimic a strange kind of computational logic, where pure identification takes the place of actual interpretation. Strangely enough, his hermeneutics of suspicion on steroids—plumbing the depths of texts for hidden meanings—depends on a shallow style of reading that ignores both content and context.

As an anti–Critical Theory warrior with a large online following, Lindsay exemplifies the characteristics of the new

26 Theodor Adorno, *The Stars Down to Earth and Other Essays on the Irrational in Culture* (Abingdon, UK: Routledge, 2002), 222–3.

27 Lindsay, *Race Marxism*, 121.

28 Ibid., 123.

29 Ibid., 65–7.

right-wing social media intellectual.[30] These new "content creators" tend to act more like influencers or celebrities. The curation of their online persona has become almost as important as the development and dissemination of their ideas. They increasingly rely on media technologies that convey a sense of immediacy, authenticity, and intimacy. Twitter/X provides the illusion of direct and continuous communication. Patreon and other crowdfunding platforms simulate a kind of personal bond between a creator and their fans, even though this connection is ultimately a commercial transaction. Most podcasts have a conversational tone that can make audiences feel that an intellectual is their close friend. These parasocial relationships—an intense and one-sided attachment to a public figure—help the intellectual to increase engagement with their ideas and narratives. Building on this dynamic of parasociality, Lindsay has attracted a digital constituency of bitter anti-woke followers who feel like they are participating in his endless battle against the left.

During the Biden administration, the anti-CRT movement also latched onto the contentious issue of LGBTQ+ rights. When DeSantis signed his controversial "Don't Say Gay" bill in 2022, critics argued that this vaguely worded legislation could possibly prevent LGBTQ+ students and teachers from even mentioning their gender identity or sexual orientation. Rufo, Lindsay, and other prominent right-wing pundits proclaimed that anyone with concerns about DeSantis's bill was a "groomer" who wanted to sexualize young children. This equivalence between predatory sexual behavior and LGBTQ+-inclusive education presumes that people are deliberately tricked or coerced into adopting non-heteronormative sexualities and identities. In his more recent work, Lindsay even contends that a new religious cult based on "gender ideology" has infiltrated and overwhelmed the American education

30 Maly, *Metapolitics, Algorithms and Violence*, 10–13.

system, where it seeks to convert healthy children into queer activists.[31] Like the attack on CRT, this "groomer panic" portrays even mild and reformist efforts to secure inclusion and diversity as the consequence of a deeper, hidden Marxist conspiracy. What drives the anti-woke coalition in the United States is the constant need for these new targets—corporate diversity, equity, and inclusion programs or pro-Palestinian encampments on college campuses—that permits them to manufacture more and more content for a growing reactionary audience. It is impossible to foresee how long this dynamic will last. Ironically, the American anti-woke movement, with all its talk of placing individual agency over group belonging, has become a self-propelling force that may never lose momentum until it destroys the rights and freedoms it once feigned to love.

## The United Kingdom: A War on Woke

On November 9, 2020, *The Daily Telegraph* published an open letter from a faction of the Conservative Party called the Common Sense Group. Following the George Floyd protests, many cultural institutions in the UK chose to reflect on Britain's colonial past. Some people welcomed these moves as a necessary corrective to an excessively triumphalist narrative of British history. The Common Sense Group's letter, however, condemned a National Trust report about colonialism and attacked the National Maritime Museum's decision to review its exhibition on Admiral Lord Nelson. The letter's signatories warned that these "institutional custodians of history and heritage" were embracing "cultural Marxist dogma" and

31 Logan Lancing with James Lindsay, *The Queering of the American Child: How a New School Religious Cult Poisons the Minds and Bodies of Normal Kids* (Orlando, FL: New Discourses, 2024).

denigrating "British values."[32] They claimed that "privileged liberals" were rewriting "our history" to suit "'snowflake' preoccupations."[33] From their perspective, British history had become a battlefield that needed to be protected from an unjustified ideological assault.

Founded by Sir John Hayes MP in 2020, the Common Sense Group represented the most anti-woke wing of the Conservative Party. The group's name implied that their project was non-ideological. Commitment to "common sense" thinking—or being sensible—is held up as a virtue in everyday British life. People make jokes about unnecessary health and safety guidelines and advise others to simply "use their head." The Common Sense Group played on these connotations to legitimate their agenda of promoting a range of contested propositions —that the British Empire was a force for good, that the UK is not systematically racist, that climate change is not a serious problem —as the "taken-for-granted" assumptions of the British mentality. According to this highly politicized notion of common sense, Cultural Marxist dogma—or wokeness—was a form of irrationality that threatened to destroy the very essence of Britishness.

In his contribution to the Common Sense Group's 2021 pamphlet *Common Sense: Conservative Thinking for a Post-Liberal Age*, the Conservative MP Gareth Bacon attempted a definition of wokeism.[34] For Bacon, wokeness was neither a coherent doctrine nor a set of policy objectives. Woke ideology could not create anything new or improve the lives of ordinary people, because it was inherently destructive, nihilistic, and divisive. Wokeness was a jumble of oppositional positions—

32 The Common Sense Group, "Britain's Heroes," *Daily Telegraph*, November 9, 2020.

33 Ibid.

34 Gareth Bacon MP, "What is Wokeism and How Can it be Defeated?," in *Common Sense: Conservative Thinking for a Post-Liberal Age* (Common Sense Group, 2021), 19–26.

anti-British, anti-Western, anti-capitalist—that spread through social media like a contagion. It functioned as a quasi-religious pseudo-Marxism: a totalitarian orthodoxy that crushed dissent or disagreement. As the hearts of "woke-ists" were full of jealousy and malice, they needed to direct their hatred against the symbols of British heritage. Within the logic of Bacon's argument, the so-called War on Woke was an act of self-defense to save Britain from a deadly and diffuse threat.

Although the term "wokeness" originated in an American context, it fit almost seamlessly into an existing vocabulary of anti-leftist buzzwords that have long circulated in British political discourse. In the Thatcherite 1980s, the right-wing press popularized the term "Loony Left" to ridicule the activities of Labour Party–run local governments.[35] Reporters confected various scandals—most famously, the so-called anti-racist ban by the Hackney Borough Council of the nursey rhyme "Baa Baa Black Sheep"—to imply that Labour councillors were irrationally obsessed with issues of race, gender, and sexuality. These fabricated stories were designed to implicitly discredit the causes of anti-racism, feminism, and LGBTQ+ rights. In the pages of right-wing newspapers, these struggles for equality were not legitimate forms of political action and expression but, rather, wild outbursts of lunacy.

In the 2010s, "the Blob" became the British right's new term for their "Marxist" enemies. According to the Conservatives, the Blob was the result of the Loony Left's "long march through the institutions." In 2013, the then–Education Secretary for the Conservative-led Coalition government Michael Gove wrote an op-ed for *The Daily Mail* to describe teachers and civil servants who opposed his reforms as "the Blob."[36] For Gove, the Blob

35 James Curran, Ivor Gaber, and Julian Petley, *Culture Wars: The Media and the British Left*, Second Edition (Abingdon, UK: Routledge, 2019).

36 Michael Gove, "I Refuse to Surrender to the Marxist Teachers Hell-bent on Destroying Our Schools": Education Secretary Berates

was a vast and stealthy Marxist establishment that wanted to lower British school standards. Over the past decade, this metaphor was expanded to include anyone—union leaders, bankers, lawyers, university staff, regulators, charity workers, police chiefs—who did not fully support the regressive, and sometimes law-breaking, agenda of the Conservative Party.

The latest stage of this War on Woke—or the Battle Against the Blob or the Lampooning of the Loony Left—was partially a by-product of the 2016 Brexit referendum. Debates about Brexit raised difficult questions about the politics of British identity. The Leave campaign evoked a nostalgic vision of Britain's former glory to suggest that leaving the European Union would lead to a revival of national greatness. Despite their denials of racism and xenophobia, the Leave campaigners' rhetoric about "taking control of our borders" scapegoated immigrants as the main source of the UK's problems. Following the referendum, Remain voters were repeatedly portrayed as members of an out-of-touch urban elite who lacked any loyalty to their country. However, the Leave vote was interpreted as a (white) "working-class" revolt against an establishment that had imposed multiculturalism on the "native" population. (Closer analysis of Leave voters demonstrates that this interpretation is misleading).[37] As the Brexit negotiation process dragged on, the British people were split into two broad camps: "Remainers" (known derisively as "Remoaners") or "Brexiteers." The so-called Brexiteers managed to turn support for Brexit into a yardstick for one's Britishness. Those who voted Remain were categorized as "anywheres" who did not conform to a narrow or "patriotic" definition of what it means to be British.[38] This

'the New Enemies of Promise' for Opposing His Plans," *Daily Mail*, March 23, 2013.

37 Aurelien Mondon and Aaron Winter, *Reactionary Democracy: How Racism and the Populist Far Right Became Mainstream* (London: Verso, 2020), 182–90.

38 David Goodhart, *The Road to Somewhere: The Populist Revolt and the Future of Politics* (London: C. Hurst, 2017).

hyper-politicization of Britishness contributed significantly to the UK's discourses of anti-wokeness.

Despite these histories, the War on Woke was rarely treated as a serious topic of discussion in the UK. Commentators often dismissed culture wars as an American import. Many people on the left suspected that right-wing attacks on wokeness were an attempt to distract voters from the real failures of the Conservative government. Between 2010 and 2024, the UK had been trapped in a cycle of stagnant wages, public sector cuts, and political scandals. A series of Conservative-led governments failed to address significant socioeconomic challenges, such as housing shortages, hospital waiting times, and child poverty rates. The last Conservative prime minister, Rishi Sunak, was hastily thrown into power after his predecessor Liz Truss introduced a calamitous "mini budget" that devastated the British economy. Instead of resolving these issues, Sunak's programme amounted to what the sociologist Phil Burton-Cartledge termed "the stewardship of a depleted state."[39] Burton-Cartledge wrote that:

> The running down of public institutions nudges those with means to find private alternatives and leaves everyone else with substandard services crippled by underfunding and staff shortages. And the intended outcome is an attenuation of the political imagination – of not seeing the state as a means for improving living standards and making life better.[40]

To many of those who were forced to rely on these substandard services, the War on Woke felt like an indulgence that they could not afford.

Nonetheless, this culture war was not just a diversion tactic; it was a broader cultural and political strategy to establish mastery over the entire ideological terrain. In this conjunctural situation,

39 Phil Burton-Cartledge, *The Party's Over: The Rise and Fall of the Conservatives from Thatcher to Sunak* (London: Verso, 2023), 311.

40 Ibid., 311.

anti-wokeness became a discursive-ideological mechanism for restricting the limits of political imagination—for ridiculing anyone who believed that the state was a potential tool for helping the lives of the marginalized, disenfranchized, and disadvantaged. As Bart Cammaerts points out, the War on Woke worked to "abnormalize" anyone who supported anti-racist, anti-sexist, pro-LGBTQ+, pro-union, or pro-environmentalist causes.[41] It denied that this activism was an actual response to genuine social problems and dismissed expressions of solidarity as mere "virtue signaling."

Instead of taking progressive demands seriously, the War on Woke was an effort to mobilize and redirect popular energies toward a right-wing vision of British society. It spoke to various attitudes and sentiments that are deeply embedded in the national mindset. The fondness for stiff-upper-lip stoicism—encapsulated in the wartime slogan "Keep Calm and Carry On" or the common exhortation to simply "put up with it"—was rearticulated as the claim that woke people, or snowflakes, are too delicate to cope with the hard realities of adult life. The polite aversion to conflict, as well as scorn for showing off, was twisted into an active hostility toward protest and public disruption. In this way, the War on Woke was not a distraction from real issues but, rather, a project to reshape the very nature of the British subject. To borrow a line from Stuart Hall, it provided "a recipe for everything: for remodelling not only how we behave as citizens and voters, but as mothers, fathers, children, teachers, doctors and lovers."[42]

Although the War on Woke was ostensibly a defense of British culture, the Conservative Party's policy agenda was

---

41 Bart Cammaerts, "The Abnormalization of Social Justice: The 'Anti-woke Culture War Discourse in the UK," *Discourse and Society* 33, no. 6 (November 2022): 730–43.

42 Stuart Hall, "Some 'Politically Incorrect' Pathways Through PC," in *The War of the Words: The Political Correctness Debate*, ed. Sarah Dunant (London: Virago Press, 1994), 170.

devastating for cultural life in the UK. Under fourteen years of Tory rule, the budget for Arts Council England was repeatedly slashed. Nearly eight hundred local libraries closed. Higher education funding for creative degrees was cut by 50 percent. Universities were forced to drop what former Education Secretary Gavin Williamson once called "dead-end" courses, such as English literature, history, and philosophy.[43] This assault on the arts and humanities meant that fewer people from working class backgrounds could sustain careers in cultural fields, such as theater and publishing. Access to arts and culture was limited to those who could afford it. Conservatives may have bemoaned the woke elite, but they simply wanted to replace it with an un-woke elite. Their War on Woke was a conflict about who gets to sit at the top rather than an effort to cultivate a truly popular democratic culture. Complaints about wokeness merely obscured the fact that the biggest threat to British culture was the politics of austerity. In the final years of Conservative government, the War on Woke belittled all forms of imagination—political, artistic, historical—and worked to convince people that a better and fairer society was just not common sense.

What were the forces that drove the War on Woke? On the political level, the Conservative Party implemented significant acts of legislation to tackle "woke nonsense." The Policing, Crime, Sentence and Courts Act (2022) and Public Order Act (2023) criminalized a range of protest tactics, such as "locking on" or blocking transport infrastructure, that had been used by pro-environment activist groups like Extinction Rebellion and Insulate Britain. The Higher Education (Freedom of Speech) Act (2023) allowed visiting speakers to sue for damages if they believed that a student union or a university failed to adequately secure their right to free speech. To promote this legislative agenda, Conservative MPs formed

---

43 Anna Fazackerley, "Ministers Could Limit Student Numbers on Lower-earning Arts Degrees in England," *Guardian*, October 23, 2021.

far-right party factions like the Common Sense Group and the New Conservatives that pushed anti-woke talking points on human rights, gender identity, and environmentalism. Reform UK—originally founded as the Brexit Party by former United Kingdom Independence Party leader Nigel Farage—was the Conservative Party's main electoral competitor. It promised to ban "transgender ideology," restrict immigration, and scrap clean energy projects. To those on the right who believed that the Conservatives were not doing enough to combat wokeness, Reform UK offered a satisfying alternative.

On the ideological and institutional level, the War on Woke involved a panoply of right-wing publications, think tanks, and pressure groups. Despite claims that "the left" dominates British media, the right-wing press remains a powerful force in the UK. Traditional conservative newspapers and magazines, such as *The Daily Telegraph* and *The Spectator*, turned relatively banal incidents—the renaming of the Brecon Beacons, for instance—into overblown scandals about woke excess. In June 2021, the right-wing television channel GB News—or National Empowerment Television with an English accent—was set up to provide an anti-woke alternative to the British public service broadcaster (BBC). The lineup of GB News presenters included Farage, then–Conservative Party MPs like Jacob Rees-Mogg and Lee Anderson, Monty-Python-star-turned-free-speech-fanatic John Cleese, and anti-lockdown archaeologist Neil Oliver. The casual viewer of GB News is left with the disturbing impression that Britain has fallen to the forces of "woke totalitarianism" as they are subjected to anecdote after anecdote about social justice madness. Dozens of other online platforms, such as *spiked* and *Triggernometry*, add to this seemingly never-ending stream of culture war content in the UK.

Like the American New Right, the British right required a standing army of think tankers and campaigners who were eager to be deployed in the War on Woke. The think tanks of

55 Tufton Street, such as New Culture Forum and Institute for Economic Affairs, pumped out publications that traced the rise of wokeness to the doctrines of the Frankfurt School. Several advocacy groups were established to tackle specific fronts in the culture war. For instance, History Reclaimed worked to downplay the horrors of British imperialism and attacked efforts to "decolonize" the study of Western history and philosophy. Following the example of the Heritage Foundation's media activism, these groups and institutions maintained a lively online presence and manufactured a range of media products—podcasts, interview series, short documentaries—to popularize their positions.

In their anatomy of the War on Woke, Huw C. Davies and Sheena E. MacRae mapped the associations between various anti-woke politicians, writers, campaigners, and organizations.[44] Their research revealed a multilayered anti-woke community with specific common beliefs and interests: unconditional support for Brexit, opposition to state intervention (with the exception of protecting right-wing free speech or repressing left-wing protest), climate change denial, anti-immigration, and so on. While the members of this coalition may not agree on all political or economic issues, their shared antipathy to woke binds them together. Wokeness acts as a capacious umbrella term under which one can place any ideology, phenomenon, or movement that one disfavors: "cultural socialism," "cancel culture," "cultural totalitarianism," "radical progressivism," "liberal individualism," "utopian perfectionism," "decolonization," "radical trans ideology." The kaleidoscopic quality of this anti-woke discourse means that every facet of British life can become a potential battleground for cultural conflict. A small change in public policy can take

44 Huw C. Davies and Sheena E. MacRae, "An Anatomy of the British War on Woke," *Race and Class* 65, no. 2 (October-December 2023): 3–54.

on civilizational proportions. Nothing is too trivial for the War on Woke—not even a vegan sausage roll.

The term "Cultural Marxism" rarely turns up in this anti-woke discourse. Unlike the American right, British conservatives lack a clear and plausible narrative about the rise of Cultural Marxism in the UK. As the Frankfurt School did not spend their exile in England (except for Adorno's brief stay at Oxford), it is harder to convince people that Marcuse or Horkheimer personally injected Critical Theory into British universities. However, the scattered uses of Cultural Marxism/s reveal one of the key dynamics of the UK's War on Woke—a dynamic that allows us to understand the trajectories and consequences of anti-wokeness.

In the 2000s, the far-right British National Party (BNP) introduced Cultural Marxism/s to the UK.[45] Founded in 1982 by John Tyndall, the BNP was initially a neo-Nazi group. When Nick Griffin became BNP leader in 1999, he tried to moderate the party's image by shifting from race science to cultural racism. In response to the 9/11 attacks and the UK's "War on Terror," the BNP pivoted from antisemitism and anti-Blackness to Islamophobia. The enemy was no longer racial threats but, rather, cultural Others. Whereas Griffin's 1997 booklet *Who Are the Mind Benders?* accused Jewish journalists of brainwashing white Britons, the BNP's post-9/11 propaganda claimed that Cultural Marxists were using political correctness to stifle criticism of Islam. In a 2011 interview for the BNP's YouTube Channel, Griffin argued that the second-generation Frankfurt School philosopher Jürgen Habermas legitimated the European Union's efforts to increase immigration and dilute (white) national identity.[46]

45 Richardson, "'Cultural Marxism' and the British National Party," 202–26.

46 "EU-Frankfurt School Neo-Marxism," YouTube, 10:50, posted by bnptv, March 16, 2011.

While the BNP was gaining popularity in local and European elections, the phrase "Cultural Marxism" made its way into the working vocabulary of the right-wing press. Like Griffin and the BNP, the long-serving *Daily Mail* editor Paul Dacre and reactionary opinion-monger James Delingpole (who would later join *Breitbart)* saw the BBC as a Cultural Marxist propaganda machine. BBC journalists, according to Dacre, were hostile to British values, the countryside, big business, Christianity, and the traditional family.[47] Similarly, Delingpole interpreted the BBC's decision to replace the Gregorian calendar with "the terms CE (Common Era) and BCE (before Common Era)" as proof that the broadcaster was dismantling the Judeo-Christian foundations of British culture.[48] In a 2013 article for *The Times*, Tim Montgomerie—founder of Conservative activist blog *ConservativeHome* and founding editor of anti-woke magazine *Unherd*—declared that Cultural Marxists had entirely infiltrated government departments, universities, and newsrooms.[49] It is unlikely that these journalists picked up the term "Cultural Marxism" from a BNP pamphlet, but it is undeniable that these articles show a growing use of Cultural Marxism narratives in the more respectable corners of the British right.

In the late 2010s, several anti-woke think tanks tried to lend greater credibility to these warnings about Cultural Marxism. In 2018, the Battle of Ideas festival—an annual event run by the Academy of Ideas—hosted a debate called "Cultural Marxism: Threat or Myth?" in London. The Academy of Ideas was founded by *spiked* contributor Claire Fox as a forum for discussing "controversial" topics. Although the Battle of Ideas

---

47 Paul Dacre, "The BBC's Cultural Marxism Will Trigger an American-style Backlash," *Guardian*, January 27, 2007.

48 James Delingpole, "How the BBC Fell for a Plot to Destroy Western Civilization from Within," *Daily Mail*, September 16, 2011.

49 Tim Montgomerie, "The Right Won on Economics. Now for Act II," *Times*, April 15, 2013.

festival is touted as a space for free thought, it tends to favor right-wing or libertarian perspectives. Most of the "debates" in this festival function as platforms for legitimating reactionary ideas and discourses. During the debate on Cultural Marxism, panelists suggested that it was absurd to immediately dismiss the term as a far-right or conspiratorial idea. One of the speakers—Mark Littlewood, director general of the Institute for Economic Affairs—even characterized Cultural Marxism as a real coordinated attack on free speech at universities.[50] Littlewood concluded that no-platforming policies in higher education should give way to a "free market of ideas" model, in which the offerings of right-wing think-tank intellectuals (like himself) would be valued as equal to the peer-reviewed research of qualified academics.

In 2018, the Bruges Group published a white paper called *Moralitis: A Cultural Virus* by Robert Oulds and Niall McCrae. Drawing on classic immunological language, the authors represented Cultural Marxism as a disease—a fictitious cultural virus called *moralitis*—that had infected the British population.[51] The symptoms of this aliment included rigid thinking, self-loathing, and a hysterical emotional response to conflicting opinions. Student Unions, according to Oulds and McCrae, were the most significant spreaders of moralitis, because they implemented no-platforming policies and campaigned for gender-neutral bathrooms. The metaphor of moralitis, like the idea of the Loony Left, implies that people who hold progressive beliefs lack agency, consciousness, and principles. It suggests that the refusal to platform an Islamophobic or transphobic speaker is not a rational position or legitimate political tactic but, rather, a symptom of a diseased mind. It hints that Student Unions—democratically elected

50 "Cultural Marxism: Threat or Myth?" *Academy of Ideas*, Soundcloud, 1:01:25, posted by Academy of Ideas, October 13, 2018.

51 Robert Oulds and Niall McCrae, *Moralitis: A Cultural Virus* (London: The Bruges Group, 2018).

representatives of the student body—are too irresponsible to be trusted to shape what happens on their campuses. For Oulds and McCrae, the Conservative Party needed to introduce measures that would immunize universities against the Cultural Marxist virus and thus restore the ideological health of the nation.

Although the Conservative Party openly criticizes wokeness, it maintains a fraught relationship with Cultural Marxism. When the Conservative MP Suella Braverman used this term at a meeting of the Bruges Group, the Board of Deputies of British Jews admonished her for using "an antisemitic trope."[52] A year later, the All-Party Parliamentary Group Against Antisemitism issued a briefing paper to all Conservative Party MPs to discourage them from saying anything about Cultural Marxism. Andrew Percy, the MP who headed this group, warned his colleagues that the term was a "dog-whistle for the far-right" that must be avoided.[53] Despite this attempt to "gatekeep" the discursive walls of respectable conservatism, Conservative MPs continued to use the phrase. For instance, the MP Miriam Cates slipped a quick reference to Cultural Marxism into her speech at the 2023 National Conservativism conference as she suggested that discussions of gender identity and climate change were "destroying" children's souls.[54]

These debates about Cultural Marxism/s in the Conservative Party illustrate one of the central dynamics of the War on Woke. Even when Cates uses a "forbidden" term, British conservatives—like *The Spectator*'s Douglas Murray—will spring into action and shelter her from accusations of using a far-right

---

52 Andrew Woods, "The 'Braverman Incident': Mainstreamings of the Cultural Marxism Conspiracy Theory," *Patterns of Prejudice* 58, no, 1 (2024): 1–22.

53 Lee Harpin, "Tory MPs and peers warned over use of the term 'Cultural Marxism,'" *Jewish Chronicle*, November 24, 2020.

54 Peter Walker and Pippa Crerar, "Low Birthrate is UK's Top Priority, Tory MP Tells Rightwing Conference," *Guardian*, May 15, 202.

trope. In this specific conjuncture, the meaning of the phrase "Cultural Marxism" has become less important than the sheer fact that one can now get away with saying it. To denounce Cultural Marxism in public is proof that one has the guts to defy wokeness. Yet the War on Woke does not simply represent this mainstreaming of far-right ideas (that journey from the BNP to Braverman); it also serves to downplay the threat of the far right. Whereas left-wing beliefs are demonized as criminal or pathological, the far right is regarded as a figment of the woke elite's imagination. The far right's demands are treated as the legitimate concerns of normal people; left-wing campaigns are dismissed as the illogical ravings of abnormal activists. Consequently, the War on Woke shifts the entire political spectrum to the right and insists that certain leftist positions are beyond the realm of legitimate politics—and thus subject to punitive measures.

In 2023, the Conservative government enlarged the scope of counterterrorism to target the left. Introduced in 2003, the Prevent policy was part of the government's strategy to prevent people from becoming radicalized and recruited into "extremist" ideologies. People who work in the fields of education, healthcare, and criminal justice must undergo Prevent training to learn about different extremist ideologies and ensure that they can identity the early "warning signs" of radicalization. The strategy has been criticized for demonizing Muslim communities. In late 2023, the government updated its definition of "terrorist ideologies" to include left-wing politics and anarchism. The new Prevent training materials categorized socialism and communism as "grievance narratives" and characterize anti-fascism and animal rights as "single-issue ideologies."[55] By representing these progressive positions as potentially terroristic, the Conservative government empowered itself with the

55 Vikram Dodd, "Socialism, Anti-fascism and Anti-abortion on Prevent List of Terrorism Warning Signs," *Guardian*, March 7, 2024.

ability to track and punish people with socialist or anti-fascist leanings. No left-wing terrorist attacks have taken place in the UK since this policy change.

Following Israel's genocidal response to the Hamas-led October 7 attacks, hundreds of thousands of British citizens took to the streets to demand a ceasefire and express their solidarity with the Palestinian people in Gaza. Students set up encampments on their campuses to force universities to divest from the defense industry. Campaigners staged demonstrations outside arms manufacturing sites, such as the L3Harris Factory in Brighton, that produced parts for the Israeli war machine. Instead of reflecting on the wider context of the Israel-Palestinian conflict, the foot soldiers of the War on Woke branded this activism as an expression of antisemitic lunacy. Days before the Palestinian Solidarity March on Armistice Day in 2023, Braverman—then home secretary—publicly declared that the event should be banned. She argued that the Metropolitan Police force had been absorbed into the Blob, and that senior officers judged protestors according to a double standard: "Right-wing and nationalist protestors who engage in aggression are rightly met with a stern response yet pro-Palestinian mobs displaying almost identical behaviour are largely ignored."[56] (Braverman neglected to mention that people across the UK had been arrested during pro-Palestinian marches, including one protestor who was taken into custody for merely wearing a Palestinian flag.) Her comments prompted far right activists and football hooligans to gather in central London to "defend" the Cenotaph—a war memorial in Whitehall—from what one participant called "the Palestinian mob."[57] Ironically, this Braverman-inspired counterprotest engaged in more hateful conduct and anti-police

56 Suella Braverman, "Police Must Be Even-handed With Protests," *Times*, November 8, 2023.

57 Mark Townsend, "Far-right 'Defends' the Cenotaph to the Echo of Home Secretary's Words," *Guardian*, November 11, 2023.

aggression than the so-called "hate marchers" that the home secretary wished to banish from London's streets.

On July 5, 2024, the Labour Party defeated the Conservatives in a general election. In her first speech as culture secretary, Lisa Nandy announced that "the era of culture wars was over." Whereas the Conservative Party encouraged "polarization, division, and isolation," Nandy promised that Labour would turn the UK into a "self-confident, outward-looking country which values its people." Less than a month later, a teenager named Axel Rudakubana walked into a dance studio in Southport and murdered three young girls (and injured ten others). Misinformation about the attacker—since Rudakubana was not an adult, the police could not reveal his identity—spread quickly on social media. Many of these online posts claimed that the killer was an Islamic terrorist or an asylum seeker. Although Rudakubana was neither a migrant nor a Muslim, a handful of violent anti-immigration riots broke out across the country—several of them targeting mosques and hotels that housed asylum seekers. In the aftermath of the riots, tens of thousands of anti-racist demonstrators came out in multiple cities and towns to counter the threat of further far right violence. As rioters were dragged to court, anti-woke warriors justified the unrest by (inaccurately) comparing the summer riots to the 2020 BLM protests and by claiming that the far right did not really exist in the UK. Claims of "two-tier policing" echoed Braverman's complaint that the police were soft on left-wing protestors and tough on "innocent" or "misguided" right-wing patriots. Nandy may have hoped that the culture wars were over, but it turns out that a ministerial statement would not be enough to bring an end to the War on Woke.

It must be remembered that a Labour government is not necessarily a left-wing government. The current Labour leader and prime minister, Keir Starmer, may express tepid support for socially progressive causes, yet he has continually excluded left-wing MPs and activists in his own party. He has dismissed the demands of BLM, Just Stop Oil, and the pro-Palestinian movement. He has also refused to retract the Conservative Party's Public Order Bill (2023). Under his premiership, climate activists have received the longest ever sentences for non-violent protest in British history. Starmerism, if such a thing exists, seems to be nothing more than a project to pivot the Labour Party to the right. As Farage and Reform UK gain popularity in the polls as a supposedly "anti-establishment" vote, Starmer and his colleagues have felt more pressure to adopt increasingly hardline positions on immigration, welfare, and cultural debates like transgender rights. Instead of addressing the underlying issues that aggravated the 2024 riots (joblessness, regional inequality, poverty), Labour is parroting some of the rhetoric that caused rioters to channel their anger and frustration against minorities. Starmer's "soft" turn to the right may be praised by some as a shrewd electoral tactic, yet it will not appease the forces of anti-wokeness. For them, Starmer is practically a reincarnation of Joseph Stalin. The right will not be satisfied until every museum and every university and every street (and every hospital and every library and every pub) is cleansed of wokeness. A glorious restoration of British common sense; the death of political imagination.

## Brazil: The Language of Bolsomitology

In 2018, the then–PSL presidential candidate Jair Bolsonaro presented his vision for Brazil in *The Path to Prosperity* (*O Caminho da Prosperidade*). In a section of this plan called "Our Flag is Green and Yellow," Bolsonaro argued, "Over the past thirty years, cultural Marxism (*Marxismo Cultural*) and its derivatives like Gramscianism joined with the corrupt oligarchs to undermine the values of the Nation and the Brazilian family."[58] Bolsonaro's claim implied that, since the end of

58 Jair Bolsonaro, *O Caminho da Prosperidade* (2018), 8.

Brazil's military dictatorship and the enactment of the Citizen's Constitution in 1988, a secret communist conspiracy had been meddling with familial and national life. The democratic pact of 1988 partially widened the terrain of the public sphere to acknowledge the interests of workers, women, Black Brazilians, Indigenous populations, and LGBTQ+ people. Yet Bolsonaro's use of *marxismo cultural* recontextualized this process of redemocratization as a symptom of a deeper social disease. In the 2018 Brazilian general election, Bolsonaro pitched his platform as the magical cure that would revive Brazil's pre-1988 glory.

When Jair Bolsonaro became Brazilian president in 2019, many authors tried to make sense of the strange phenomenon known as *Bolsonarismo*.[59] This was not an uncomplicated task. The term denotes more than simply the personal beliefs and policy decisions of Bolsonaro himself—the man that his supporters call *Bolsomito* (or, to translate, "Bolso-Myth" or "Bolsonaro-the-Legend"). *Bolsonarismo* brought together a medley of social and ideological tendencies that were deeply rooted in Brazilian society: social conservatism, anti-leftism (or *antipetismo*, which refers to a dislike of Brazil's left-wing Workers' Party or PT), militarism, anti-intellectualism, neoliberal entrepreneurialism, and evangelicalism. What united these varied and sometimes contradictory elements under the banner of *Bolsonarismo* was an underlying desire for order.

In the years before Bolsonaro's presidency, Brazil experienced an onslaught of economic and sociopolitical crises. In 2013, millions of citizens participated in a series of rallies and marches called "the June Days" to protest transit fare hikes, low investment in public services, and extravagant government

59 Esther Solano, "'It's All Corrupt': The Roots of Bolsonarism in Brazil," in *The Emergence of Illiberalism: Understanding a Global Phenomenon*, ed. Boris Vormann and Michael Weinman, (New York: Routledge, 2021): 210–23; Rodrigo Nunes, "Of What Is Bolsonaro the Name?," *Radical Philosophy*, no. 209 (Winter): 3–14.

spending on sports events (the 2014 World Cup and the 2016 Olympics). The 2014 economic downturn resulted in a sharp rise in rates of unemployment. Many Brazilians, especially those whose standard of living had risen under the PT's redistributive policies in the 2000s, were struggling with the stress and humiliation of downward mobility. As this economic crisis was unfolding, a major corruption scandal known as "Operation Car Wash" engulfed the political establishment. In 2016, then-President Dilma Rousseff was impeached for her alleged involvement in this corruption. The immensity of this scandal caused some Brazilians to feel that the whole political system was corrupt. Other social problems, such as increased levels of urban violence, only reinforced the perception that Brazil was descending into chaos.

Although Bolsonaro had been a politician for nearly three decades by the time he announced his presidential campaign, he rebranded himself as a political outsider who could clean up government corruption and social turmoil. He scapegoated different groups—Afro Brazilians, Indigenous communities, students, LGBTQ+ people, left-wing politicians, feminists, the Landless Peasant's Movement—to blame them for the nation's decline. He condemned efforts to remedy gender and racial inequality and demanded the revival of a traditional order. Yet Bolsonaro's promise of order was ultimately little more than a defense of existing hierarchies.

Despite the PT government's efforts to tackle poverty and discrimination, Brazil remains a deeply unequal country. The enduring legacy of slavery and colonialism, which profoundly shaped Brazil's social and economic structures, deposited what the anthropologist Lilia Moritz Schwarcz calls an "idiom of social disparity" that allows Brazilians to justify and become accustomed to deep-rooted inequality.[60] National statistics

60 Lilia Moritz Schwarcz, *Brazilian Authoritarianism: Past and Present* (Princeton, NJ: Princeton University Press, 2022), 112.

reveal the full extent of this inequity. The wealthiest 1 percent of Brazilians receive almost a third (28.3 percent) of the country's income. Wage disparity between men and women, as well as white and Black Brazilians, continues to perpetuate gender and racial imbalances. Brazil's rate of femicide—the gender-based killing of women—is the worst in Latin America. Similarly, its rates of violence against transgender people are the highest in the world.

During his presidency, Bolsonaro fought to preserve these levels of inequality and to recreate the so-called "natural" order of Brazil. He cooperated with the broad right-wing congressional alliance known as the "beef, Bible, and bullets caucus" (or Bancada BBBs) to promote restrictions on environmental protections, welfare provisions, and civil liberties. His administration cut public education budgets, promoted the deforestation and illegal mining of protected Indigenous lands, reduced spending for programs that addressed gender-based violence, attacked labor standards and trade union rights, defunded government-led affirmative action initiatives, and threatened to criminalize social movements. A variety of provocative catchwords—*marxismo cultural*, Gramscianism, gender ideology—worked to rationalize this legislative assault on Brazilian civil society. These terms circulated through a dense and multilayered right-wing organizational infrastructure that ranged from major institutional players to small WhatsApp groups. The leaders of large Pentecostal churches, such as the pastor and televangelist Silas Malafaia, urged their congregations to support Bolsonaro's mission to protect the traditional family from the spread of "gender ideology" in Brazilian schools. Instituto Mises Brasil and other libertarian think tanks endorsed the Bolsonaro administration's privatization of public industries and services to overturn the rule of *marxismo cultural*. The digital "counterpublics" of the New Right—WhatsApp groups, YouTube and Telegram channels, Twitter accounts—claimed to broadcast "truths" that the Gramscian hegemony in Brazil wanted to suppress.[61] Within the mythos of *Bolsonarismo*, the Brazilian New Right needed to expose and eradicate the leftist militants that had infiltrated the country's institutions. Just as "Operation Car Wash" revealed financial corruption in the highest levels of government, the forces of *Bolsonarismo* hoped to reveal the *ideological corruption* at the heart of Brazilian education, media, and culture.

Every critique of *marxismo cultural* in Brazil can be traced back to a single intellectual source: Olavo de Carvalho. Although he would later dismiss the term as inaccurate, Carvalho was the first author to introduce Cultural Marxism/s to Brazilian audiences. As João Cezar de Castro Rocha reveals, Carvalho's writings often drew on the existing frameworks of anti-communist conspiracy theorizing that were developed within Brazil's military establishment.[62] As a mainstream journalist in the 1990s and 2000s, Carvalho published dozens of caustic articles and books that anticipated and influenced the Brazilian New Right's attacks on Cultural Marxism.

His 1994 book, *The New Age and Cultural Revolution*, argued that Gramscianism—a well-established cognate of Cultural Marxism—had imperceptibly turned Brazil into a communist state. According to Carvalho, this Gramscianism did not "rely so much on rational persuasion to propagate itself as on the effectiveness of a subtle penetration into the unconscious of the masses."[63] The Brazilian intelligentsia—journalists, filmmakers, musicians, psychologists—were the agents of this Gramscian cultural revolution. They converted citizens into communists through millions of tiny adjustments

---

61 Camila Rocha, "From Orkut to Brasília: The Origins of the New Brazilian Right," in *A Horizon of (Im)possibilities: A Chronicle of Brazil's Conservative Turn*, ed. Katerina Hatzikidi and Eduardo Dullo (London: University of London Press, 2021), 81–101.

62 João Cezar de Castro Rocha, *Guerra Cultural e Retórica do Ódio* (Goiânia: Caminhos, 2021).

63 Olavo de Carvalho, "A Nova Era e a Revolução Cultural: Capítulo II," *Olavo de Carvalho*, Marc 9, 1994.

to common sense. Even if someone has never heard of Gramsci, they may have unconsciously absorbed Gramscian mental attitudes (like moral relativism).

When one reads Carvalho's writings, it can feel like Gramscian ideology is everywhere. "Gramscianism" becomes a conspiracy that no longer needs conspirators, a sort of cultural second-hand smoke that people inhale without even realizing it. The very diffuseness and indistinctness of this revolution imply that the Brazilian public needs someone like Carvalho just to tell them what is happening in the world. In other words, this theory of Gramscianism casts Carvalho in the role of an all-seeing guru whose powers of perception allow him to glimpse the true nature of social reality. If you do not believe him, then you are simply not looking hard enough.

In the early 2000s, Carvalho built on these earlier arguments to propose his own notion of Cultural Marxism/s. Although Carvalho rarely cites his sources, many of his claims seem to be borrowed from Buchanan's *The Death of the West*. His 2002 article "On Cultural Marxism," which was published in the conservative newspaper *O Globo*, rehearsed standard right-wing claims about Lukács's and Gramsci's supposed hatred of Western culture.[64] Like Lind, he said the Frankfurt School was established as a think tank to devise techniques for undermining the West. For instance, Adorno developed the concept of the "authoritarian personality" to pathologize the ideals of Western civilization.

Carvalho defined the Frankfurt School's ideology as a self-inversion of Marxism. Instead of accepting Marx's proposition that material conditions determine consciousness, the Frankfurt School decided that it was possible to transform society by merely changing the "mentalities" of the masses.[65] In this idealist variant of Marxism, the intellectuals replaced the proletariat

64 Olavo de Carvalho, "Do marxismo cultural," *Olavo de Carvalho*, June 8, 2002.

65 Ibid.

as the revolutionary class. During their exile in the United States, Adorno, Horkheimer, and Marcuse disseminated the "macabre dogmas" of Critical Theory to foster an "atmosphere of suspicion, confusion and hatred."[66] Later in the twentieth century, the French postmodernists continued the Frankfurt School's work and popularized the malicious idea that all white men "oppress" women, Black people, LGBTQ+ communities, animals, and plants.

Cultural Marxism, according to Carvalho, had become the ruling ideology in higher education, media, business, the church, and publishing. He estimated that nearly every contemporary novel, film, play, and textbook espoused the beliefs of Cultural Marxism. Unlike Carvalho, most people could not recognize that these cultural products were full of Marxist propaganda. As Carvalho put it, the clueless masses failed to see that Western culture had degenerated into a "war machine against itself."[67] Even though his work had just been printed in the most popular newspaper in Brazil, Carvalho concluded his article by declaring that conservative intellectuals faced total censorship.

During the 2000s, Carvalho decided to establish alternative institutions to combat Cultural Marxism. He founded the blog *Media Without Masks* in 2002—the same year that the PT won their first national election—to publish articles that contested the so-called leftist bias of Brazilian newspapers and television shows. In subsequent years, Carvalho launched a podcast and an online seminar series to provide students with the knowledge that would supposedly help them to see through the political correctness of Brazil's mainstream intelligentsia. The scholar Georg Wink explains that the series was intended to "form single-handedly a new generation of 'intellectuals'" who could function as multipliers of "Carvalho's truth."[68]

66 Ibid.

67 Ibid.

68 Georg Wink, *Brazil, Land of the Past: The Ideological Roots of the New Right* (Cuernavaca, Mexico: Bibliotopía, 2021), 193.

When the social network Orkut was founded in 2004, fans of Carvalho established forums to discuss their guru's philosophy. Between 2005 and 2007, Orkut was the most popular social media platform in Brazil. Most of its early users were teenagers or young adults with high levels of income and education, located in Brazil's Southeast and Southern regions, who could access computers at home or at local Internet cafes. Carvalho's digital output attracted an audience of people who felt ignored or excluded by the PT government: anarcho-capitalists and neoliberals, monarchists, militarists, and conservative Catholics. They identified with Carvalho's claim that a vast Gramscian hegemony was running Brazil. Many of Carvalho's younger supporters felt inspired to form their own alternative media platforms. A prominent example of this new Olavist generation was the media company Brasil Paralelo (BP).

BP was founded in 2016 to produce revisionist documentaries about Brazil's past. During Bolsonaro's administration, the Ministry of Education broadcast these documentaries during prime time on the state channel TV Escola. In 2018, BP expanded its operations to include a paid subscription service, described as a "training center," that featured hundreds of interviews with right-wing intellectuals and a growing list of online courses on philosophy, political science, and economics. As of 2022, BP had gained a following of roughly 276,100 paid subscribers (one of whom is allegedly Bolsonaro himself) and over 3 million YouTube subscribers. In less than a decade, BP has become the most influential cultural agent on the Brazilian New Right.

Since its release in 2019, BP's documentary *1964: Between Weapons and Books* has been viewed millions of times.[69] The film advances a revisionist interpretation of Brazil's military dictatorship and presents interviews with an array of almost exclusively white male "experts" who disclose long-buried

69 Brasil Paralelo, "1964: O Brasil entre armas e livros," YouTube, 2:07:19, posted by Brasil Paralelo, April 2, 2019.

"facts" about the 1964 military coup. BP characterized their interviewees as free of ideological bias merely because their insights contradicted the "mainstream" view of Brazilian history, as though this oppositionality did not signify any kind of political stance. While most Brazilian historians conclude that the 1964 coup was unjustified and that the threat of an imminent revolution was exaggerated, BP's experts insist that the military intervention occurred to prevent João Goulart's center-left government from turning Brazil into a communist society.[70] From 1964 onward, the military was "compelled" to impose draconian measures to counter anti-regime guerrilla fighters. Although contemporary historians portray these dissidents as pro-democracy forces who resisted an authoritarian government, BP's experts claim that the military protected the Brazilian people from an international communist conspiracy. As the guerrilla fighters could not defeat the military in armed combat, they adopted a strategy of "cultural warfare" (the titular shift from weapons to books).

Building on Carvalho's work, the documentary branded Lukács, Gramsci, and the Frankfurt School as the architects of a grand Cultural Marxist offensive against Western civilization. In Brazil, these Cultural Marxists ridiculed traditional hierarchies and encouraged resistance to the military dictatorship. New "mentalities" were disseminated through the universities, schools, and the media to influence the Brazilian youth. After a few decades, the worldview of Cultural Marxism had become the "common sense" of the post-1988 elite. According to the documentary, anyone who complained about "sexism," "racism," and "homophobia" was merely exhibiting their commitment to Gramscian attitudes rather than speaking about genuine social problems. Despite their formal and logical flaws, BP's documentaries successfully adapted Carvalho's ideas

70 Rodrigo Patto Sá Motta, *On Guard Against the Red Menace: Anti-Communism in Brazil, 1917–1964* (Eastbourne: Sussex Academic Press, 2020).

about Cultural Marxism into a form of right-wing entertainment that could be transmitted through the online channels of *Bolsonarismo*.

When Bolsonaro was elected in 2018, Carvalho's influence extended beyond the Internet and reached into the corridors of the Brazilian government. Several of Bolsonaro's ministers, such as the Foreign Minister Ernesto Araújo, were even hand-selected by Carvalho. Like Carvalho, Araújo was a prolific right-wing blogger. His blog, *Metapolitics 17: Against Globalism*, featured posts that described the theory of climate change as "Cultural Marxist" propaganda designed to weaken Western economies.[71] During his time in office, Araújo turned anti-globalism into "the official narrative of Brazil's foreign policy."[72] As Araújo saw it, a muscular pan-nationalistic politics was the only way to resist the globalist rise of Cultural Marxism.

Araújo outlined his vision of pan-nationalism in a 2017 text called "Trump and the West," in which he argued that Brazil belonged to a Western community of nations.[73] For Araújo, the West is neither a defense alliance (NATO) nor a borderless amalgamation (the European Union). It is a spiritual creation that upholds the nation as its quintessential symbol. Drawing on Oswald Spengler's *The Decline of the West*, Araújo argues that Western states are failing because they have substituted their cultural symbols for generic concepts. Globalism—the abstract ideology of humanity and human rights—constitutes a civilizational threat to the continued existence of the West.

---

71 Jonathan Watts, "Brazil's New Foreign Minister Believes Climate Change Is a Marxist Plot," *Guardian*, November 15, 2018.

72 Feliciano De Sá Guimarães, Davi Cordeiro Moreira, Irma Dutra De Oliveira E Silva, and Anna Carolina Raposo De Mello, "Conspiracy Theories and Foreign Policy Narratives: Globalism in Jair Bolsonaro's Foreign Policy," *Latin American Perspectives* 50, no. 1 (February 2023): 282.

73 Ernesto Araújo, "Trump e o Ocidente," *Cardernos de Política Exterior* 3, no. 6 (2017): 323–58.

According to Araújo, this new globalism emerged during the aftermath of the Cold War. While the capitalist West may have triumphed against the nihilistic forces of Soviet communism, it succumbed to another form of nihilism: Cultural Marxism. Globalists replaced Western ideals with Cultural Marxist values. They promoted a brand of cultural relativism that degraded the unique identities and heritages of Western peoples. Instead of protecting the West, they engineered the erosion of national borders and encouraged non-Western immigrants to relocate to Europe and the United States. In this account, Araújo ignores other structural or sociological explanations—the dislocating and contradictory dynamics of late capitalism—and embraces a semi-metaphysical narrative of cultural change that places all blame on a demonic force.

The strength of the nation, Araújo theorizes, depends on the preservation and enforcement of traditional gender hierarchies. Globalists, with their tools of Cultural Marxism and gender ideology, seek to establish a world of "gender-fluid" cosmopolitans who cannot resist the power of the state. Like Carvalho's articles and BP's documentaries, Araújo's argument reframes the efforts to reduce femicide or anti-LGBTQ+ abuse as external attacks on the nation. Brazil's backlash against "gender ideology" can be traced back to the then–Education Minister Fernando Haddad's effort in 2011 to launch an initiative to distribute educational materials in schools to combat homophobia and discrimination. Bolsonaro himself played an instrumental role in blocking this measure, which he derided as a "gay kit" that displaced traditional family values. Since 2014, Brazilian lawmakers have introduced more than 200 legislative proposals to ban "indoctrination" or "gender ideology" in schools.[74] Although LGBTQ+ people in Brazil experience an extremely high level of harassment, Araújo and other members of the

74 Cristian González Cabera, "'I Became Scared, This was Their Goal': Efforts to Ban Gender and Sexuality Education in Brazil," *Human Rights Watch*, May 12, 2022.

Brazilian right believe that this violence is simply a natural feature of Western civilization.

In November 2017, far-right Brazilian groups organized a petition to prevent Judith Butler from delivering a talk at the Social Service of Commerce in São Paulo.[75] The petition, which gathered more than 370,000 signatures, condemned Butler as a promoter of "gender ideology." It characterized this ideology as a disguised form of Marxism that sought to bring about the destruction of the family. On the day of the seminar, protestors turned up to the event and burnt an effigy that portrayed Butler as a witch. This incident revealed one of the major assumptions that motivate attacks on Cultural Marxism in Brazil: that foreign ideas and theorists are sneaking across "our" sovereign borders to disrupt the natural—and fundamentally unequal—order of "our" nation.

Bolsonaro's electoral victory in 2018 marked a turning point in the Brazilian New Right's war against Cultural Marxism and gender ideology. In early 2019, Araújo published an essay in the American paleocon magazine *The New Criterion* that characterized the recent election as an act of divine intervention.[76] Building on the political alliance between Trump and Bolsonaro, Araújo delivered a speech at the Heritage Foundation a few months later, where he reflected on the nature of Cultural Marxism.[77] Critical Theory, according to Araújo, was essentially a strange form of psychic projection. In other words, theorists criticized that which they secretly desired. For instance, the Frankfurt School thinkers may have critiqued alienation in capitalist society, but they actually wanted to

75 Scott Jaschik, "Judith Butler on Being Attacked," *Inside Higher Ed*, November 12, 2017.

76 Ernesto Araújo, "Now We Do," *New Criterion* 37, no. 5 (January 2019): 37.

77 Ernesto Araújo, "'Brazil is Back': Brazilian Minister of Foreign Affairs Ambassador Ernesto Araújo," YouTube video, 57:49, posted by the Heritage Foundation, September 11, 2019.

make people feel more alienated. To pick another one of Araújo's examples, Michael Hardt and Antonio Negri's 2000 book *Empire* demonstrated that the left wants to build its own imperial order. Like Lindsay and LaRouchites, Araújo's semi-Freudian technique of reading proposes to unearth the secret meanings that hide within the classic texts of Critical Theory. This interpretative procedure turns Critical Theory into a self-refuting mess and pre-empts any possible critique of the Brazilian right. Araújo's attacks on Critical Theory imitate Carvalho, whose own criticisms of Gramscianism were based on a sort of mystic, secret knowledge.

In 2021, Araújo resigned from Bolsonaro's administration. A year later, he followed the example of his mentor Carvalho and launched his own online course on globalism. For the price of R$500, Araújo promised to teach his students about the ideas that have led to contemporary geopolitical crises, such as war and inflation. Like Carvalho and BP, Araújo presented his course as a truthful alternative to the Cultural Marxism–dominated spheres of Brazilian education and media. These offerings formed part of what scholar Beatriz Buarque calls Brazil's far-right "active knowledge" industry—a sector of ideological entrepreneurship that questions the validity of major educational institutions and proposes to redirect Brazilian education toward right-wing ends.[78]

Before he even entered office, Bolsonaro was vocal about his desire to dismantle Brazil's educational system. On the campaign trail, Bolsonaro boasted to his supporters that he would "enter the education ministry with a flamethrower to remove Paulo Freire."[79] For Bolsonaro and his followers, Freire —the Brazilian inventor of critical pedagogy—was a deranged revolutionary who deserved to be stripped of his title as

78 Beatriz Buarque, "How Brazil's Far-Right 'Active Knowledge' Industry Supports Jair Bolsonaro," *Open Democracy*, March 10, 2021.

79 Andrew Woods, "Why is the Brazilian Right afraid of Paulo Freire?," *Open Democracy*, July 2, 2020.

Brazil's patron of education. According to the New Right, Freire injected Marxist ideology into Brazil during his stint as municipal secretary of education in Sao Paulo between 1989 and 1992. Although the methods of critical pedagogy were never formally or widely applied in Brazilian schools, the use of Freire as a leftist bogeyman provided Bolsonaro and his administration with an excuse to persecute their opponents in education.

Bolsonaro's first education minister, Ricardo Vélez Rodríguez, littered his inauguration speech with all the anti-leftist buzzwords of the Brazilian New Right: "gender ideology," "Gramscianism," and "Cultural Marxism."[80] Rodríguez, who was recommended for the role by Carvalho, presented himself as a defender of Brazil's religious heritage. During his brief time in government, he proposed revising history textbooks to describe the 1964 military coup as a democratic and constitutional transfer of power.

In April 2019, Rodríguez was replaced by Abraham Weintraub, who threatened to divert funding from sociology and philosophy departments to other disciplines, such as engineering and medicine, that would offer an "immediate return" to the taxpayer.[81] Critics of this policy claimed that Weintraub sought to defund these fields of study because he saw them as hotbeds for left-wing activism. Several days later, Weintraub declared a 30 percent budget cut for all federal universities. These funding cuts were part of a larger campaign to demoralize resistance to the Bolsonaro regime. Weintraub hoped that these actions would discourage federal universities from hosting political organizations, such as the Landless Workers' Movement (MST), on their campuses. Yet Brazilian students

80 Amurabi Olivira, "Public Universities in Brazil Today: Fake News, Attacks on Autonomy and Bolsonarization," *Revista de Sociología de la Educación* 16, no. 3, 269.

81 Andrew Woods, "The Cultural Marxism Conspiracy Thrives in Bolsonaro's Brazil," *Fair Observer*, October 16, 2019.

and teachers refused to tolerate Weintraub's assault. In response to the proposed cuts, mass protests took place in over 200 cities across the country, described as "education tsunamis." Before he resigned from his post, he revoked a 2016 ordinance that required federal universities to provide affirmative policies for Black people, Indigenous people, and people with disabilities in graduate school. (This decision was later annulled.)

Although Bolsonaro promised to clear up corruption in the Brazilian government, his third and fourth education ministers were involved in significant scandals. Shortly after he had appointed Carlos Alberto Decotelli da Silva, it was discovered that Decotelli had lied about his qualifications. Bolsonaro's fourth education minister, Milton Ribeiro, was arrested on charges of bribery and misuse of public funds as he had deliberately prioritized giving grants to municipalities run by his friends (including two prominent pastors).[82] A few days before the 2022 general election, Bolsonaro took advantage of his last few moments in office to attack his enemies in education and slash hundreds of millions from the budget for federal universities. Demonstrations erupted in seventy cities across Brazil to express dismay about this vindictive move.

On October 30, 2022, Bolsonaro narrowly lost the second round of the Brazilian presidential election. His opponent, Luiz Inácio Lula da Silva (known popularly as Lula), received 50.9 percent of the vote. However, Lula—the leader of the PT party and the former president of Brazil (2002–10)—was not a universally popular figure. He had been accused of involvement in a series of corruption scandals, such as the 2005 Mensalão scandal and Operation Car Wash. In the aftermath of the 2022 election, Bolsonaro declared that Lula and his allies had corrupted the electoral process. He claimed that Brazil's electronic ballot system, which has been used in elections since 1996, had been rigged against him. He insinuated that members of the

82 Amurabi Olivira, "Public Universities in Brazil Today," 271.

Superior Electoral Court—an independent judicial body that protects electoral integrity in Brazil—manipulated the election to guarantee Lula's victory.

Supporters of Bolsonaro erected hundreds of roadblocks to protest the result of the election. They camped outside army bases and urged military leaders to stage a coup against the president-elect. Although Bolsonaro affirmed that he would respect the Brazilian Constitution, he never acknowledged his defeat. On January 8, 2023, thousands of Bolsonaristas stormed the presidential palace, as well as the buildings of Congress and the Supreme Court, in Brasilia. In this bizarre homage to the January 6 US Capitol attack, rioters vandalized artworks, assaulted journalists, smashed glass panels, stole government property, urinated in the corridors, and defecated in offices. They unfurled banners that called for military intervention. Instead of preventing the unrest, police officers reportedly fraternized with the Bolsonaristas and took pictures of the carnage. Following the riot, Brazil's electoral authority prohibited Bolsonaro from running for public office for eight years (on charges of abuse of power and misuse of media). In September 2025, he was sentenced to twenty-seven years and three months in prison after the Supreme Court declared him guilty of plotting a military coup.

The fate of *Bolsonarismo* without Bolsonaro remains unclear. The Brazilian New Right maintains a significant presence in the Congress. While Lula has relaunched several progressive social programs and reversed some of the damage caused by Bolsonaro's regime, he has been forced to negotiate and compromise with reactionary political representatives. Lula's modest achievements—raising the minimum wage and reducing the rate of inflation—have not cooled the militance and ambition of the Bolsonaristas. Various far-right politicians, such as federal congressman Nikolas Ferreira and governor of São Paulo Tarcísio de Freitas, compete for the title of Bolsonaro's successor. But other Bolsonaro allies—Flavio Bolsonaro, the former president's eldest son and senator from Rio de Janeiro—propose a shift to the "center-right" to attract voters outside the *Bolsonarismo* base. It is difficult to anticipate whether the Brazilian New Right will ever recover from the reputational harm of the January 8 riots or even whether they will rally behind an appropriate candidate for the 2026 presidential election. Bolsonaro's defeat, however, did not bring an end to conspiratorial talk about the threat of Cultural Marxism. BP, the ever-industrious ideological factory of *Bolsonarismo*, continues to manufacture videos and articles about *marxismo cultural* as they ready the troops for the next confrontation.

## What's Left

The current conjuncture seems to trap us in a maze of false exits. In their pursuit of power, the transnational right positions itself as an "anti-establishment" political force. Instead of honoring existing institutions, reactionaries denounce the "deep state," "Big Tech," "Big Pharma," and the "mainstream media." Of course, this attitude of right-wing oppositionality is not new. The conservative movements of the 1960s, especially in the United States, felt that they were fighting to displace a firmly entrenched liberal power elite. Even if the right's critiques of "the Establishment" seem self-serving and hypocritical, they should still prompt some reflection among those of us who consider themselves to be on the left.

In his 1979 essay "The Great Moving Right Show," Stuart Hall offers the intriguing observation that it "is always the case that the Right is what it is because of what the Left is."[83] According to Hall, Thatcherism succeeded as a political project partly because it exploited the weaknesses and contradictions of postwar Labourism. The major flaw of the Labour Party's social democratic corporatism was its use of the state to

83 Stuart Hall, *The Hard Road to Renewal: Thatcherism and the Crisis of the Left* (London: Verso, 2021), 56.

contain and reform British capitalism rather than surpass it. Labour may have been willing to operate the state "on behalf of the people," yet it became increasingly hostile to the demands of popular mobilization (trade unions, for example). As the crisis of the 1970s set in, Labour relied on the state to "discipline, limit and police the very classes it aimed to represent."[84] Hall contends that the anti-socialist messages of Thatcherism managed to tap into this experience of the state "not as a benefice but as a powerful bureaucratic imposition on 'the People.'"[85] To expand and clarify Hall's compelling adage, the right is what it is because the aims and aspirations of the left have been confined to the preservation of the existing order.

Woke capitalism represents the latest containment of the left. Although several radical authors have ably critiqued this new configuration of capitalist power, many people continue to perceive corporate wokeness and leftism as broadly identical phenomena. Corporate wokeness may be a parody of actual anti-racist or anti-sexist organizing, yet it has become the dominant framework through which most people encounter and experience discussions about social justice. It represents the absorption of left-wing concerns into a range of managerial procedures. In this light, something rings true about Rufo's framing of DEI discourse as a kind of "critical theory as farce: the ideology of the revolution passed through the human resources department."[86] That HR departments can somewhat convincingly be portrayed as strongholds of the left is symptomatic of deeper contradictions. As Carl Rhodes points out, the causes of radical politics have been instrumentalized and rearticulated in a way that "will further cement the concentration of political power among a corporate elite."[87]

84 Ibid., 50.

85 Ibid.

86 Rufo, *America's Cultural Revolution*, 66.

87 Carl Rhodes, *Woke Capitalism: How Corporate Morality is Sabotaging Democracy* (Bristol: Bristol University Press, 2022), 13.

While it may offer limited benefits and opportunities for members of marginalized groups, woke capitalism constitutes an antidemocratic and anti-popular articulation of progressive values. It seeks to contain and reform capitalism rather than implement a vision of social transformation that will dismantle the oppressions it claims to address. It may embrace LGBTQ+ inclusion (pinkwashing) and environmentalism (greenwashing), yet it remains silent about other so-called woke causes like Palestinian solidarity and higher corporation taxes. Instead of building a more equitable future, it wants to shift our desire toward the continuation of a consumerist neoliberalism, where we can "buy into" the struggle for justice merely by purchasing "ethical" products (or by supporting companies with the right ESG rating). The current political successes of the right can be attributed to its ability to exploit these contradictions: It mobilizes popular discontent with the "patronizing elite" to motivate an agenda for reinforcing the old inequalities.

Can the left place any hope in the available political options? A return to so-called normalcy—Biden, Starmer, Lula—was not necessarily a major victory for the left (or a crushing defeat of the right). The leaders of social democratic, or slightly-left-of-center, parties remain subject to the same contradiction as 1970s Labourism: to improve the conditions of ordinary people without endangering, or seriously interfering with, the logic of capitalist accumulation. Their solutions to the enduring problems of late capitalist society must operate within ever-tighter limits as the symptoms of crisis worsen: climate disasters, increasing inequality, the hollowing out of democratic rights, declining productivity. The failure to overcome these fatal contradictions provides more space for the right to peddle its authoritarian and regressive solutions. This is the conjunctural terrain on which we are forced to organize and act. We can no longer retreat to the safety net of the status quo. We must find a way out of this maze.

# Conclusion: Politics in the Age of the Chainsaw

*When a conjuncture unrolls, there is no "going back." History shifts gears. The terrain changes. You are in a new moment. You have to attend, "violently," with all the "pessimism of the intellect" at your command, to the "discipline of the conjuncture."*

—Stuart Hall, "Gramsci and Us"

On January 20, 2025, Donald Trump returned to the White House. In his inaugural address, he promised a "revolution of common sense." Over the next few days, he delivered a blitzkrieg of anti-woke executive orders. He reinstated the 1776 Commission and cut funding for any aspect of K-12 education that promoted "radical, anti-American ideologies." He terminated all DEI programs in the federal government, rescinded Biden's legal protections for transgender people, and eliminated civil rights–era affirmative action legislation. With each new stroke of his pen, Trump went after "gender ideology extremism," "radical environmentalism," and "discriminatory equity ideology." The American right rejoiced. The Heritage Foundation's Mike Gonzalez hailed Trump's anti-DEI executive actions as "the policy equivalent of the Romans salting the Carthaginian fields."[1] Without the taxpayer dollars of the "DEI bureaucracy," Cultural Marxism would—allegedly—never again take root in America.

---

1 Mike Gonzalez, "Trump's Dismantling of DEI is Deeper and Bigger Than You Even Know," the Heritage Foundation, January 24, 2025.

Not only did Trump "depoliticize" the social, but he also deregulated the economic. In a practical sense, Trump's anti-regulatory orders were gifts to the constituencies that had endorsed his 2024 presidential campaign. To pay back the oil and gas companies, he withdrew from the Paris Agreement, lifted restrictions on fossil fuel production, and scrapped appliance efficiency standards. To say thanks to the crypto industry, he repealed Biden's efforts to build a framework for the responsible development of digital assets. And, to reward the school choice movement, he instructed federal administrators to redirect funds toward a voucher program that would get parents to put their children in private or faith-based schools (a step toward the right's long-anticipated abolition of the Department of Education). However, Trump was not alone in his crusade against government regulation. With the help of far-right tech bro Elon Musk, he established the Department of Government Efficiency (or DOGE) to tackle wasteful spending—especially on woke causes—in the federal bureaucracy. Under this whirlwind Trump-Musk co-presidency, DOGE emerged as the sharp edge of an ideological project to shrink the state. Even after Musk left the Trump administration in May 2025, the White House continued its rampage against "woke" by withholding funding from major universities to reprimand them for their handling of student-led pro-Palestinian protests.

This Trumpian blitzkrieg appears to take inspiration from the libertarian (and anti–Cultural Marxist) Argentinian President Javier Milei, whose "Government by Chainsaw" approach drastically reduced his country's rate of inflation. At his electoral campaign appearances in 2023, Milei wielded a chainsaw to symbolize his commitment to slashing public expenditure and getting rid of the "shit leftists." In the first year of his presidency, he halved the number of government ministries (including the agencies for education, culture, and women and gender), scrapped transport and energy subsidies, and dismantled labor protections. He defunded cultural institutions, cut off existing channels for expressing dissent and solidarity, and exposed the country's resources and population to the desires of a rapacious global market. Trade unions and social movements have fiercely opposed these stark neoliberal reforms, pointing out that these policies will exacerbate the divide between the "haves" and the "have-nots." Over the past two years, Milei has turned Argentina into a laboratory for testing out an extreme form of libertarian economics. Consequently, Milei's aggressive chainsawing has become a template for the contemporary transnational right. During a Conservative Political Action Conference event in February 2025, Milei gleefully handed his signature chainsaw over to Musk. In a scene that would not have felt out of place in a 1970s slasher movie, Musk brandished the chainsaw above his head like a deranged killer of the night. If you want a picture of the future, imagine a chainsaw.

Whether we like it or not, the chainsaw is now the political symbol of our age. Its appeal lies in the promise to sever the "dead weight" from society: the work-from-home bureaucrats, the welfare scroungers, the unwanted refugees, the whiny minorities, the "shit leftists." It expresses a raw macho desire for individual freedom—the right to shred all the obligations that make up the social fabric and clear a way for the pursuit of profit and self-interest. In the Chainsaw Society, nothing is safe from privatization or austerity. No one can escape the violence of the market. Contrary to some sympathetic accounts of right-wing "national populism," this Orgy of the Chainsaw reveals that Milei and other emerging far-right leaders are not the enemies of neoliberalism—they are, to borrow a phrase from historian Quinn Slobodian, "the bastard offspring of neoliberalism itself."[2] They are not interested in saving the environment, protecting workers' rights, or addressing historical injustices. In the Age of the Chainsaw, the state is not a tool

2 Quinn Slobodian, "Elon Musk's Hostile Takeover," *The New Statesman*, January 15, 2025.

for improving people's lives but, rather, a service provider for facilitating the needs and demands of capital.

How have the histories of Cultural Marxism/s fed into this conjuncture? Decades of intellectual agitation, paired with conditions of crisis and decline, have transformed the political landscape. The thoughts of mainstream and marginal figures —Minnicino, Lind, Breitbart, Carvalho—have inspired ideological programs to crack down on protest, dismiss the demands of minorities, and weaken cultural and educational institutions. The critics of Cultural Marxism have successfully convinced people that left-wing beliefs are the result of top-down Frankfurt School–led manipulation rather than the product of genuine aspirations and well-reasoned principles. Progressives, according to this view, are useless appendages waiting to be amputated. This long-running campaign against a phantasm of the Frankfurt School has also helped to build a cultural agenda with serious economic consequences. Echoing Lind's own brand of fusionism, the leaders of the contemporary right have implemented coercive measures on gender, abortion, and labor rights to produce a culture that best suits the expansion of the free market. And in what many have called a "vibe shift," several multinational corporations have axed their DEI and environmental commitments. After a brief affair with woke capital, neoliberalism has returned to its first true love: cultural conservatism. It seems that the War on Cultural Marxism has finally culminated—no surprise—in another major triumph for capital.

What can we do to resist and overcome this onslaught? There are no easy or pre-packaged answers. Cultural Marxism/s, as explored in this book, have informed a wide range of political projects—each with their own identities, interests, and ideologies. It is not exactly helpful to draw a direct parallel between, say, Minnicino's obscure writings and Musk's late-night tweets. We must focus on what is specific or new about these emerging anti–Cultural Marxism forces before we can develop more situated and effective strategies for countering them. We should acknowledge that the right's new tactic of "flooding the zone"—a relentless bombardment of policy decisions, public announcements, and online posts—is designed to overwhelm our capacity to fight back. It breeds panic, bewilderment, and hopelessness. We are left feeling immobilized. And even when we turn away from the headlines, we still face the inevitable daily routines, that dull and isolating reproduction of a restrictive capitalist reality: the wages to be earned, the bills to be paid, the dishes to be done. Instead of succumbing to defeatism or settling for individual survival, we need to frustrate this game of shock and awe. We need to locate potential openings for a radical politics that confronts both oppression and exploitation. We need to jam up the chainsaw.

Is there anything that we could possibly learn from the right's assault on progressive values? In a 2021 talk at the Claremont Institute, Rufo stressed the use of narrative in ideological struggle.[3] He pointed out that parents were not turning up to school board meetings to complain about CRT because they had read a cerebral critique of neo-Marxist thought in a conservative magazine. Rather, they had decided to participate in this anti-CRT movement because they had heard a story that moved them emotionally. Most responses to Rufo's anti-CRT campaign tended to operate at the level of pure fact-checking. They tried to replace Rufo's distortions with accurate information. However, debunking is not enough to displace a powerful and memorable story. One cannot defeat a narrative by simply listing the facts. The success and effectiveness of Rufo's stories did not lie in their capacity to dupe ordinary folk but, rather, in the fact that they addressed people's stated values and yet represented them—to quote Stuart Hall—within "a logic of discourse which pull[ed] them systematically into line with

3 "Christopher Rufo: Critical Race Theory and Woke Capital," YouTube, posted by Claremont Institute, 24:35, June 1, 2021.

[the] policies and class strategies of the Right."[4] Freedom and equality in the service of book bans and privatization. Opposition to "race and sex stereotyping" as fuel for racism, misogyny, and transphobia. It is pointless to "debunk" Rufo and co.'s misinformation if we do not also offer a compelling counter-narrative. We need a counter-narrative that enters people's lives and transforms the way they act in the world, a vision of the future that redirects their desire toward other kinds of freedom and equality. It should speak to their deeper aspirations and allow them to see themselves as part of a broader emancipatory project.

Of course, a narrative cannot act on its own behalf. It must take root in a social movement or political organization to have material effects. There is no guarantee that a socialist message will suddenly jolt some pre-existing constituency of support into action. Political majorities, as Hall reminds us, "have to be 'made' and 'won'—not passively reflected."[5] In the Age of the Chainsaw, it is still possible to organize defensive struggles against the relentless slashing of the social safety net—but more is needed. Fighting the right should never simply be a matter of negating the threat but, rather, a project to fundamentally transform the structures that give rise to inequality and prejudice. This task requires a coalitional approach to organizing that combines range of grassroots struggles: anti-racism, anti-fascism, refugee and immigration organizing, feminism, labor unions, tenant unions, Indigenous and "Land Back" movements, trans liberation, pro-Palestine protests, and so on. We must articulate an internationalist vision that attends to the necessity of forming alliances and exchanging ideas with anti-fascist researchers, activists, and social movements around the world to contest the campaigns of the transnational right.

Certain figures on the left have decided to learn a different lesson from the right. They have treated the backlash against

4 Hall, *The Hard Road to Renewal*, 57.

5 Ibid., 281.

wokeness as an opportunity to ditch identity politics and return to more foundational class-based struggles. For some, this is an honest attempt to draw more people into a progressive coalition. For others, it is a way to promote a class-reductionist conception of left-wing politics that, at best, regards culture war issues as epiphenomenal (and, at worst, parrots far-right positions on race, gender, sexuality, and the environment). Instead of looking for more effective forms of anti-racism and anti-sexism, this tendency has merely accepted the right's framing of DEI as the epitome—the only possible outcome—of social justice organizing. However, this dismissal of identity politics is not necessarily a consequence of bigotry or opportunism. It is a reaction to the major contradiction of woke capitalism: the absorption of some progressive concerns insofar as they can expand the reach of corporate power over public life. Under the Rule of the Chainsaw, some on the left believe that they must make a difficult choice—to either protect the partial gains of a corporate wokeness (and, in some embarrassing cases, justify the levers of America's neo-colonial soft power) or abandon certain social groups—immigrants, minorities, transgender people—that have become the main targets of the right's anti-woke rampage. We must reject the conceptual framework that underpins this false binary. So-called woke issues cannot be detached from the struggle to transcend class society.

In their 2023 *Novara Media* essay "The Culture War Doesn't Exist," the writer and organizer Amardeep Singh Dhillon questions the logic of categorizing certain debates as "cultural" battles. As Dhillon explains, the left regularly distinguishes between culture wars and class struggles, as though these cultural matters are independent of capital. However, the so-called culture war is not just a cynical divide-and-conquer tactic. Although anti-immigrant political rhetoric ("Send Them Back," "Stop The Boats," "Build That Wall") may appear to be a staple of culture warring, it is "part of an internally coherent strategy to maintain the production of a migrant underclass and discipline citizens by manufacturing consent for law and order."[6] For Dhillon, the culture war does not exist, because there are no cultural struggles in contemporary society that take place in a context outside racial capitalism. The attempt to frame certain concerns as culture war issues obscures, as Dhillon puts it, the "material effects of right-wing politics on minoritized communities; dismisses white supremacy as a distraction from economic decline, rather than an ideology that serves capital in concrete ways, and fails to distinguish between material struggle and media outrage over how such a struggle is discussed."[7] Following Dhillon's analysis, we must push back against a politics that relegates some demands to the realm of the "irrelevantly cultural." No one deserves to be left behind.

But what of culture itself? The fight against Cultural Marxism is not just a squabble about politics. It is a conflict over the books people read, the music they listen to, the movies they watch, the people they kiss in public, the spaces where they gather, the knowledges they produce, and the worlds they imagine. The practices of art, culture, and education are not mere adjuncts to human existence; they are integral to our ways of life. The right's position on these areas was perfectly summed up in a 2021 Fox News segment when the Republican Senator Marco Rubio was asked about University of Central Florida's Graduate Certificate in "Social Justice in Public Service." Rubio replied forthrightly that colleges should not teach students "Cultural Marxism." He claimed that universities should instead focus on teaching technological fields, such as engineering, biology, and math, to ensure that more people will "find a good paying job, contribute to their community, their family, and country."[8] This is a classic example of the

6 Amardeep Singh Dhillon, "The Culture War Doesn't Exist," *Novara Media*, April 19, 2023.

7 Ibid.

8 NRSC, "Sen. Marco Rubio: 'Social Justice' and 'Wokeness' Are Really Just Nice Names for Cultural Marxism," May 26, 2021.

right's desire to limit institutions to the task of reproducing a capitalist economy and a normative cultural community. Although the proponents of Cultural Marxism/s pay lip service to "Western Civilization," they hope to enforce an impoverished notion of learning and culture that subjects all forms of human expression to a capitalist logic. They want a culture that consolidates the traditional norms that they define as the strict boundary of human experience, a culture that imposes a mere repetition of pre-existing perceptions and patterns. The convergence between reactionary politics and techno-futurism has intensified this trend. The phenomenon of AI-generated art and writing expresses a similar desire to restrict culture: it seeks to devalue the labor of actual artists and writers, supplant the products of human expression with the plagiarized fantasies of an inhuman machine, and stifle the cultural and political possibilities that can only come from using your own imagination. In a reversal of vulgar Marxist economism, reactionaries place their faith in a kind of cultural determinism: once they re-take their favored institutions (and destroy the ones they detest and replace cultural workers with algorithms), they can fully dominate the culture and finally stamp out all disruption and difference. They are afraid of culture precisely because they do not know how to control it.

We must passionately defend an open, rather than deterministic, conception of culture. We cannot act as commissars who can dictate an artistic line that painters, writers, or filmmakers must follow. As Raymond Williams once put it in his daring essay "Culture is Ordinary," it is "stupid and arrogant to suppose that any of these meanings can in any way be prescribed."[9] Instead, Williams recommended that "all the channels of expression and communication should be cleared and open, so that . . . actual life, that we cannot know in advance, that we can know only in part even while it is being

9 Raymond Williams, *Resources of Hope: Culture, Democracy, Socialism* (London: Verso, 1989), 8.

lived, may be brought to consciousness and meaning."[10] We need to support the material infrastructure that allows new cultural meanings, practices, and expressions to emerge. We must protect arts schemes for working class and marginalized youth, local galleries, music venues, bookshops, community centers, theaters, and libraries. Culture is not a bourgeois pastime; rather, it is essential to a way of life that expands the capacity of people to do more for themselves and with others in the places where they actually live. In a 2017 speech at Glastonbury Festival, the former Labour leader Jeremy Corbyn offered a glimpse of what this world might look like: "In every child there's a poem, in every child there's a painting, in every child there's music . . . I want all of our children to be inspired, all of our children to have the right to learn music, write poetry and to paint in the way that they want."[11] This is not about some utopia, for, as Corbyn reminded us, politics is about "everyday life . . . [and] about all of us, what we dream, what we want, and what we want for everybody else."[12] If we are "Cultural Marxists," then this is what Cultural Marxism should be all about.

Our future may look dark, but our fate is not predetermined. Although the global rise of the right may feel inevitable, politics is not a closed system. It is an open process of turning individuals, whose identities are fragmented, into new political subjects who feel that their interests and desires are represented, on some level, in particular demands and positions. If we want to counter the right's lies about the Frankfurt School, we cannot count on some law of history—we must throw ourselves into the openness of political struggle. The strongest possible counterargument against Cultural Marxism/s is the collective mobilization of people who are willing to stand up

10 Ibid., 9.

11 Alex Flood, "Read Jeremy Corbyn's Glastonbury 2017 Speech in Full," *NME*, June 24, 2017.

12 Ibid.

for one another and fight for a better future. These people will not agree about everything; they will not even look like each other. Yet they will share in a vision of a world where freedom is no chainsaw and where equality is no dream. Only when we show that this human solidarity is more powerful than any conspiracy will we finally refute the right's facile talk of Cultural Marxism/s.

# Acknowledgments

Thank you to the short-lived Portland Critical Theory Meeting Group: Chris O'Kane, Jan Mieszkowski, Kirstin Munro, James W. Russell, and Johannes Wankhammer. Our beer-fueled conversations back in 2017 inspired me to write this book.

Thank you to the mentors who pushed me to write better and think harder: Antonio Calcagno and Michael E. Gardiner, Anne-Marie Oliver and Barry Sanders, Joan Handwerg and Marie-Pierre Hasne, and Brian Lobel and Ian Hornsby.

Thank you to the various people whose insights guided me in the right direction: Ian Gardner (who discovered the links between the LaRouchites and Raymond V. Raehn), Hylozoic Hedgehog (Kevin Coogan), Jeremy R. Smith, Devin Daniels, Marah Nagelhout, Martin Jay, Douglas Kellner, Sam Hoadley-Brill, Bruce Wilson, Johannes von Moltke, Moira Weigel, Robert MacDougall, Robert F. Carley, and Andreas Huyssen.

Thank you to my editor, Sebastian Budgen, for your faith in me and this book.

Thank you to the staff at the libraries and archive collections where I did much of the writing and research for this project: the Rauner Special Collections Library at Dartmouth University, the St. Peter's House Library at the University of Brighton, the Jubilee Library in Brighton, the Radicalism Collection at Michigan State University, and the D. B. Weldon Library at Western University.

Thank you to the participants of University of California, Berkeley's Center for Right-Wing Studies working group for your rich and informed feedback on early drafts of this book.

Thank you to John Woods for the paper, the printer ink, and the pints.

Thank you to everyone who distracted me while I was trying to finish this book and got me to go outside and enjoy life a little: Alexandrea Marsh, Emily Oliver, Morgan Oddie, Paris Wilder, Alice Chia, Jacqueline Trevino, Frank Newsome, David Bennett, and Olivia Judah.

And thank you, Natalie Treviño, for all the ways you work to build a world where many worlds fit.

# Index